THE BLACK ANGELS

The Story of the Waffen-SS

THE
BLACK ANGELS
The Story of the Waffen-SS

Rupert Butler

PEN & SWORD MILITARY CLASSICS

First published in 1978 by Hamlyn Paperbacks
Published in 2003, in this format, by
PEN & SWORD MILITARY CLASSICS
an imprint of
Pen & Sword Books Limited
47, Church Street
Barnsley
S. Yorkshire
S70 2AS

© Rupert Butler, 1978, 2003

ISBN 0 85052 968 9

A CIP record for this book is
available from the British Library

Printed in England by
CPI UK

CONTENTS

ILLUSTRATIONS

Grateful acknowledgements are due to the Imperial War Museum for the use of all the illustrations in this book.

BIBLIOGRAPHY

Aitken, Leslie, MBE, *Massacre on the Road to Dunkirk* (William Kimber 1977)

Carell, Paul, *Scorched Earth: Hitler's War on Russia*, vol. 2 (Harrap 1970)

Clark, Alan, *Barbarossa: The Russian-German Conflict 1941–45* (Hutchinson 1965)

Elstob, Peter, *Hitler's Last Offensive* (Secker & Warburg 1971)

Höhne, Heinz, *The Order of the Death's Head* (Secker & Warburg 1966)

Jolly, Cyril, *The Vengeance of Private Pooley* (Heinemann 1956)

Keegan, John, *Waffen-SS: The Asphalt Soldiers* (Macdonald 1970)

Kruuse, Jens, *Madness at Oradour* (Secker & Warburg 1969)

Lucas, James and Matthew Cooper, *Hitler's Elite: Leibstandarte-SS* (Macdonald & Jane's 1975)

McKee, Alexander, *Caen: Anvil of Victory* (White Lion 1964)

Manvell, Roger and Heinrich Fraenkel, *Heinrich Himmler* (Heinemann 1975)

Meyer, Kurt, *Grenadiere* (Schild Verlag 1957)

Neumann, Peter, *Other Men's Graves* (Weidenfeld and Nicolson 1958)

Preston, Anthony (ed.), *Decisive Battles of Hitler's War* (Chartwell Books, Inc. 1977)

Reitlinger, Gerald, *The SS: Alibi of a Nation* (Heinemann 1956)

Russell of Liverpool, Lord, *The Scourge of the Swastika* (Cassell & Co. 1954)

Sauer, Karl, *Die Verbrechen der Waffen-SS* (Roderberg 1977)

Seth, Ronald, *Jackals of the Reich* (New English Library 1972)

Shirer, William L., *The Rise and Fall of the Third Reich* (Secker & Warburg 1960)

Stein, George H, *The Waffen-SS* (Cornell University Press 1966)

Trevor Roper, Hugh (ed.), *The Goebbels Diaries: The Last Days* (Secker & Warburg 1978)

Tulley, Andrew, *Berlin: Story of a Battle* (Simon & Schuster, New York 1963)

Weingartner, James T., *Hitler's Guard* (Southern Illinois University Press 1968)

Whiting, Charles, *Hunters from the Sky* (Leo Cooper 1975)

Whiting, Charles, *Massacre at Malmédy* (Leo Cooper 1971)

Wyles, Alan, *Himmler* (Pan/Ballantine 1972)

Second World War, History of the: Waffen-SS (Purnell & Sons)

World War II Special: 'The Warsaw Ghetto No Longer Exists' (Orbis Publishing Ltd)

ACKNOWLEDGEMENTS

In preparing this book I owe a great debt to Mr James Lucas, Mr Terry Charman, and Mr George Clout and the staff of the Imperial War Museum, London, for their patience in supplying material, answering countless questions and reading the final manuscript. No story of the Waffen-SS can be written without reference to 'Hitler's Elite: Leibstandarte SS' by James Lucas and Matthew Cooper (Macdonald & Jane's, 1975). I am grateful for Mr Lucas's permission to consult his history of the campaigns of Hitler's élite. I am in equal debt to the Institute of Contemporary History and Wiener Library, London. Its staff gave me access to translations of evidence submitted at the International Military Tribunal, Nuremberg, and other documents relating to the Waffen-SS. My thanks also to the staff of Wandsworth Library who allowed me to consult its large collection of books on World War II. Valuable research and assistance has also been given by Mr Malcolm Hudson, Mr Mel Bray, Mr William Fowler and Mr Michael Gunton.

'I swear to you, Adolf Hitler, as Führer and Reich Chancellor, loyalty and bravery. I vow to you, and those you have named to command me, obedience unto death. So help me God.'

The oath sworn by members of the Leibstandarte SS Adolf Hitler in November 1933 and after that by every man who entered the ranks of the Waffen-SS.

'A new man, the storm soldier, the élite of Central Europe. A completely new race, cunning, strong and packed with purpose ... battle proven, merciless both to himself and others.' Ernst Jünger, German poet and novelist.

THE BLACK ANGELS

1

The tall, striking men in black stood out from the crowd on that exciting, unforgettable day in Berlin which seemed to many a nightmarish re-run of a superbly staged pageant from the Middle Ages.

The uniform of these men included the Death's Head insignia on the caps, a runic flash of double S on the sleeves – and an inscription on the belt buckle which read *'Meine Ehre heisst Treue'* – *'My Honour is Loyalty.'*

That runic flash belonging to the SS (Schutzstaffel; Protection Squad) was to become a symbol of power and terror throughout occupied Europe, rivalling even the most fevered imaginings of Nordic myth-makers. Those who supported the flash were to grow sharply in numbers between the years when Adolf Hitler came to power and the start of World War II – from 52,000 to 240,000. By the time of Germany's defeat in 1945 there were something like one milion men owing some form of allegiance to the armed offshoot of the Schutzstaffel.

The growth of the Waffen-SS – the armed SS – was to spring out of the cumbersome organisations within the Schutzstaffel (SS) proper. But during the remarkable last weekend of 1933, all this was still a long way off and the SS was but one force of the legions coming to pay homage to their Führer.

To the people of Berlin on that day, it seemed as if all those legions were stuffed into an endless procession of army trucks which rumbled through the boulevards and sidestreets of the city. In the surrounding countryside there had been hasty mobilisation of every available company, not only of the SS but of the organisation that was to prove its deadly rival. This was the grouping of brown-shirts, the SA (Sturmabteilung; Storm Troopers).

Even to the most stolid and politically indifferent Berliner it was obvious that something rather special was happening. Crowds watched the troops gravitate towards the main assembly point of the Charlottenburger Chaussee. It was not just that Germany had a new Chancellor; there had been a seemingly endless succession of saviours of the Republic since November 1918. But this time, it seemed that an entirely new era was being ushered in for a country whose nose had been rubbed continually in the ashes of defeat, and who had known little but economic depression and political violence since Kaiser Wilhelm II had taken his withered arm and shattered dreams into exile in 1918.

It was certainly to be a new era. The movement of troops which turned Berlin into a veritable fortress on 28 January 1933 was providing a dramatic curtain-raiser to the birth of the Third Reich.

Austrian-born Adolf Hitler took the oath of office administered by President von Hindenburg, who but a short time before had declared contemptuously that the 'Austrian Corporal' was barely fitted to be Minister of Posts.

Earlier Hitler and his colleagues, in a positive delirium of joy at the scent of power, left their headquarters at the Hotel Kaiserhof and moved across the road to the Reich Chancellery, Wilhelmstrasse 77. As Hitler himself entered the inner courtyard there occurred an event of profound significance for the future of Germany, even if few realised it at the time.

A detachment of the Reichswehr, members of the country's standing army acting as Chancellor's Guard, snapped to attention and saluted. There was nothing remarkable in that: a Chancellor was fully entitled to such courtesies.

But Hitler's response was something entirely new. His salute was a partly raised right arm. This, of course, was the salutation of the Nazis and, as such, a direct challenge to the proud independence of the established military machine.

It was to be the first challenge of many.

On the evening of Hitler's appointment as Chancellor, it was as if some half-crazed operator of a time-machine had flicked a miracle switch and catapulted Germany back down the long corridor of the centuries.

As darkness settled over the city a million torches were ignited and a cavalcade of triumphant Nazis wound its way through the Brandenburg Gate. And German history was recalled in song: the heady glories of the days of the Bavarian kings, Frederick the Great and Bismarck. There was the voice of the new Germany, too – the songs of the SS, orchestrated by the brutal crunch of the jackboot.

> Clear the streets, the SS marches,
> The storm-columns stand at the ready.
> They will take the road
> From tyranny to freedom.
> So we are all ready to give our all
> As did our fathers before us.
> Let death be our battle companion.
> We are the black band.

Hitler's eyes, according to close observers, were filled with tears throughout the procession. He leant from a window to acknowledge 'Sieg Heil'. The groups that passed below the Führer's gaze consisted of SA, Hitler Jugend (Hitler Youth), Stahlhelm (ex-servicemen), National Socialist party members – and SS. Of the Schutzstaffel, its Reichsführer-SS (Reich SS leader) and Grand Master of the Order, Heinrich Himmler, was to comment with pride: 'I know that there are many in Germany who feel uncomfortable when they see this black tunic; we under-

3

stand that and do not expect to be beloved by over many people.'

Let the image of the marching bands of the SS be frozen for a while. We have need of our own time-machine: one to take us back to a very different Germany, on the eleventh day of the eleventh month of the year 1918 . . .

The imperial ambitions of Kaiser Wilhelm II, German Emperor and King of Prussia, had brought Europe to its knees in four years of war. The flower of British, German and French manhood had perished in the mud of France and Flanders. At the end of it all, the Kaiser fled to Holland and his generals scuttled thankfully into retirement.

The Great Powers were very far from being magnanimous to a defeated Germany. The terms of the Treaty of Versailles were severe. Germany had to accept the surrender of all her colonies, submit to militarisation of the Rhineland for fifteen years, and pay heavy reparations to those countries over-run in the four years of war.

For the Army, the loss of pride was devastating. In what can only be described as a positive orgy of cashiering by the victors, the strength of the Army was cut to a puny one hundred thousand. There was to be no General Staff, no conscription, no tanks, no heavy artillery, no poison-gas supplies, no aircraft, no Zeppelins. No vessels of the German fleet were to exceed ten thousand tons. There were to be no submarines and no airforces.

To many, emasculation could go no further. Resentment and anger smouldered in the breasts of the politically conscious. But, nevertheless, there were men of goodwill in the new Republic who had an image of democracy that they hastened to try to solidify; it was by no means the fault of every German that peace and sanity were to be but mirages.

The Republic's first Parliament met at Weimar, a town on the river Elbe which had a long tradition of liberalism.

4

On paper, there looked nothing whatever wrong with the new constitution which provided for universal suffrage and the establishment of civilian control over the subdued Army. But hatred of Weimar, a fierce determination to avenge the surrender of 1918, was, from the start, a powerful force.

The move was on to strangle democracy at its birth. Carefully planned campaigns of subversion turned the streets of every city in Germany into a miniature battlefield. Terrorist groups such as the Spartacists (forerunner of the German Communist party) did battle with the Reichswehr and irregulars of the Freikorps (paramilitary units consisting of disgruntled ex-officers, adventurers and louts).

In Bavaria a soviet-style regime assumed power with a programme that had all the familiar trappings of land reform, workers' control and popular participation in government. Combined forces of the Reichswehr and Freikorps defeated it with savagery – but left behind the germs of a new movement and, incidentally, two of its foremost architects.

Outwardly there was little that was intimidating about Heinrich Himmler. He was the Munich-born son of a pedantic, painfully respectable secondary schoolmaster with social pretensions.

Young Heinrich looked every inch the painfully conscientious, totally unimaginative clerk in a civil service backwater – shunted with his beloved files and his dirty fingernails into some mundane section of petty bureaucracy. Pince-nezed, narrow-chested and weedy, he was nevertheless destined to become head of an organisation to procreate the blond, blue-eyed true Nordic species, typified ideally by the SS man.

Despite his unimpressive physique, Himmler had dreams of becoming a successful soldier, but his service in the 11th Bavarian Infantry had been as an officer cadet. To his considerable annoyance, the soldier *manqué* had just missed service in the First World War, but he did have the fleeting satisfaction of belonging to one of the Freikorps which had 'liberated' Munich. In 1922 he had qualified as an industrial chemist, and become much dedicated to the pseudo-scientific pursuits of homeopathy and herbal cures.

Another man who also found himself in the Bavarian capital in 1918 was Adolf Hitler, awaiting demobilisation. At Munich the eventual meeting of these two men was to herald the formation of the SS and its various branches.

Before discharge, Hitler attended one of the soldiers' indoctrination classes with which the Reichswehr corps supplemented its armed combat of left-wing subversion. Evidently he showed promise.

Hitler found himself appointed a Bildungsoffizier (Instruction Officer) with the job of protecting the men from such pernicious influences as socialism, pacifism and democracy generally. One group was worrying his employers particularly. It was called the National Socialist German Workers' Party. Adolf Hitler found it to consist largely of beer-swilling nationalists with working-class sympathies, but not much political maturity. Ruthless and astute, Hitler managed to infiltrate the party, rising within the ranks and, by January 1920, emerging as its leader.

It was not long before he was establishing a fiery reputation for rabble-rousing, most of it distinctly anti-Semitic. The Weimar Republic was quickly denounced as 'Jew-ridden', and Hitler peddled a message of hate from countless platforms around Munich.

Hitler was soon revealed as not merely an impressive orator but a superb stage-manager. He recognised that it was not enough to talk about violence, one had to create an appropriate atmosphere. So squads of only too willing bully-boys were imported.

The new leader was full of brutal advice to his party workers. He informed stewards at his meetings: 'None of us will leave this hall unless we are carried out as corpses. If any coward shrinks back I will personally rip off his arm-band and cap-badge.'

In such an intimidating atmosphere it obviously made sound sense to establish a personal bodyguard. Party member Ernst Röhm, an industrious drinker and flagrant homosexual, mustered a stationery salesman, an amateur wrestler, a watchmaker and a beer-hall bouncer to act as the Führer's protectors. This new bodyguard was known as Stosstrupp (Storm Troopers) by Adolf Hitler but it was no more than a sub-unit of the SA, a 2,000-strong private army which Röhm had created.

Predictably, with that sort of membership, the Stosstrupp soon consisted of a roster of out-and-out thugs who liked nothing better than laying about crowds and property with their boots and rubber truncheons.

On 9 November 1923 a 600-strong group of SA led by Hitler, and with the ecstatic Heinrich Himmler as standard-bearer, made an astonishing bid for power from the nationalist and rigidly independent leaders of Bavaria to proclaim a new government. The move failed; it cost around a dozen Stosstrupp lives and SA casualties and resulted in short-term imprisonment for Adolf Hitler. At the same time it emblazoned his name and that of the totally obscure National Socialists across the headlines of Germany and the world.

Whatever may have been the intention of the Munich Putsch, it almost spelt total disaster for Hitler's movement and its various factions, all of which were fragmented while he was in jail. To recreate the Stosstrupp as it had been before was clearly impossible; something entirely new was needed.

Conscious of this, Hitler wrote: 'I told myself then that I needed a bodyguard, even a restricted one, but made up of men who would be enlisted unconditionally, ready even to march against their own brothers, only twenty men to a city (on condition that one could count on them absolutely) rather than a dubious mass.' In April 1925 eight men came together to create the Stabswache or Headquarters Guard. Within two weeks the unit was renamed the Schutzstaffel; the SS had begun the twenty years of its life.

A new recruit was number 168: Heinrich Himmler. By 1929 the industrious Heinrich, the eternal subaltern, had attained an ambition to become not simply a soldier but a very special warrior serving an élite force. He had the grandiose title of Reichsführer-SS now, was in charge of thirty men, but remained firmly subordinate to Röhm and his much larger SA. Himmler most certainly did not care for this state of affairs, but he had the born bureaucrat's gift of patience. Meanwhile he set about building up the black-uniformed SS to be his emperor's praetorian guard, outranking the more plebeian formations of the SA.

For Adolf Hitler the problem of personal safety remained, even after he became Chancellor. Hitler was under no illusion that he was greatly loved, and the opposition, he recognised, could prove formidable.

The Nationalist Party, with which he had been forced to forge a political alliance, had its own military force, the Stahlhelm, which could very likely turn nasty. There was also the Communist party which, although cowed, was far from beaten. And supposing the traditional military caste in the Reichswehr decided to overthrow the Nazis? There could be no question yet of locking up the more tiresome members of the opposition; President Hindenburg, although becoming progressively senile, was still alive and a considerable symbolic force of the old order. Hitler, a ruthless opportunist with his own brand of cool courage, still felt all the insecurity of the dictator who could trust no one. Thus it is hardly surprising that in 1933 he raised yet another Headquarters Guard, drawing from the SS.

The armed SS can be said to have had its origins from that moment with the creation of the Führer's personal bodyguard, the Leibstandarte SS Adolf Hitler, élite of the élite, knight errants of the Schutzstaffel. At the time of its formation the Leibstandarte had a very clear-cut function: it was to be the sole property of its master, swearing allegiance to him. In the wake of the creation of the Leibstandarte came another full-time armed organisation. This was the SS Totenkopfverbände, at this time completely separate from the Leibstandarte and originally formed to guard the concentration camps. By 1937 the Totenkopfverbände, with additional duties to maintain internal security, could boast three regiments.

But in 1934 Hitler had other things on his mind besides building up a succession of private armies. Suddenly the whole prestige of National Socialism was threatened, undermined by the increasing belligerence of Ernst Röhm and the SA. The Leibstandarte was given its key role: to crush Röhm and his followers before they brought down the whole elaborate structure which Hitler had created.

Some regard for legalities and diplomatic niceties have to be observed by even the most appalling gangster states. The apologist, the public relations officer and the official spokesman must either emerge or be appointed. A brand image of sorts had to be created. In the months after Hitler came to power, Nazi Germany's absence of suave front-men became only too obvious. There was nothing remotely suave about the brawling, bullying brownshirts. In the election which Hitler had called after becoming Chancellor, the SA frequently swooped down on political opponents and beat them to death. Stegerwald, leader of the Catholic Trades Unions, was pulverised when he attempted to address a meeting. Killer squads from both the SA and SS tumbled over each other to arrest political opponents and even intrigued to get rid of each other. Artur Nebe, head of the Criminal Police and a rising member of the SS hierarchy, would slip the safety-catch of his revolver as he entered his office building through the back door, and he would hug the walls as he climbed the staircase.

But the man who really worried Hitler was Ernst Röhm. The 'socialism' in National Socialism was a shrewd political label on the swaggering road to power, but once in office the Führer found it awkward. Röhm and his SA hit-men claimed to take socialism seriously and, worse, stumped about talking of the 'People's Army of Nazism' – dangerous in an organisation over which the leader lacked complete control.

One of the first principles in the manual of dictatorship is to secure the continuing support of the Army. And the German Army, the rigidly traditionalist Reichswehr, had no confidence in Röhm which, in practical terms, meant no confidence in Hitler either. As chief of staff of the SA, Röhm now had under his control two and a half million Storm Troopers, plus a seat in the Cabinet which the outwardly conciliatory Hitler had given him. It was very far from being sufficient to keep Röhm quiet.

In February 1934, Röhm flung down on the Cabinet table a bulky memorandum which was nothing short of dynamite. It proposed the setting up of an entirely new Ministry of Defence which would embrace a new People's Army, the SS, the SA and all veteran groups. It needed no imagination to realise who would step in as supreme commander.

Was the German officer corps, the present-day heirs of Frederick the Great, of Bismarck and of the Kaiser, to be subordinated to a riff-raff of street thugs, sadists and perverts? Was this to be the new Germany which was seeking to redress the humiliations suffered by the old? Plainly not. Hitler had to act fast: he could not afford to lose the confidence of the Army. Equally, Röhm was a dangerous man to cross. The moment to strike had to be picked carefully; meanwhile the inflammatory proposals remained on the Cabinet table with no one daring either to pick them up or throw them away.

To tread lightly was not Hitler's style. Diplomacy would never work with a man like Röhm. He needed to be taught a lesson by someone who understood him and would therefore know the best method. Hitler's choice fell on one of his most loyal followers, a rock-hard Bavarian named Josef ('Sepp') Dietrich. It would be fitting, Hitler reasoned, that Röhm should go under a plan concocted by Dietrich. There would be few scruples about this former butcher, paymaster sergeant, petrol-pump attendant, and chauffeur to the Führer. When it came to brutality, there was not much to choose between Röhm and Dietrich.

But Dietrich had another qualification which eclipsed all the rest. In 1933 he had formed the cadre which became the SS Bodyguard Regiment Adolf Hitler – the élite Leibstandarte.

No longer was it to be a mere ornament: the smart and efficient guard for the Führer, two of whose rifle-bearing, helmeted members stood like statues before the bronze doors of the Führer's office in the Chancellery. The Leibstandarte was to be blooded in battle.

On 27 June 1934, Sepp Dietrich requested the Reichswehr authorities for arms so that the Leibstandarte could carry out what he called 'a secret and most important mission ordered by the Führer'. This meant no less than the slaughter of dissident elements within the SA, an occasion to settle old scores and stifle simmering resentments. It was to be Germany's equivalent of America's St Valentine's Day Massacre; the ghost of more than one Chicago thug was to squat on the shoulders of Adolf Hitler.

The early dawn of 30 June was shattered by motorised SS units roaring through towns and villages on a high-speed drive towards Bavaria.

At the Hanslbauer Hotel at Weissee on the shores of the Tegernsee, some top SA leaders slumbered in each other's beds. Action was swift and brutal: Edmund Heines, SA Obergruppenführer of Silesia, was dragged from the arms of his male lover, taken outside the hotel and summarily shot on the personal orders of the Führer. Ernst Röhm, the scar-faced brawler who had shared all Hitler's hopes and ambitions in the early days but had dared to make his own personal bid for power, was brought back to Munich and thrown into Stadelheim jail where he had been imprisoned after the 1923 putsch.

Here, Sepp Dietrich, flanked by former railway clerk and psychiatric clinic inmate Theodor Eicke, came into his own as saviour of the Reich. Röhm, stripped to the waist and his eyes filled with contempt, stood to attention and faced the firing party.

Röhm could only mutter: 'Oh, my Führer!' Eicke riposted: 'You should have thought of that before!' Then the revolvers were emptied into the SA leader's body.

The same evening, at 17.00 hours, Sepp Dietrich received instructions to select one officer and half a dozen men as an execution squad for six prominent SA leaders. One hour later Dietrich was at Stadelheim with 'six good shots to ensure that nothing messy happened'. With the Leibstandarte in direct control of these executions, there was at least some semblance of civilised procedure. Those about to die were led one at a time in front of the firing squad in the grey prison courtyard. There a polite Leibstandarte officer greeted the condemned with the words: 'The Führer and Reich Chancellor has condemned you to death. The sentence will be carried out forthwith.' And that was how the enemies of the Reich died: there had indeed been 'nothing messy'.

Just exactly how many were shot by the Leibstandarte firing squads will never be known; there is no record of the number of corpses piled like rotting vegetables at the Lichterfelde barracks which had been converted into a dumping ground.

The removal of Röhm and the more troublesome elements of the SA revealed Nazi Germany as a gangster state, but it had one overwhelming value for Hitler. In its first major undertaking the armed SS had shown that it was capable of obeying orders blindly and displaying total loyalty. To Hitler these were the virtues that counted. Heinrich Himmler, the racial crank, might extol the Aryan perfection of his fine blond beasts. Hitler saw them as bastions against treachery.

No attempt was made to hide what had happened in the bloodbath. Himmler was later to express it: 'We did not hesitate to stand comrades who had lapsed up against the wall and shoot them. . . . It appalled everyone, and yet everyone was certain that if it is necessary and such orders are issued he will do it again.'

As for the Army, it could not but agree that Hitler had removed the most serious threat against it. The officer corps shut its eyes to the methods which had been used. Nazi mythology was henceforth to refer to the 'Putsch', supporting Hitler's allegation that 'a clique of perverts around Röhm' had plotted to seize the state by force in collusion with foreign powers.

But, as is often the way, the man in the street came up with a description of the events which was far nearer the truth. From henceforth what had happened in June 1934 became known as the 'Night of the Long Knives'. And there was no doubt just which faction had wielded the dagger and twisted it most effectively: the initiative of brute force now belonged to the SS.

And plain to see as one of the supreme instruments of the Schutzstaffel was the Leibstandarte whose men, in 1933, had sworn the oath which was soon to be common throughout the armed SS: *'I swear to you, Adolf Hitler, as Führer and Reich Chancellor, loyalty and bravery. I vow to you, and those you have named to command me, obedience until death. So help me God.'*

It was an oath, let it be noted, sworn not to the Army, not even to the Reich, but to Hitler personally.

From the bloodbath which had engulfed the SA, the SS emerged as the supreme arbiter of terror in Hitler's Germany. It was to have three militarised, full-time formations: the Leibstandarte SS Adolf Hitler; the SS Verfügungstruppe (SS-VT, Special Purpose Troops) and the Totenkopfverbände (Death's Head detachments) – separate strands to be woven together by 1939 to form the Waffen-SS.

13

The oath of the Leibstandarte gave Hitler complete sovereignty over the destinies of the German people, particularly over anyone who dared to oppose him. After the death of Hindenburg in 1934, Hitler merged the offices of President and Chancellor and became supreme dictator.

The routing of the SA opposition did not remove the jealousies, rivalries and jockeying for position of various factions within the SS. Himmler had gained the initiative from Hermann Göring, the former fighter ace from World War I, by seizing the Gestapo (Geheime Staatspolizei; Secret State Police). The two men – one a puritan crank and the other a self-indulgent vulgarian with a liking for garish uniforms and jewelled batons – regarded each other with contempt, but were forced to sink their differences. The man of the hour, though, was undoubtedly Heinrich Himmler.

Göring once declared with engaging frankness: 'I joined the party because I was a revolutionary, not because of any ideological nonsense.' But to Himmler ideology was all; he embraced the pseudo-mystic trappings of the Nazi creed root and branch. In the black uniform of his SS he saw shadows of an earlier Germany which he had half digested from undirected, over-credulous reading: a Germany of forests and hunters, of supermen who lived by the dagger, products of a twilight world of ferocious gods and lion-hearted heroes.

Had not the Teutonic Knights carried out crusades of cleansing liberation against the inferior Slavs? And was not the symbol of the oakleaf and the eagle a potent memory of the former empires of the Romans? With what trembling joy Himmler dipped into the pages of the superman philosopher Friedrich Nietzsche, and read deep of the glorification of brutalism.

'The strong men, the masters, regain the pure conscience of a beast of prey; monsters filled with joy; they can return from a fearful succession of murder, arson,

14

rape and torture with the same joy in their hearts, the same contentment in their souls, as if they had indulged in some student's rag. When a man is capable of commanding, when he is by nature a master, when he is violent in act and gesture, of what importance are treaties to him? To judge morality properly by two concepts borrowed from zoology: the *taming* of a beast and the *breeding* of a species.'

The armed SS man was, Himmler decreed, to be godless – and, what is more, to revel in his godlessness. The Christian message of reconciliation and tolerance was to be renounced as 'unGerman'. From the outset, young men of *all* branches of the SS were to abjure Christianity as destructive, effeminate and – all reasoning departed sharply here – 'Jewish'.

On leaving the cadet schools, young officers were required to write essays on such choice subjects as 'Responsibility of Christianity for the decline of the Ostrogoths and Vandals' or 'Effect of Christianity on Ancestor Worship among our people'. To Himmler, such exercises for the armed SS man were deemed 'advanced education'.

By insisting on what he regarded as the flower of German manhood to serve this patchwork ideology, Himmler was to entrust to his lieutenants, early in 1933, the setting up of two regiments (Standarten): Deutschland, stationed in Munich; and Germania which was based in Hamburg. Already in existence, of course, was the Leibstandarte which was to preserve jealously a measure of independence.

Hitler was notoriously loyal – too loyal, some said – to the more pliable of his old cronies, and one of the first to receive his reward after the 'Night of the Long Knives' was Sepp Dietrich. Of him, the Führer said: 'He is a man unique, under whose swashbuckling appearance is a serious, conscientious, scrupulous character.'

To the traditional officer corps, Dietrich was a foul

15

loud-mouth, an ill-educated thug who should never have risen above the rank of sergeant. But the Army did as it was told by then, and had to suffer Dietrich's promotion.

A natural choice to command the first of Himmler's SS cadet training centres (*Junkerschülen*) was the Verfügungstruppe commander, Paul Hausser, a man who knew nothing and cared less about the abstractions of Nietzsche and the nutritious virtues of garden herbs, but was a staunch believer in turning out rock-hard troops to defend a modern state.

While Dietrich was bull-necked and brutal, Hausser seemed everyone's ideal of the true Prussian officer. Merciless, certainly, but he was also elegant and educated, with a gift for sarcasm which endeared him to few. A career soldier with a healthy gift of cynicism and contempt for politicians, Hausser had climbed the military ladder in classic progression. He had gone through infantry training and staff college. He had been a staff officer on the western and eastern fronts in World War I and had retired, a Lieutenant-General, one year before Hitler came to power.

Like many of the rootless, discontented members of the officer corps in the Germany of the 1920s and 1930s, he had joined first the Stahlhelm and, when that was amalgamated with the SA, had teamed up with Röhm and had gained the rank of SA-Standartenführer.

What more natural – and more prudent – than to accept a job from Himmler at the right time and become SS-Standartenführer?

Hausser's troops had the initial advantage, admittedly, of being almost perfect physical specimens, flawless to the extent, it was claimed, of not having so much as a single filling in their teeth. In January 1937 Himmler declared: 'I insist on a height of 1.70 metres. I personally select a hundred or two a year and insist on photographs which reveal if there are any Slav or Mongolian characteristics. I personally want to avoid such types as the members of the "Soldier's Councils" of 1918-19, people who loc'x somewhat comic in our German eyes and often gave the impression of being foreigners . . .'

They were hard, these supposed racial paragons, very hard indeed, and they needed to be. The SS recruit was aroused at six and put in an hour of physical training before a breakfast of – Himmler's touch – mineral water and porridge. After breakfast came weapon training. Then there was an interlude which must have been welcome to many of the recruits, if not precisely on ideological grounds. Everyone was subjected to lectures on the all-wisdom of the Führer, the tenets of National Socialism and the supreme rightness of racialism and Nordic superiority. For light reading there was always *Myths of the Twentieth Century* by the Reich's resident philosopher, Alfred Rosenberg.

Training exercises were made as realistic as possible – often frighteningly so with live ammunition and artillery fire. Inevitably, there were casualties and even fatalities. The Army, to whom the armed SS was, after all, supposed to be subordinate, protested vigorously. Himmler conceded that it was 'a shame to lose each good German lad' but went on to point out that 'every drop of blood in peacetime saves streams of blood in battle'.

There resulted a hard, heartless fighting animal: a deadly technician of dictatorship who, because he was totally uninhibited by any of the conventional 'rules of war', was often a decidedly more aggressive proposition than his Army counterpart.

Physical fitness through sport was encouraged, but what gave the armed SS its particular identity was not just its physical prowess. Among officers, NCOs and other ranks a sense of fellowship and mutual respect existed. This led to a form of democracy quite unknown in the Army. The traditionalists frowned on all this – at least openly. Many, however, confessed in private that they envied a form of comradeship that they would have found very attractive if it had existed when they were young soldiers.

17

But of course the SS Panzer Grenadier School at Keinschlag and later the SS Artillery School at Glau produced more than finely-tuned Fascist barbarians. The drift and impotence of the Weimar Republic, moribund with the class attitudes and barriers of the past, had produced a rootless, defeated generation. The armed SS helped to change all that. Even the private soldier was given a sense of purpose, of belonging. Himmler himself had written: 'The point is that in his attitude to discipline the man should not behave like an underling, that his gait, his hands, everything should correspond to the ideal which we set ourselves.'

Above all, serving in the SS was a career open to the man of ability and not one just from a caste; a quality of leadership was considered paramount. All potential officers had to serve at least two years in the ranks before they could even be considered for the military academies. Although obedience from superiors became second nature, the officers were not remote beings. Sepp Dietrich for example often ate with his men who discussed their personal problems with a frankness that would have been considered almost indecent in the Army.

Moreover, the men of the SS lived in conditions of some style that would have been envied by the troops of other countries used to sullen barrack blocks. The great showpiece was Lichterfelde Barracks which owed their existence to Dietrich who told Hitler that his men must have a setting worthy of them.

Lichterfelde was entered from a pleasant, tree-lined street. The main gate was dominated by two heroic-sized statues of German soldiers in overcoats and coal-scuttle helmets. At each corner of the enormous rectangle which made up Lichterfelde were large dormitory blocks, designated 'Adolf Hitler', 'Horst Wessel', 'Hermann Göring' and 'Hindenburg'. Within the rectangle were the classrooms and instructional facilities; there was a barracks chapel to which civilians from the Lichterfelde-West suburb were admitted on Sundays.

There was an enormous mess hall which absorbed up to 1,700 men at a single sitting. But still more striking was the dining hall of the officers' home. Even here where they ate and drank and where the mess parties were decidedly boisterous, the men of the Leibstandarte were not allowed to forget their Führer. He gazed down at them from an enormous oil portrait topped by a hand-wrought metal eagle.

Furnishings in the reception area of the barracks were of the finest oak, the walls inscribed with Nordic runes inlaid in silver, together with their translations. There were magnificent frescoes which lionised the achievements of Germany and, above all, of the Führer's own personal inspiration, Frederick the Great. Lichterfelde had some of the very finest stables in the whole of Germany, an underground shooting-range and a garage filled with the most modern equipment.

Hitler was almost childishly proud of this magnificent showpiece of his armed SS, and liked nothing better than showing foreign visitors around and regaling them for hours with his own highly individual view of world history and Germany's place in it.

A revolutionary barracks, certainly – but then it was a new sort of army that the architects of Nazism were anxious to create. While Himmler toyed with his racial fantasies, a former Reichswehr officer, now SS-Sturm-bannführer, Felix Steiner, dedicated himself to more practical matters. He was prepared to place himself in head-on opposition to the advocates of the 'old-fashioned' Army. A mass army, he argued, was outmoded: what the new German state demanded were mobile operational formations of élite troops of the highest class – a force which 'by blows of lightning rapidity would split the enemy in fragments and then destroy the dislocated remnants'. To create that sort of soldier entailed iron discipline in all things. That meant going on leave with a handkerchief folded with the required number of creases. If a paybook produced an unsightly bulge in a uniform, then the wearer was deprived of his pay.

If the recruit of the future Waffen-SS considered himself hard done by, his rigorous preliminary training was as nothing compared to what awaited him in the academies – if indeed he ever passed into them. If his record was considered worthy, he was permitted to take the SS oath and had the option of withdrawing if he wished to. A man not considered to have reached the required standard would be dismissed. At this stage Himmler could afford to be fastidious: the élite guard was not yet fighting a war where sheer weight of numbers would prove of paramount importance.

Critics of the armed SS were prepared to concede that these new-fangled paramilitary formations knew all about square-bashing and how to look smart, but surely when it came to the battlefield they would be severely out of their depth? Many of these critics did not know what went on at the infantry training schools. Here a man could be required to dig himself into the ground, knowing that within a prescribed time a tank would drive over him – whether or not the hole had been completed.

By the end of 1937 the military academies were producing around four hundred officers a year from original volunteers: men hardened by their aggressive training and ready for action. Neither were they to fail their Führer and SS-Reichsführer; by 1942, for example, nearly all of the first fifty-four cadets who had passed out of the Junkerschule Bad Tölz in 1934 had been killed.

Before and in the early stages of the war, these armed aristocrats of the new Germany were of a physical perfection that was everything Himmler desired. And of course they were racially spotless. From the end of 1935 all SS men were required to produce a record of ancestry, for other ranks back to 1800, for officers to 1750. A trace of Jewish blood, if discovered, meant instant expulsion.

To Sepp Dietrich of the Leibstandarte this was a

mixed blessing. A man could be a superb soldier with magnificent battle potential, but if it was discovered that his great-aunt had married a Jew, then he was ineligible for the SS. It was scarcely likely that the fact could be concealed: Himmler's files, his beloved files, bulged with minutiae pointing to possible racial traits. No one knew when the Reichsführer-SS, spectacles primly on nose, would pounce. Dietrich had more sense than to complain too stridently, but he was known to have grumbled: 'Some forty good specimens at least are kept from joining the Leibstandarte every year due to doubt concerning racial ancestry.'

The SS of course was to breed beautiful blond beasts for tomorrow. Therefore, any woman wishing to marry an SS man – fornication was frowned on – had to submit her ancestry for examination, as well as a photograph of herself in a bathing costume.

It all looked marvellous on paper. An SS instruction could outline with brisk no-nonsense: 'A decision to join the Führer's military force is equally nothing less than the expression of a voluntary determination to continue the present political struggle on another level.' The transformation from bodyguard duties to full military status might appear to have gone smoothly: in the Leibstandarte minimum enlistment was for four years for enlisted men, twelve for NCOs and twenty-five for officers. Rates of pay would, it was promised, correspond eventually to those of the Army.

And yet all was not well, and Hitler remained uneasy. There were still dissident elements in the Reich and there was still the slow, cautious, tradition-bound mentality of the 'old-style' soldier, typified by the officer corps that the Führer had always hated. Hitler was sensible enough to realise that he could not continue indefinitely putting everyone who disagreed with him up against a wall. This was Germany in the twentieth century, not France in the eighteenth. The tumbrils could not continue to roll without some word reaching the outside world and tarnishing the image of respectability that Hitler desperately craved. Other methods had to be found of putting the Army firmly in its place and making it less of a threat to the infant dictatorship. Obligingly, the Army was to provide the weapon for its own partial destruction.

2

Two of the most seemingly impregnable members of the old guard were Field Marshal Werner von Blomberg, the Minister of War, and General Werner von Fritsch, the Commander-in-Chief of the Army. Once again out came Himmler's files, to be scanned line by line by those blackened finger nails. The task of discrediting Blomberg and Fritsch was turned over to yet another branch of the SS, the SD (Sicherheitsdienst; Security Service). The SD went to work with dedication, the operation masterminded by one of Himmler's most deadly lieutenants, Reinhard Heydrich.

Most attention was concentrated on Blomberg. The Minister of War, it appeared, liked women. That was no crime in the Third Reich, but it could be a convenient blackmail weapon if the need arose. Blomberg, so Heydrich's agents soon discovered, was not over particular in his tastes, enjoying nothing so much as an evening in mufti around the more exotic of the Berlin nightspots. Needless to say, these expeditions from now on were shadowed by Heydrich's men.

By the autumn of 1937 Heydrich was able to report to Himmler that the Blomberg dossier was building up in a most satisfactory way. Then the SD was saved quite a lot of work when Blomberg put the pistol to his own head. He confided to Göring that he wanted to marry, as he delicately put it, 'a girl of the people'. There were complications, he explained. The lady in question already had a lover with whom she was maintaining a friendship. What should he do? Göring relished the role of adviser. He exuded bonhomie and, slapping Blomberg on the back, assured him that these affairs could be arranged quite easily by men of the world. A much-relieved Blomberg departed – presumably leaving the two-faced Göring to go straight to Hitler. Inevitably this choice titbit got to the ears of Himmler – and then Heydrich. Researches were instituted forthwith into the background of a certain Erna Gruhn.

What emerged was a story that would have delighted any journalist with an ear close to the gutter. Erna had indeed been 'a girl of the people', but not in the way Blomberg had meant. She had a record as a prostitute. That was bad enough; but then the agents of the SD stumbled across evidence that the lady had posed for indecent photographs.

That should have been enough for anyone. But soon Himmler was licking his lips even more; really, Blomberg had done all his work for him.

Erna Gruhn was undeniably interesting, but then so was her mother. This lady was well known to the Berlin police as the proprietor of an establishment masquerading as a massage parlour. Hitler reportedly flew into a horrified rage when he heard the news, particularly as Blomberg had already gone ahead and married Erna with the Führer and Göring as witnesses. Hitler's main concern was not so much with morality, but that he had been made to look a fool for not knowing of the background of the Field Marshal's young wife.

At first, the whole thing was kept discreetly within Army and Nazi circles, but soon the tide of rumour became a surge. A standard joke circulating in Berlin was that the Army was so low on talent that it was now recruiting girls from cafés, coffee shops, nightclubs and, of course, massage parlours.

Blomberg was confronted with evidence showing that his young wife was a tart with some rarified services to offer. This time Göring was present; a very different Göring, however. The bonhomie had departed; he was now a ruthless opportunist who had, all along, seen the enormous possibilities which the affair offered.

Coldly, he told Blomberg that he must resign. That, however, would have been an incomplete triumph for Hitler: no, Blomberg must be sacked with the maximum disgrace.

The dismissal and disgrace wrecked the career of Field Marshal Blomberg, whose name was stricken from the Army records. He and his wife settled in the Bavarian village of Weissee for the whole of World War II. His utter devotion to the wife who had inadvertently smashed his career would seem to be the only redeeming feature of this sleazy episode.

Blomberg had played into the hands of Himmler; Fritsch was the victim of a frame-up by the gangster state of Nazi Germany. This affair was to be even more sleazy than the indiscretions of the Minister of War. A sculptor, seeking a model to typify the General Staff Officer of the old school, could have done no better than pick on this Prussian aristocrat who had been a professional soldier since the age of eighteen. Fritsch had made the initial mistake of dismissing the Nazis as mere exuberant schoolboys whose excesses would be curbed eventually by their betters. On discovering his error, the General had switched to an attitude of outspoken contempt for the vulgarity of the Third Reich and the excesses of the SS. That was a mistake, too, but for different reasons.

In Nazi Germany, as in other countries, sexual offences, including homosexuality, came under the province of the civil police. The difference was that in Germany the Kripo (Kriminalpolizei; Civil Criminal Police) was responsible to Heydrich who had not been slow to see the potentialities of Paragraph 175 of the German Civil Code, which concerned homosexual offences. In 1934–35 a valuable titbit fell into the hands of the SD.

It seemed that a notorious criminal named Schmidt had been arrested, and had admitted that he had made a lucrative living from blackmailing well-known homosexuals. Some of the names Schmidt mentioned made even the well-informed members of the SD raise their eyebrows. But only one name interested them then. Schmidt alluded casually to an officer named 'von Frisch' or 'von Fritsch'. The blackmailer claimed to have seen an elderly gentleman wearing a monocle, a short coat with a fur collar, and carrying a silver-headed cane, entering Potsdam station. In the lavatory the officer had picked up a known homosexual and gone with him into a dark lane. Schmidt followed them and pounced at an appropriate moment.

The officer threatened and blustered but in the end agreed to pay Schmidt several hundred marks. Needless to say, there had been other blackmail demands since.

Once again Hitler was confronted with what looked like the makings of a first-class scandal. But Hitler was a superb tactician. To rub the Army's nose in it too obviously would alienate him from the officer corps. So in high dudgeon he stated that he did not wish to hear about 'such filth', and in any case did not believe it. Furthermore he ordered that the blackmailer's testimony be destroyed.

Possibly Hitler felt that Heydrich and his minions had gone too far. No doubt the Führer could also detect, not too far in the background, the hand of Heinrich Himmler on behalf of the SS and its ambitions.

Whatever the reason, Heydrich was not a man to pass up this chance. When Fritsch took some well-advised leave, Heydrich's agents followed him.

As the investigations progressed, the SD made a startling and decidedly awkward discovery. Whatever may or may not have been the truth about his sexual proclivities, Fritsch was *not* the man involved in the Potsdam station incident. The unfortunate blackmail victim in that case was named 'von Frisch'.

Heydrich's men had seemingly blundered. The Army was jubilant. This surely would spell the end of Hitler, the SS and the whole unsavoury band. Once again rumours gripped Berlin, and it was said that the Army was planning a takeover.

Hitler moved fast. At a court of inquiry the wretched Fritsch was found not guilty. By way of reparation he was hastily made an honorary colonel of his regiment. But the memory of his disgrace never left this taciturn but basically honourable Prussian. When war broke out in 1939 he was killed following his regiment into a suburb of Warsaw.

Then came the hasty announcement that Blomberg and Fritsch had resigned for 'reasons of health'. This did not stem the rumours, although it was a brave man who would have discussed such things in the possible hearing of the SS or the SD. In the case of Fritsch, it was widely alleged, the SD had even gone to the extent of bribing or threatening stables of homosexual youths to make false testimony.

As far as Himmler and the SS were concerned, the rumours were of no consequence. To the Reichsführer-SS the issue was simple: the Army had always stood in his way and had hated him. Now its power had been broken and the SS had emerged as a more formidable force than ever.

Hitler had used the indiscretions – or manufactured indiscretions – of the old school of officers to bring the Army under his direct control.

On 4 February 1938, Hitler stated that there would be no successor to Blomberg. Instead, he announced: 'Henceforth, I will personally exercise immediate command over all the armed forces. The former War Ministry becomes the High Command of the Armed

Forces (Oberkommando der Wehrmacht, or OKW) and comes directly under my command.'

From now on, Hitler's immediate lieutenants would be pliable characters who would carry out the Führer's demands, and would have little scruples as to what these might be. The new Commander-in-Chief of the Army, in succession to Fritsch, was Walther von Brauchitsch, a man who was no proof against the mercurial character of Hitler. One of the Führer's most ardent admirers was General Wilhelm Keitel, who became Chief of Staff of the newly created OKW, and was to be one of the very few senior Nazis who held the same job from the beginning of the war until its end.

A clutch of generals who might have proved tiresome if kept in their jobs were dismissed. Göring, somewhat disgruntled that his role in the Blomberg-Fritsch affair had not been given what he considered proper recognition, was mollified with yet another baton to add to his collection. He became a Field Marshal.

Hitler had routed a good deal of the opposition and had cleared the decks for an infinitely more aggressive foreign policy. The Army had been the last stronghold of independent power with the capacity to challenge the Nazis.

The instrument of its immolation was the SS. The initiative had passed into new hands in Nazi Germany; tomorrow belonged to Heinrich Himmler.

The oath which had been sworn by the Leibstandarte, and subsequently by every man who entered the ranks of the SS, had held profoundly important implications for the future of all the armed forces in Germany.

Hitler had personally laid claim to the hearts and minds of all who served him. The son of an Austrian customs official, he had been a down-and-out in Vienna and a denizen of its numerous flop-houses, and eventually a gas-stricken lance-corporal in the 16th Reserve Bavarian

Infantry of the Kaiser. He had now risen to be dictator of Germany: a man with an historic mission who was not going to be deflected by any old-fashioned notions of law or morality.

Hitler's various 'private armies' – the Leibstandarte, the SS-VT and the Totenkopfverbände – greatly worried the hard core of the Army which had managed to survive. Hitler hastened to assure the officer corps that the crack Leibstandarte, used to quell Ernst Röhm, was his own personal security force. The SS-VT was not envisaged as having a military role. In August 1935 the Führer assured worried Army chiefs that they were to be 'the sole bearer of arms'.

Himmler, keeping his own ambitions under wraps, gave Hitler a certain degree of support, and in 1936 claimed to be quite prepared for the Wehrmacht to guarantee 'the safety of the honour, the greatness and the peace of the Reich from the exterior'.

As far as the SS-VT was concerned, the Army – always provided, of course, that it behaved itself – was to be allowed a fair degree of control over the Special Purpose Troops. True, in the event of war, SS-VT formations would buttress the armed forces and would be subject to their commands.

It appeared therefore that each group had its own watertight function, but Germany was still at peace. The reality of the battlefield was to change all this; for the moment the Army professed itself reassured.

In 1936, though, cracks began to appear. It was suddenly realised that there was a fine shade of distinction between being involved in domestic anti-terrorist duties at home and suddenly having to switch to military duties. For example, on 7 March 1936, the Leibstandarte had played a leading role in Hitler's first act of belligerence outside Germany, the reoccupation of the Rhineland, that part of the Reich which bordered Belgium, Luxembourg and France.

In 1918 the Treaty of Versailles had stipulated that the

Rhineland, although remaining German, was to be occupied by Allied troops for fifteen years, and that a thirty-mile-wide demilitarised zone was to be created on the right bank of the river. The permanence of the demilitarised zone had been emphasised by the Treaties of Locarno in 1925, but after the advent of Hitler, relations on the whole question became strained. The Führer alleged that the French were planning the encirclement of Germany, and he ordered his troops to take up positions in the demilitarised zone. The British and the French, preoccupied at the time with Mussolini's war in Abyssinia, contented themselves with empty protests.

The Army had been uneasy over such an act of naked aggression. Hitler, never one to mince words, proclaimed: 'If the Army is reluctant to lead the way, a suitable spearhead will be provided by the Leibstandarte.'

And so it was that on the early morning of 7 March 1936 a company moved across the Rhine and proceeded unopposed to Saarbrücken on the French border. A local newspaper marked the event with a florid headline: 'Hitler's men – they are gods come to show us the way to the new Germany.'

As a military operation – three German battalions across the Rhine bridges – it was a puny affair compared to what the vast military machine of Nazi Germany was capable of some while later, but it was a sharp illustration of the way Hitler's mind was working.

The next act in a drama which was leading inexorably to the outbreak of World War II was once again to see the favoured Leibstandarte in a leading role. On 12 March 1938, Hitler set off for his native Austria as a conquering hero. He received a tumultuous welcome as he proclaimed that his earthly mission had been fulfilled – to return Austria to Germany. Two days later he was in Vienna, the old Imperial capital which he felt had consigned him to the gutter in his youth, but was now strewing flowers in his path.

This was the city that he had always deeply hated. In *Mein Kampf* (*My Struggle*) he had fulminated: 'This motley collection of Czechs, Poles, Hungarians, Ruthenians, Serbs and Croats and always . . . the Jew, here there and everywhere – the whole spectacle was repugnant to me . . . The longer I lived in that city, the stronger became my hatred for the promiscuous swarm of foreign peoples which had begun to batten on that old nursery ground of German culture.'

The union of Austria with Germany had long been a dream of many people in the two countries sharing a common language. After the dissolution of the Holy Roman Empire in 1806, and until 1918, Austria had been the head of a separate vast empire under the Habsburg monarchy, and when that in turn was dissolved there were certain fresh yearnings for unity with Germany. Austria, shorn of its power and provinces, had felt lonely, powerless and not a little apprehensive in the post-war world. Hitler's Germany, seemingly prosperous and set firmly on the road to expansion, appeared to many to offer the security Austria badly lacked.

Into Austria with Hitler went the sinister figure of Reinhard Heydrich and the whole bureaucracy of Nazi terror. The apparently delirious, almost hysterical reception which the Führer received in the streets concealed the other side of the story: the knock on the door at midnight, the arrest and disappearance of thousands of 'unreliables'.

And the military role? According to Hitler's plans, units of the German Army and the SS-VT were to be despatched to Austria to 'establish constitutional conditions'.

In charge of the motorised elements of the invasion force was Major-General Heinz Guderian, recently appointed Commander of these elements of the invasion force. He was informed by General Ludwig Beck, Chief of the Army General Staff, that his forces were to include his earlier Command, 2nd Panzer Division, and the

Leibstandarte SS Adolf Hitler – the latter at the express and personal order of the Führer.

Shortly before midnight on the 12th, Guderian in Berlin communicated the news of the mobilisation direct to Sepp Dietrich. Guderian secured Hitler's permission to bedeck the tanks with green foliage – an earnest of the peaceful intentions of the invader.

The assembly area for 16th Corps was Passau at the point where the Danube and Inn rivers join, and just over the border from Upper Austria. At 9.00 am, Guderian's columns began to flow across the frontier with Dietrich's Leibstandarte bringing up the rear. By noon Guderian's Corps had reached Linz and remained there for Hitler's triumphant entry into the city. The black-and-silver uniforms with the distinctive white belts and the SS runes on the right collar made the Leibstandarte stand out, both eyecatching and sinister.

The sinister side was something that propaganda tended to play down – but it was there nonetheless. By the time World War II arrived, the Austrians were to get more than an indication of what to 'establish constitutional conditions' could mean. The role of the armed SS in Austria was a small one; a single instance of behind-the-scenes terror need suffice.

As late as 14 November 1939 a report was forwarded from the SD in Vienna to SD, Berlin: 'Mobile detachments of the Verfügungstruppe drove up to the synagogues and placed stocks of hand-grenades in position preparatory to setting fire to buildings.'

But this was still some time off on the day of Hitler's *Anschluss* (Union with Germany). The SS, along with everyone else from Germany, was regarded by many almost as angels – black angels maybe, but among the men of the Leibstandarte there seemed almost a festive air about this first act of conquest.

Could it be that their mere presence was all that was required? After all, had not the Führer walked through what was virtually his back door without the slightest trace of opposition?

The Leibstandarte, which was to remain in Vienna until April, could reflect with not a little contemptuous satisfaction that it had showed up well in comparison with the Army. The much vaunted Panzer (armoured) units had experienced mechanical trouble on the road from Salzburg to Vienna, and had been stranded. Angrily Guderian denied this and defended the troops by saying that the breakdowns were trivial. But, whatever the truth, the Leibstandarte troops had covered no less than six hundred miles in some forty-eight hours. Co-operation with the Army had been total. And Guderian pronounced himself pleased with the SS-VT.

He was not the only one in a good mood. Hitler had been delighted with the scarcely credible ease of the entire Austrian Anschluss. The reception he had in Vienna and elsewhere intoxicated the Führer; he became decidely more amenable to a modest increase in the strength of the armed SS. Himmler, who had never stopped bothering him on the subject, was to be allowed a little more power. For the SS-VT, he created a new regiment named Der Führer. It was composed largely of Austrians and was stationed in Vienna and Klagenfurt. Another Totkenkopf regiment was also set up, bringing the strength of the Totenkopfverbände to some 8,500 men.

Although Hitler was keen to stress that the armed SS should never forget that ultimate authority was vested in the Army, he was now setting out to put the record straight and (in the words of a highly important top secret decree of 17 August 1938) to 'delineate the common tasks of the SS and the Wehrmacht'.

It was very necessary. There had been many jealous mutterings in the Army about the relationship of the SS-VT to the Army. It could with fair accuracy be described as cool; at times it was downright hostile.

By 1938 the rivalry was getting decidely awkward.

Hitler, for obvious reasons, did not want the SS-VT competing with the Army. Hence the need for the directive. The SS-VT was, he stated flatly, to form no part of the Wehrmacht or of the police. 'It is a permanent armed force at my disposal.' In ideological, political terms, and in a domestic role, it was to be in the hands of Himmler. If the Army wanted to make use of the SS-VT within the Army framework, than the SS-VT would be subject to military law and instructions.

That, on paper at least, was the position of the Verfügungstruppe (soon to be swallowed up by the Waffen-SS whose title was not yet official). There is no reason to suppose that at this time Hitler wanted it any other way. But this was peacetime. Decrees could be made, laws passed and orders given without outside pressures. But war, like politics, was the art of the possible. Hitler, buffeted by the fortunes of the battlefield, was to commit more and more of his armed SS to the frontline, and to give them increasing powers. Realities of combat ultimately outweighed all theories and desk plans.

All this lay ahead, but there were indications of how Himmler's power was to grow and one item of the Führer's directive must have struck fear in the minds of many. Himmler's emotions can only be described as those of delirious joy.

The paramilitary Totenkopfverbande, made up originally of concentration-camp guards, had already grown into the strength of several battalions. It would, said the directive with grisly delicacy, be maintained 'to clear up special tasks of a police nature'. It would also reinforce the SS-VT with volunteers and picked men.

Hitler considered that he had tidied things up very nicely. The more questionable elements in the Army had been got rid of without too much scandal; the feathers of the officer corps would be a little less ruffled now that it had been made clear that the SS-VT was under the ultimate control of the Army. As for Austria, what had the little mice among the Allies done about it? Precisely nothing! It was now time to move on to something else.

Next came the turn of Czechoslovakia. It had all the characteristics necessary for conquest by the Nazis.

The Czechs, so Hitler's argument ran, were racial inferiors. Their country, as a modern state, was the creation of the hated peace treaties. Their constitution was democratic. The country had treaties with France and Italy, had an efficient army, the Skoda armaments factories and strongly built fortress defences along the frontier with Germany. In addition Berlin itself was in easy reach of Czech airfields. The conclusion was obvious: Czechoslovakia must be destroyed.

The country contained a German minority of something over three million. These Germans or Sudetens – from the name of the area along the frontier where they lived – had been subjects of the old Austrian Empire, but had never been subjects of the recent German Reich. Nevertheless this did not stop the massive machinery of Nazi propaganda humming. The tune this time was 'Come home to the Reich'. There was a Sudeten Nazi party in existence which was being subsidised by Germany. The Czech government tried hard to make a satisfactory accommodation with the Sudeten leader, the former gymnastics instructor Konrad Henlein, who as early as 1935 had demanded 'full liberty for Germans to proclaim their Germanism and their adherence to the ideology of Germans'.

In February 1938 Hitler fanned the flames when he addressed the Reichstag and called attention to 'the horrible conditions of the German brethren in Czechoslovakia'. This rhetoric was, predictably, orchestrated by the Nazi press which denounced a whole string of atrocities against the Sudeten Germans by the Czechs.

The stage was set for the execution of Czechoslovakia and the Allies proved themselves utterly powerless; indeed the French and the British at Munich virtually gave Hitler *carte blanche* to annexe the Bohemian Germans.

In the military adventure which followed, the armed

34

SS was for the first time to be employed in a military role at more than token strength. During the German mobilisation preceding the occupation of the Sudetenland in October, four SS Totenkopf battalions and the entire SS-VT were, on the direct orders of Hitler, placed under the Army's command.

Three SS regiments – Leibstandarte Adolf Hitler, Germania and Deutschland – actually took part in the occupation, while two battalions of the SS Totenkopf Regiment Oberbayern, which had been operating on Czech soil in support of the SS-controlled Henlein Freikorps even before the invasion, were also made part of the occupation Army.

Things were still very far from being well between the Army and the SS, who were regarded openly as interlopers. The role of Himmler's men in the Czech occupation was still small, but both the Reichsführer-SS and Hitler were determined that the conventional military were not to overlook it. A draft Order of the Day which announced the successful completion of the Sudeten operation was amended specifically to include the SS and the SA.

The OKW had unbent only to the extent of mentioning 'the Army, Air Force and the Police'. That was very far from being enough for Hitler whose version of the order, later released to the press, stated specifically that 'the operation was carried out by units of the Army, the Air Force, the Police, the Armed SS (SS Verfügungstruppe), the SS and SA'.

The Army had been put in its place, and with some justification. After all, the three regiments *had* taken part, admittedly largely to fill gaps in the number of the Panzer divisions. But no more could they be regarded as the spit-and-polish, exquisitely tailored dummies, as depicted so often with a sneer by the Wehrmacht.

With the help of the SS, German troops poured into Bohemia and Moravia at 6 am on 15 March 1939. Hitler slept that very night at Hradcany Castle, ancient seat of the kings of Bohemia. The next day, the Führer proclaimed his Protectorate. The shadow of Himmler fell across a conquered land: he made the notorious Karl Hermann Frank, a fanatical Sudeten German, chief of police and an officer in the SS. The long night of terror for the Czechs, 'the degenerate Slavs', had begun.

As the war progressed, that terror became even more pronounced and was eventually to be total. Within two years of the Czech operation, memoranda like this, submitted as evidence at the Nuremberg Trials, were to become only too common:

Kommandoamt of the Waffen-SS   Berlin –
(Command Office)   Wilmersdorf 14
    Kaiserallee 188
    14 October 1941

Sect Ia
NR. 4116/41 Geh.   *SECRET*

SUBJ: Intermediate report on the civilian state of emergency.

TO: The Reichsführer-SS

I deliver the following report regarding the commitment of the Waffen-SS in the Protectorate Bohemia and Moravia during the civilian state of emergency:

In the mutual changes, all Battalions of the Waffen-SS in the Protectorate Bohemia and Moravia will be brought forth for shootings and the supervision of hangings.

Up to now there has occurred:

In Prague:
99 shootings
21 hangings

In Bruenn:
54 shootings
17 hangings

Total: 191 executions (including 16 Jews)

A complete report regarding other measures and on the conduct of the officers, non-coms and men will be made following the termination of the civilian state of emergency.

Official stamp of   signed
Personal Staff of
Reichsführer-SS   JUETTNER

SS Grupppenführer
(Major General)
and Generalleutnant
of the Waffen-SS

Immediately after the Czech occupation the training of the armed SS was intensified. It is doubtful whether at this time even Hitler was really aware of the true calibre of the crack fighting machine he had ordered Himmler and his lieutenants to set up. The Reichsführer-SS was determined that his chief should be left in no doubt. When he told Hitler 'These are men who glory in battle', he was telling the truth.

During the early summer of 1939, Adolf Hitler, accompanied by Himmler and various high-ranking OKW officers, visited a combat exercise of the SS-VT. The star of this particular event was SS Regiment Deutschland and it was required to carry out at the Münsterlager manoeuvre grounds a full-scale assault on a prepared defensive position. Here was no popgun pantomime of the type that might have formed an amusing diversion at a military tournament. Supported by actual barrages from Army military batteries, the SS troops used live ammunition.

The whole enterprise was, of course, designed to impress Hitler. It worked even beyond the wildest dreams of Heinrich Himmler. According to eyewitnesses, Hitler watched with open-mouthed astonishment. The former corporal from the trenches of World War I knew front-line combat when he saw it. He gasped: 'Only with such soldiers is this sort of thing possible.'

The demonstration had an even more salutary outcome. Orders soon came that the SS-VT was to be provided with the equipment necessary to make it an SS regiment of artillery, integrated, it was stressed, with the Army.

On the morning of 1 September 1939, Adolf Hitler drove from the Chancellery to the ornate hall of the Kroll Opera House – on the very day that German armies were pouring across the Polish frontier and converging on Warsaw. Overhead the might of Göring's Luftwaffe rained bombs on soldiers and civilians alike.

Hitler declared: 'From now on I am just the first soldier of the German Reich. I have once again put on that coat that was the most sacred and dear to me. I will not survive the outcome.'

The Führer's uniform was not the customary brown jacket familiar to millions, but a field-grey uniform blouse. It bore a distinct resemblance to those worn by officers of the armed SS.

The invasion of Poland, which was to unleash World War II, was undertaken in a very different atmosphere from that which had accompanied the rape of the Czechs. 'The little worms', as Hitler had called the leaders of France and Britain, had done nothing when the Nazi heel had crushed down so ruthlessly on Prague. This time, Britain had made guarantees not only to Poland but to Greece and Rumania; France had echoed them. Appeasement was at an end.

Undoubtedly, the happiest man in Nazi Germany was Heinrich Himmler. At last, the power of his SS was growing and with it his own prestige as a statesman. Himmler's almost childish delight in his own achievements in building up the Schutzstaffel was never to leave him. As late as 1943, when the tide was already turning ominously against the Reich, he was able to describe to assembled senior officers of the SS how 'fantastic' had been the expansion of the armed branch after the outbreak of war; it had been carried out 'at an absolutely terrific speed'.

In 1939, Himmler explained, the armed SS had consisted of only 'a few regiments, guard units, 8,000 to 9,000 strong – that is not even a division; all in all, 25,000 to 28,000 men at most'. Yet the war was only a year old and the strength had become 150,000 men. It was an expansion that was soon to establish the armed SS 'as the fourth branch of the Wehrmacht'.

The invasion of Poland was short, sharp and bitter. The contribution of the armed SS, when viewed overall, was small – an adjective that must bring a wry smile to survivors of what was a nightmarish campaign, and which showed once and for all that the men of the armed SS were among the most brave as well as heartless fighting units that any military machine had ever produced.

The SS Regiment Deutschland, the newly created artillery regiment, the SS Reconnaissance Battalion (Aufklärungs Sturmbann) and an Army tank regiment were brought together to form the 4th Panzer Brigade, commanded by an Army staff of which Major General Werner Kempf was the Commander. The SS Regiment Germania was attached to the 14th Army massing in the southern part of East Prussia. Another regiment battle group was made up of members of the Leibstandarte and supported by the SS Combat Engineer Battalion (SS Pioneer Sturmbann) which formed part of General Walter von Reichenau's 10th Army, moving into Poland from Silesia. The SS Totenkopf Sturmbann Götze, which had been formed originally for operations of a 'police nature' in and around Danzig, became a reinforced infantry battalion, Heimwehr Danzig, and was sent into battle under Army command.

On 29 August 1939, Hitler had summoned the three leading representatives of his armed forces – Walther von Brauchitsch, Hermann Göring, Grand Admiral Raeder – together with the Army commanders, to his mountain villa in the Obersalzberg. The gathering followed a predictable pattern with the Führer doing most of the talking. Furthermore, he talked at very great length, holding forth for a full two hours before releasing his wilting underlings for a brief lunch.

What the harangue actually amounted to was an announcement that Foreign Minister Ribbentrop had been sent to Moscow to sign a non-aggression pact which would lead to the carve-up of Poland. As far as his plans for that unhappy country were concerned, Hitler made it clear that it would be isolated, attacked and generally blasted out of existence in just four days. Hitler envisaged a new German eastern frontier and possibly a protectorate state as a buffer against Russia.

The SS, Hitler further proclaimed, would be expected to carry out 'special tasks'. Just what these tasks were remained somewhat vague, but the Führer stressed that 'they would not be to the taste of German generals'. Hitler then gave a sinister clue by stating that the Army had its instructions: to get on with smashing Poland with the forces at its disposal. Anything that the SS did was strictly its own business, particularly among the Polish intelligentsia and church leaders.

There had never been anything but a poor outlook for Poland. The predicament of its army could only be described as dire. The material which the Polish commanders had at their disposal was mostly slow-moving, foot-marching infantry. Alongside thirty Polish infantry divisions there were only two motorised brigades and eleven cavalry brigades.

And the Germans? From north and south two gigantic Army groups were to strike in a three-pronged operation. The Polish Field Army was to be encircled in a double envelopment east and west of Warsaw. It would then be held and destroyed in a killing-ground in the bend of the Vistula river. The third stage would be the seizing of Warsaw and its fortress areas.

Throughout that menacing summer of 1939 the vast might of the German Army confronted the Poles. The Poles had only nine companies of 8-ton tanks and twenty-nine companies of armoured weapon carriers. Ninety-two per cent of their military wheeled transport was horse-drawn.

On 30 August the German High Command sent out the code-words which set action-day as 1 September and H-hour as 04.45 hours. Under the light of a waning moon the Army commanders kept their eyes firmly on their watches which were ticking away the last precious hours of peace. Then positions were being taken up for the first stage of the campaign in an inexorably moving river of men and machines. Long columns of guns, vehicles and men surged forward towards Poland.

All was quiet now. The last cigarettes were extinguished along with the headlights of the leading vehicles, and the formations merged into the dark forests enclosing the concentration and assembly areas. The assault detachments were positioned.

Thus had been set in motion a campaign which was to catapult at a sadly defenceless Poland a terrifying strike-force of fifty-five divisions, including every armoured, motorised and light division that the Reich possessed. The countryside in which they were to fight might almost have been made for them. It was open and rolling terrain: ideal for tanks whose commanders itched impatiently for the word of command to roll.

The SS military honours in the Polish campaign must go largely, if not exclusively, to the Leibstandarte which was part of Army Group South. The fighting record of some SS formations was to be bitterly criticised by certain sections of the Army, but the spectacular showing of Hitler's élite guard was not in dispute; its services were called on early in the campaign. The group Commander, von Rundstedt, badly needed extra reconnaissance strength for his 10th Army's left wing. Leibstandarte was quickly infiltrated into the line to act as a link between 8th and 10th Armies.

Its brief was to approach from Breslau and slice through the fortified frontier line, grabbing an important height behind the Prosna river.

To the eager, clean-limbed products of the barrack squares and the academies, all those months of cruelly vigorous training made sense at last. There was no fear at the sight of the menacing 37 mm anti-tank guns of the Polish 10th Infantry Division which barred the way and put up a fierce resistance. The SS troops crossed the river and punched into the frontier positions. Now there was nothing to stop the infantry assault upon the heights. The Leibstandarte kept going, knifing with ease and speed through intense Polish fire and fortifications.

It had been a testing, daunting baptism of fire, but Adolf Hitler's 'black angels' came through it with particular distinction; the Poles were swept away in devastating disorder.

Then it was on to the next objective, the town of Boleslavecz. Here the Poles stood and fought the Leibstandarte. If the Polish horses looked as if they had strayed out of the 1914 war, the fighting methods of the soldiers seemed to hark back a century or so.

Vast waves of Poles in their khaki uniforms hurled themselves at the Leibstandarte, their officers yelling the battle cry 'Forward'. The men attacked in line after line, bayonets suddenly flashing for bouts of hand-to-hand combat. Losses for the Poles were appalling; by 10.00 hours the town was in the hands of the Germans and dispirited columns were surrendering in droves.

However, the Poles were to be no easy enemies, even

for the SS. Their countryside was ideal for defence and the troops knew the sort of cover which they could exploit to the full. Not a clump of bushes was neglected that could conceal a man with a machine-gun. If the methods of the Leibstandarte were brutal, so was the reaction of the Polish troops. For instance, at the small market town of Pabianice, a road and railway junction on the river Ner, which was on the way to the Lodz region, the SS encountered a garrison with a healthy complement of heavy tank guns. These Polish troops were in belligerent mood and soon they had marshalled posses of riflemen who knew the wooded area intimately and were able to bring into play the skills of the huntsmen. These well-camouflaged fighters became adept at picking off single motor-cycle despatch riders or staff cars without escort.

While the Leibstandarte was fighting with implacable bravery well matched by its hopelessly outnumbered opponents, the overall strategic plan of the German High Command was yielding highly satisfactory results. The 10th Army had cut as a knife through butter north of Chestakova and on 3 September units from two Panzer divisions, slicing through a gap between the Lodz and Cracow armies, stormed across the Pilica river and headed north-eastward in a rapid advance towards Warsaw. The Polish armies around the west of the capital were now to feel the jaws of the pincers slowly but surely snap down on them.

Slowly but surely because the resistance of the Poles continued to be fierce and unrelenting. The Lodz region, an area with vast fields containing a riot of sunflowers and maize, was perfect cover for the men with the Eagle of Poland symbol in their field caps. They knew the land and they stood and fought; often there were small groups, even individuals, stalking each other through tall plants, like avenging gunmen in a Western.

The Poles became expert at holding their fire until an eager member of the Leibstandarte was at point-blank range. Inevitably, though, sheer weight of numbers began to tell and it was not very long before the Germans became wise to the Poles' tactics.

But soon the Leibstandarte was remembering all its earlier training in camouflage and was able to take a leaf out of the Poles' book when it came to patience. The enemy in the maize field had to show himself at some time and when he did he was picked off with ease.

The 23rd Panzer Regiment had been confident of plucking the particular plum of Pabianice for itself, but the Poles had proved adept at dealing serious blows to the Mark I and Mark II tanks and the more heavily armoured Mark III and Mark IV. Indeed, these tanks had found the going very heavy indeed.

There was nothing for it; the Panzers would have to be withdrawn and their place taken by the SS. Swift set-piece attacks were just the thing for which the Leibstandarte had been trained. Hand-picked, hard-trained troops – 1st and 2nd Companies of Hitler's élite – overcame all resistance with astonishing speed. They continued walking through a hail of bullets and shells from automatic weapons, field guns and anti-tank weapons. The Poles went on fighting like tigers and at one time it seemed that they might wear down the SS advance. The Poles threw in all available resources for counter attacks with the prime object of holding the town.

Infantry and cavalry were strained to the uttermost and the Leibstandarte found itself edged back – at one point dangerously near the field in which its HQ was situated. But the Poles in fact were only putting off the inevitable hour and there came a point when the Leibstandarte defence was able to stand firm.

Even now there was no admission of defeat. The Poles are a proud race and never looked prouder than on this day. Indeed, one German eye-witness scarcely concealed his admiration when he stated later: 'They came with their heads held high as if they were swimmers breasting the waves.'

They walked through the German fire, trampling over the bodies of their dead comrades, but they fell thick and fast under a relentless barrage. The Pabianice garrison went into death and captivity in a blaze of glory, and their equally brave and resourceful opponents, though they gave no quarter and expected none, admired them for it.

The speed and ruthless efficiency of Blitzkrieg (lightning war) allowed for no pity, but the tragedy of the ultimate Polish defeat was manifest in the terrible scenes of carnage which accompanied it.

The Leibstandarte had moved on. This time, 1st Battalion had orders to deal a decisive blow at Oltarzev, a town on the road to Warsaw. The other two battalions were positioned to capture Blonie which was also on the road to the Polish capital – a road which the Poles were desperately anxious to keep open.

By now it was evening and the mist which gathered was made even more of a hazard by the smoke from the guns. Through this miasma catapulted the troops of horse artillery, but for the Poles it was nothing but a death ride.

The butchery was total; it enveloped not only horses and men. Victims also were the civilians and refugees who had been withdrawing, hopeful of cover from the Polish troops. But now they all lay dead and dying along the road which was so soon to be lost. The reduction of the Polish divisions continued and in every significant phase of the adventure there was a role for the Leibstandarte.

It was in the forefront, for instance, of the lorry-borne assault crossing the Bzura river where it was fully integrated with 35th Panzer Regiment and 12th Rifle Regiment. This mechanised might did not even wait for the engineers who were working feverishly to construct a convenient bridge for it. From the eastern bank, in plunged the armoured vehicles, wading straight into a barrage of Polish artillery.

For a time things looked decidedly ugly – not helped by the sudden change in the weather and the onset of rain which muddied hopelessly the exits from the Bzura river. News came that part of 36th Panzer Regiment and 1st SS Battalion had encountered heavy resistance and was in danger of being overrun. Furthermore, ammunition and petrol were in short supply. The Leibstandarte swooped to the rescue. Two battalions and 35th Panzer attacked with such precision that within an hour the threat had been seen off decisively. Indeed, the constant harrying by artillery and Luftwaffe were beginning to signal the end for the entire Polish army. The final battles were fought for the possession of the road near the Vistula river in the north, which connected with Warsaw.

The scenes were sickeningly familiar: the dead and the dying, the smashed carts, the blackened vehicles, the screams of the horses which went on ceaselessly because no one was left alive to put the animals out of their hideous misery. Above it all rose a cloying stench; the weather had changed yet again and the corpses blackened under the rays of the sun.

It was to be nearly a month before the rain came again, but by then the campaign in Poland was over and Warsaw had surrendered.

On 25 September, Hitler visited detachments of the Leibstandarte and inspected No. 13 Company in encampment near Guzov. Now Hitler's Guard was ordered to move. Rumours began to course through the ranks that they would all be on the Western Front within days. Instead, though, they were sent to Prague for recuperation, there was work indeed for the Leibstandarte. Its men would need all their strength for the battles that lay ahead.

The first campaign of the armed SS of any significance had been highly creditable, but the Army was far from willing to give unqualified praise. The fact that the Leibstandarte had been needed to help out the 23rd Panzer Regiment at Pabianice did not endear it to the diehards.

In addition there had been widespread and quite genuine disgust in certain sections of the Army over a number of atrocities allegedly committed by the armed SS. The most notorious of these in Poland concerned a sergeant-major in the Military Police, assisted by a gunner from the SS Artillery Regiment, who had collected fifty Jews in a synagogue and then shot them.

Both men, it seemed, had carried out the slaughter for no better reason that they had not known what to do with the Jews. The local Army commander had insisted that the men be tried by court-martial. Although the prosecution demanded the death penalty, the two men in fact served only short prison sentences for manslaughter – even these were commuted after strong pressure from Himmler.

The Reichsführer-SS went even further. He prevailed on Hitler to amend certain sections of previous decrees which placed the armed SS under the jurisdiction of military courts during wartime.

On 17 October 1939 there appeared the 'Decree relating to a Special Jurisdiction in Penal Matters for Members of the SS and for Members of Police Groups on Special Tasks'. It was the work of the Ministerial Council for Defence of the Reich. Its purpose can be summed up quickly: to free the armed SS from the legal jurisdiction of the Wehrmacht.

To critics it was pointed out soothingly that members of the SS were still subject to the provisions of the military code. A particularly brave critic, though, might have riposted by asking: *Which* military code? Courts martial of the SS were now the job of SS courts, not military ones. And SS courts martial were, as was only natural, staffed only by those previously approved by the Reichsführer-SS . . .

Certainly the SS was beginning to make itself felt in the few countries which Hitler had occupied so far. But the role of the armed Schutzstaffel was still very small. There had been only eighteen thousand fighting men of the SS in Poland, distributed between the Leibstandarte, Totenkopf and Verfügungstruppe. The vast majority of these were withdrawn after the ceasefire and, although three regiments of Theodor Eicke's Totenkopfverbände, numbering some 7,400 men, were kept for a time in Poland, they left eventually and were replaced by German policemen who were too old to be conscripted for the Army. The Leibstandarte and the rest were going to have to wait a little longer for the bulk of the action and a fair share of the glory.

Himmler, his intelligence fogged by Nordic mists, was delighted to receive from his Führer permission to increase the number of SS divisions from one to three. The Reichsführer, however, may not have appreciated that ideological considerations were very far from being Hitler's motive. Himmler, herbalist and racial crank, could afford to dream. Hitler, with a war to prosecute, could not. He wanted soldiers itching for battle.

3

Himmler set about raising the new formations with his customary zeal. But soon he found himself severely frustrated. The barrier was the Army which made it clear that there were to be strong limits on the independence of the armed élite. The Army had an enormous say in the whole question of recruiting, backed by legal machinery. The Reich recruiting laws laid down specifically that no German of military age could join the armed services until he had been given clearance by the local military establishment. That clearance would be determined only by the needs of the Army, Navy and Air Force. In other words, no provision whatever was made for the SS!

Himmler and his minions could extol endlessly the virtues of the SS. They could and did conduct the most vigorous recruiting campaigns, but this could not conceal from volunteers that there was no guarantee for them whatever of a posting. That would depend very much on the goodwill of the Wehrmacht – an emotion in somewhat short supply after the Polish campaign.

Heinrich Himmler, despite the awesome power which he was to gather before the war's end, had a massive social inferiority complex. He regarded the Army, of which he had scant experience, with a mixture of respect and contempt; to take it on became a personal challenge.

The Army was prepared to unbend only to the extent of limiting the SS to recruits who would fill out its prescribed 'division' strength. The announcement of the raising of two new divisions altered things somewhat: volunteers were indeed thrown in the direction of Himmler's upstarts. But what was the use of raw recruits on the eve of a major war?

The question remained: how was it possible to get round those irritatingly restrictive laws which prevented the SS from taking its rightful place in the fighting ranks of the Führer's anointed? More specifically, how was it possible to procure a manpower supply already partly trained for combat?

The answer of Himmler and his recruiting chief, SS Brigadeführer Gottlob Berger, was of classic simplicity. It would, if it succeeded, bring into being two battle-worthy divisions in time for the forthcoming campaign in the west and, simultaneously, double the strength of the armed SS.

And, what was particularly exquisite to Himmler, there was not a thing that the Army could do about it!

As Reichsführer-SS and Chief of the German Police, Himmler would simply transfer sufficient Totenkopf and police personnel – neither group was under military jurisdiction – to the armed SS for the purpose of manning the two divisions. Then the SS would go ahead and recruit splendid young Nordic specimens to bring the Totenkopf and police formations back to strength. The plan had all the hallmarks of the first-class civil service mind undoubtedly possessed by Heinrich Himmler; he knew how to manipulate a set of rules in favour of his own empire in the making.

Hitler's decree of 18 May 1939 enabled Himmler to call up older men on the outbreak of war to replace the permanent units of concentration camp guards. These units, particularly Totenkopf 1st, 2nd, and 3rd Regiments were drafted into the second of the new divisions (to be called Totenkopf) and their place was taken by newly formed units of volunteers. There was now a reserve pool for the field divisions – and one over which the Wehrmacht had no control.

The 3rd Division was the least satisfactory. Somewhat bewildered policemen found themselves forced into field-grey and faced with vigorous military training, a good deal of it decidedly beyond their advanced years: the Division, called Polizei, was not to be counted among the élite.

SS Brigadeführer Berger, who had already shown impressive organisational ability during the Sudeten occupation, busied himself in the closing weeks of 1939 with setting up the Waffen-SS Recruiting Office, although in fact the title 'Waffen-SS' was not yet official. Recruiting stations mushroomed across Germany and the aim was obviously to set up a recruiting organisation which exactly paralleled that of the Army.

The old rumblings between Army and SS continued, most of the bitterness this time surrounding the Totenkopf units which the Army flatly refused to recognise as soldiers. This blank refusal defeated even Himmler who took it as a personal slight. In fact, the precise status of the Totenkopf formations could not have mattered less to Hitler – what was important to him was their strength, and that was considerable. By June 1940 nearly thirty thousand men were serving in these units and, even before the war was half over, most of the Totenkopf personnel, like their 6,500 colleagues in the Totenkopf Division, were serving in the field units of the Waffen-SS.

The situation was intriguing, to say the least, for these units came under the ultimate control of an Army which refused to recognise their existence!

Indeed, many former members of the German Army and of the Waffen-SS have claimed since the war that they did not even know of the existence of this 'illegal organisation'; furthermore they knew nothing of a Führer's Decree of 18 May 1939 which authorised specifically an increase in SS Totenkopf regiments; nor were they aware of the number, strength and disposition of the units.

It was not until May 1940 that the Army went so far as to put its grumbles on paper, and file a formal complaint that the Totenkopf was going as far as wearing the Army's field-grey uniform. The SS replied smoothly that it was all quite legal simply because the Führer had said so. Besides, the official riposte added disarmingly, 'It is too late to do anything about it now.'

In his *Waffen-SS* (Oxford University Press, 1966), George Stein writes: 'It is difficult to avoid the conclusion that the Generals were only feigning ignorance in matters concerning the Totenkopfstandarten. It is true that the SS leaders made every effort to keep secret the size of these formations, but it is hard to see how entire regiments of Death's Head troops stationed in Poland, Czechoslovakia, Norway, Denmark and Holland could have escaped notice.'

Whether or not blind eyes were turned, the truth was that by the summer of 1940 one SS Totenkopf regiment was installed in each of these non-German cities: Oslo,

Stavanger-Bergen, Radom, Brno, Cracow, Breda and Prague. Another was being formed in Copenhagen.

Not that the ingenious official jugglings of Himmler and Berger solved the manpower problem entirely. Himmler had other plans for expansion and these were entirely in line with his racial theories and beliefs. This was to enlist volunteers from among the Polish and Slovakian *Volksdeutsche*. These Volksdeutsche were the German-speaking communities which the Nazis had 'taken under their protection'. The whole Nordic gospel, after all, they believed was something that had to be spread among other nations whose impure denizens needed to be educated.

As the Nazis overran more and more countries, so the number of co-opted SS men increased. But in 1940 it was very much a case of 'Ethnic Germans only'. By the first month a total of 109 of these ethnic Germans from Slovakia were examined as potential SS soldiers. Fifty-eight of them survived the tests and were found suitable; numbers were to increase substantially throughout the war.

To many eager young men of Austria, to whom the Germans were represented as true national parents, and to many youths of a 'protected' Czechoslovkia, the SS seemed to offer a glowing career. If the stuffy Army would not recognise them as Germans, the SS, with its fine sense of comradeship, had no such scruples. The recruiting drives were stepped up. Soon Himmler had a new problem: just what to do with all this bursting talent that the Army could not or would not find room for. The solution hit upon was to set up a replacement (*Ersatz*) regiment for each of the field divisions. There were also smaller Ersatz formations for specialised troops such as artillery, tank destroyers and combat engineers.

After ten thousand men had been found postings in this way, there came a highly significant directive from the Army, regulating the wartime status of the SS. It must have been a gigantic exercise in pride-swallowing, because it gave virtually complete control over the Ersatz formations to Himmler; the Army had some say in training and – exquisitely vague phrase – 'the right of inspection'.

A delighted Himmler lost no time in putting replacement units wherever he could and looked forward impatiently to the coming war when the process could be continued.

On 1 December 1939 the title 'Waffen-SS' became official. This organisation embraced the SS Verfügungs Division, the Leibstandarte, the SS Totenkopf Division, the SS Polizei Division, the SS Junkerschülen (training schools), together with their replacement and training units. Service in these formations would count as active military duty.

Further, added a decree of OKW, the SS Totenkopfverbände were now recognised officially as part of the Waffen-SS. However, it was still not a total victory for Himmler: the Army remained adamant that the ranks would not be filled with former concentration camp guards.

Hitler was still cautious. If the Reichsführer-SS saw his black legions as becoming ultimately a rival to the Army under his control, Hitler left his diabolical chief clerk with no such illusions. Although it gained judicial freedom from the Wehrmacht in 1939, the Waffen-SS never had complete independence. Hitler, 'the first soldier of the German Reich', remained firmly an Army man and ultimate control of the Waffen-SS remained with that Army.

Nevertheless, the Waffen-SS had grown and fattened; its Nordic prodigies were impatient for blood. Upon occupied Europe had fallen, in Churchill's phrase, 'the long night of barbarism'. What could it expect from the Waffen-SS?

In August 1940 the following 'Statement on the Future of the Armed State Police' was circulated to all Army commands:

'In its final form the Greater German Reich will include within its frontiers peoples who will not necessarily be well disposed towards the Reich. Outside the borders of the old Reich, therefore, it will be necessary to create an armed State Police capable, whatever the situation, of representing and enforcing the authority of the Reich in the interior of the country concerned.

'This duty can only be carried out by a State Police containing within its ranks men of the best German blood and identified unquestionably with the ideology upon which the Greater German Reich is founded. Only a formation constituted upon these lines will be able to resist subversive influences in times of crises. . .'

Many of these 'armed state police' were or subsequently became members of the Waffen-SS or were under the command of Waffen-SS soldiers – despite the still shrill denial of many former SS men that they were merely 'soldiers like the rest'.

The long and bitter winter of 1939-40 saw the Waffen-SS training for the series of bloody battles which were to be fought in the west. Until now Himmler's armed legions had enjoyed what was essentially only a shadow role; those days were rapidly coming to an end and the Leibstandarte in particular was to demonstrate its full capabilities, not always with complete success. Indeed, there was to be an episode of dangerous incompetence which was to bear out the Army's view that the élite formations had become decidedly too big for their boots. The outcome scarcely mattered : the Dutch forces, with their obvious weakness of artillery, were destined to taste the ashes of defeat at the hands of the Germans steamrolling through virtually undefended terrain.

During the western campaign, SS troops fought for the first time in divisional formations under the command of their own officers. The conquest of Denmark and Norway – *Fall Weserübung* – did not involve units of the Waffen-SS and was all but completed in the first week of May. Then Hitler ordered *Fall Gelb*, the western offensive.

There had been repeated postponements, most of them due to the fear of the German generals of becoming embroiled in a war of attrition; neither had their plans of operations been sufficiently clear-cut to satisfy Hitler.

The overall scheme was to penetrate the allied front deeply with armour at the point where the Maginot Line – the elaborate system of fortifications constructed by the French as Europe's major fixed frontier – petered out south of the Ardennes forest, coupled with a diversionary offensive into Holland and Belgium. The object was to reach the sea midway between Calais and Le Havre; cutting the Allied armies in two and destroying them.

There were 136 divisions marshalled for the offensive and these were divided into three Army groups – B, A and C – which were to be spread in that order along a 400-mile front from northern Holland to the Swiss-French-German border. Army groups A and B would be entirely responsible for 'Fall Gelb'. They would be assisted by a division of airborne troops. The passive role of C, which consisted of nineteen static divisions, was to stand fast opposite the Maginot Line with the exception of a feinting attack in the Saar area with its rich coalfields.

One overwhelming anxiety gripped Adolf Hitler. It was that the Royal Air Force would make full use of Dutch airfields for forays into Germany; clearly these had to be put out of action by occupying Holland and knocking Dutch defences out of the war. The success of lightning assaults had been proved amply in Poland, of course, but the west was to prove woefully unprepared for them.

Winston Churchill was to admit later: 'I did not comprehend the violence of the revolution effected since the last war by the incursion of a mass of moving armour.'

The role of Army Group B was to slice through Belgium's jugular vein. The task of A was to fling its armoured might through southern Belgium and Luxembourg and thus into northern France. The Dutch and Belgian armies would be elbowed aside and the British Expeditionary Force and a large part of the French Army would be encircled and eliminated. What was left of the French would then be crushed under the might of all German forces in a vast movement south.

Little of what was afoot had penetrated to men of the Waffen-SS undergoing further intensive training. There had been isolated hints. For example, Hitler had visited the Leibstandarte and told them they would soon be fighting 'in regions on which their father's blood had been shed'. In training there had been much emphasis on rapid movement and the seizing of bridges which seemed to suggest a fairly crucial theatre of war.

In ill-humour after its enforced rest following the Polish campaign, and impatient for action, was the Totenkopf Division with its 7,400 former concentration camp guards, and its Commander, that same irascible Alsatian, Theodor Eicke, who had been one of the chief executioners during the 'Night of the Long Knives'. 'Papa' Eicke, once saddled with the grandiose title of 'Inspector of Concentration Camps and Commander of SS Formation', was in absolutely no doubt that his men should be regarded as of the élite.

As far back as 1937 he had stated: 'We belong neither to the Army nor to the police nor the Verfügungstruppe . . . men of the Totenkopfverbände consider themselves members of the General SS and cannot therefore be commanded either by officers or NCOs . . . henceforth, commanders who act like officers, junior officers who act like NCOs and men who act like private soldiers will be posted to the General SS.'

It is scarcely surprising that the Army held out for so long before admitting followers of this sort of thinking to its ranks. This corps of thugs was to besmirch the name of the Waffen-SS for ever. A postwar generation, thanks largely to the Totenkopf, was to forget the quite genuine record of courage of many of the armed SS, and remember only the atrocious record of the followers of 'Papa' Eicke. And the role of the Totenkopf was to be particularly atrocious in occupied France.

At the start of the war in the west, however, the SS Totenkopf Division was held in Army reserve near Kassel. Held in reserve too was the Polizei Division – at Tübingen, behind the upper Rhine front of Army Group C.

And the Dutch? This was not to be a war of the old kind where two more-or-less equally matched and superbly equipped armies faced one another. The weak Dutch forces were incapable of adequately defending their 220-mile long frontier with Germany. They based their defence on a series of rivers and canal lines, lightly fortified near the border but growing progressively stronger in the west. Their last defence line was 'Fortress Holland', the five major Dutch cities of Rotterdam, Amsterdam, the Hague, Utrecht and Leiden.

Bridges were to be captured by parachute and airborne infantry who were to be relieved by motorised columns deployed before H-hour immediately in front of the Dutch frontier posts.

It was yet another application of the *Blitzkrieg* philosophy – the lightning war in which the emphasis was no longer placed on endless columns of soldiers marching a few miles a day. The static lines which had been a feature of World War I engagements, notably the bloodbath at Verdun, where opposing armies dug themselves into the ground and hurled shells at one another, had given way to mobility and fluidity.

The first stage of Blitzkrieg was the activity of fifth-columnists behind enemy lines. Next came the swift surprise blow, the opposing air force being destroyed on the ground, effectively eliminating the main obstacle to land attack. Then came the turn of the attacking air force: wave upon wave of dive-bombing on all means of communication and transportation.

Next the bombing was turned on the troops and had to be of such pressure as to throw them off balance and prevent strike-backs in any strength.

This was followed by the light forces – motor-cycle infantry, light tanks, motor-drawn infantry – which forged ahead, followed by heavy tanks with the job of carving out mechanised pockets in the rear.

Then and only then came the oldfashioned foot-slogging soldier buttressed by his artillery. But his job consisted mostly of getting rid of what puny resistance was left and only then joining up with advanced forces.

The theory of Blitzkrieg had been expounded in several places, notably in *The Army of the Future*, written in the 1930s by a 44-year-old French colonel, Charles de Gaulle. His temerity did not endear him to conservative officers who turned a deaf ear to his bold plea for mechanisation, for the concentration of armoured troops in armoured divisions. The policy had always been to use Army tank brigades in a supporting role, and why should some new-fangled scheme be even considered, merely because of the impertinent outpourings of some bumptious unknown colonel?

Hitler and his generals showed no reluctance in adopting what was patent heresy to blinkered Frenchmen; Blitzkrieg enjoyed scintillating success in the opening campaigns of World War II.

For the attack in Holland, OKW mustered a force equal to around four divisions. There were to be forty thousand paratroopers and four regiments of Army airborne infantry to secure and hold open the bridges behind the lines.

These bridges, once they were held by the attackers were to be crossed by one Army Panzer division and four regiments of SS motorised infantry. In full support were dive-bombers and fighters, the whole force to press on with the occupation of the key cities within Fortress Holland.

On 9 May 1940 all units of the Wehrmacht received the code word DANZIG. The lightning thrust to the English Channel was under way.

In the path of the Germans stood the Royal Dutch Army whose strength was sadly incomparable: the bulk of available forces consisted of only four Army corps, each of two divisions. In addition there was a light division on bicycles and motor-cycles, some infantry brigades, frontier battalions, fourteen regiments of Army artillery and a single regiment of hussars.

Smarting still under what they considered the rather parsimonous gratitude doled out to them after the Polish campaign, the men of the Leibstandarte were determined that this time they would secure a very large share of any glory that was going.

They did not have long to wait. The very start of the campaign found them in the frontier bridge area near the Dutch border town of De Poppe. An assault squad of the Leibstandarte overpowered the Dutch border guard, cut the fuses to the bridge demolition charges, and raised the barrier for the waiting column of vehicles. The Germans found that road-blocks were virtually non-existent and demolition half-hearted.

The SS vehicles rumbled swiftly over the excellently maintained roads, while overhead Junkers 52s, swollen with airborne troops, roared towards the flimsy Dutch defences.

On sped the Leibstandarte, encountering negligible opposition from the five defending frontier battalions. Opposition, so the champions of the Führer reasoned, could surely be swatted away like flies; the hour plainly belonged to them.

And so it proved until they reached Bornbroek where it soon became apparent that the Dutch were by no means as sleepy as the Leibstandarte had fondly imagined. The key bridge of the canal had been blown.

In high dudgeon the SS men pillaged a nearby farm, and barn doors were snatched as improvised rafts; the Germans crossed to a stiff hail of Dutch fire.

Soon the patrols were racing ahead to make sure that other bridges were still intact on the line of advance.

Under the growing exhilaration of the Leibstandarte, the SS pioneers were scarcely given time to finish erecting a light bridge before the forces were swarming across and sweeping all before them for the next objective which was Zwolle, the provincial capital of Overijssel and the two large bridges spanning the Ijssel river nearby. Dazed troops and frightened civilians in Zwolle greeted the advance guard.

The paucity of the general defences was yet another potent example of how the countries of the West badly underestimated the potential speed of a lightning war. True, the advance of the Leibstandarte had been more or less bloodless; even so, the SS contingent had advanced nearly fifty miles in a mere six hours.

The triumphs were to go on. The 227th Infantry Division, under whose command the Leibstandarte had been placed, was concentrated into three strike columns. Confidence was high but things began badly.

The Dutch, expecting a parachute drop, had blown the bridges of the Ijssel river, but the 3rd Battalion of the Leibstandarte forced a crossing further south, near Zutphen, eventually capturing the town of Hoven and the strength of two hundred defending it. With dreadful clarity the Germans were demonstrating what could be achieved with fully motorised units deployed against a static, under-equipped adversary.

In the process the Leibstandarte achieved for itself a highly gratifying distinction: SS Obersturmführer Hugo Kraas, who had stormed in triumph across the Ijssel and penetrated more than forty miles into enemy territory, was awarded the Iron Cross, First Class, the first to be awarded to an officer in the campaign. Krass, son of a schoolteacher from the Ruhr, was already the holder of the Iron Cross, Second Class, won during the Polish campaign.

The limelight and the laurels were not to be the exclusive property of the Leibstandarte during the Netherlands offensive. The 3rd SS Regiment, Der Führer, also secured crossings of the Ijssel.

One half of the Division found itself locked in combat with the left wing of the 1st French Army which had advanced into south Holland. The other half, with the Leibstandarte, continued the relentless drive towards Rotterdam. The French showing was brief but ultimately ineffectual; Rotterdam was now the glittering prize.

But by no means an easy one. The bridges around the town held out against the tanks and the Dutch sealed them off at the northern ends. To the fuming German High Command, Rotterdam represented a serious waste of time and resources. It was anxious to pull the troops out of puny Holland and get on with subjugating France. From Hitler came the terse directive: 'The power of resistance of the Dutch Army has proved to be stronger than anticipated. Political as well as military considerations require that this resistance be broken speedily.'

And it was. While the Leibstandarte was preparing for the assault on the city, a flight of Heinkel-III bombers appeared and reduced the centre of Rotterdam to a heap of rubble.

In just three-quarters of an hour it was all over; cold statistics were to point to the terrible effectiveness of the bombardment. Eight hundred civilians were killed, thousands wounded, and seventy-eight thousand made homeless.

The Dutch (they had no choice) finally accepted the surrender terms. In Rotterdam itself all was indescribable confusion. The city burned like tinder and there was a time when it seemed that the victors themselves would be engulfed in the holocaust. The advance of the Leibstandarte was slowed down, a state of affairs which did not commend itself to Sepp Dietrich's men. The impatience was to land the Leibstandarte in trouble and for the moment, at least, give its arrogance a shaking.

German and Dutch troops inside Dutch military headquarters were busily conferring on surrender terms when suddenly they heard a massive roar of tanks and trucks racing through the rubble towards them. Possibly unaware of the surrender, the Leibstandarte carried on fighting and emptied its machine-guns at the knot of Dutch troops which confronted it. A startled General Student, Commander of the airborne troops, ran to the windows of the headquarters building to see what was happening.

A German bullet crashed into his head and he fell back severely wounded. Strictures on the Leibstandarte were to come later; the crack SS formations, still in victorious mood, continued on their rampage, blissfully unaware that they had nearly killed one of their own side. Amateurism and high spirits aside, the Waffen-SS had shown a thirst for battle that, not for the first time, dismayed the orthodox minds of the German High Command. It was not simply that SS troops were ruthless fighters, but that their commanders, even the most conscientious of them, seemed to take for granted that the death rate would always be high. That death might come to each and every one was accepted: this had been the prime lesson of the cadet schools and academies.

One one occasion 'Papa' Eicke commented that during an attack human lives had been allowed to count for nothing. His superior officer, General Erich Hoepner of the Wehrmacht, commented coldly: 'That is a butcher's outlook.' The two attitudes illustrated very concisely the different philosophies of Waffen-SS and Wehrmacht.

The campaign in the Netherlands, meanwhile, had only a little steam left in it. More mopping-up forces needed to be left behind; the bulk of military strength switched south to support the breakthrough which was now in motion in northern France.

Then would come, it was confidently predicted, the

separation and destruction of the armies of France and England. The effervescent Leibstandarte permitted itself a quick victory jog through Amsterdam while SS Gruppenführer Hausser peeled off part of the Verfügung Division and some Wehrmacht infantry in a campaign to smash the Franco-Dutch forces holding out in Zeeland and on the islands of Walcheren and Beverland. SS Deutschland, with strong support from the Luftwaffe, cut through to the east. On 17 May, French destroyers picked up survivors and the SS were masters of Vlissingen, the principal port.

The Netherlands war was over; SS Verfügung Division turned south for France.

Adolf Hitler, as supreme war-lord, indeed had cause for satisfaction. The Netherlands was knocked out; the outer defences of Belgium had been penetrated; the French and British armies were now in Flanders; the French were in trouble on the river Meuse. Now was the time to fling all resources into a powerful, steamrolling drive to the English Channel.

4

If the Leibstandarte had been at all shaken by the near fatal attack on General Student, it would have been more than anyone's life was worth even to think such a thing in the presence of Sepp Dietrich. Repentance was not in the nature of an élite force, but the Leibstandarte had not liked giving the Army yet another excuse to be censorious at its expense. Worse, the limelight for the next week or so was to be grabbed by SS Totenkopf

Division, which on 16 May found itself pulled out of reserve and ordered forward to help exploit the salient which had been created by the spectacular advance of the German armour.

The next day, General Erwin Rommel's 7th Panzer Division reached Le Cateau and Cambrai in north-eastern France, on the direct path to the channel port of Boulogne. The advance had been spectacular, but surely an Allied attack from the north could not be long delayed? Rommel felt uneasy without the comfort of infantry reinforcements.

These came in the form of the SS Totenkopf Division whose job was to clean up the area and consolidate the conquests of Le Cateau and Cambrai. This operation earned Eicke's over-confident formations their first taste of battle: six dead and fifty-three wounded between 19 and 20 May.

It was a sharp initiation into the realities of war; just to ram home the lesson, there was worse waiting the next day. The Germans had reached the Channel coast west of Abbeville at the mouth of the Somme, but the 7th Panzer Division and SS Totenkopf Division were held up south of Arras. The Allies threw in everything they had. Seventy-four British tanks and two infantry battalions, supported by an additional sixty tanks from the French 3rd Light Mechanised Division, were hurled at the 7th Panzer and SS Totenkopf. The fighting was unexpectedly fierce; the Germans, who had almost come to take for granted easy victories and feeble opposition, learnt what it was to be matched in ferocity. Nine German medium tanks were destroyed, some light tanks and some motor transport.

In terms of casualties the 7th Panzer Division lost eighty-nine killed, 116 wounded and 173 missing. Nineteen men of the Totenkopf Division died, twenty-seven were missing and two were wounded.

For the Allies, however, this had become a time of despair. Once their line had been breached at Sedan, they found it impossible to contain the German thrust; in eleven days the Panzers of Guderian had sliced their way from Luxembourg to the sea – a distance of more than 240 miles. The capitulation of the Belgian army in the north, and the southern thrust of the tank forces, cut off British and French at Dunkirk.

The Leibstandarte, which was now under the command of the 1st Panzer Division, had by 24 May begun to arrive in position on the line of the Aa canal which was along the southern and eastern side of the evacuation perimeter at Dunkirk. To reach the canal had meant a gruelling night march, but there was to be no respite for the men of the Waffen-SS. Ahead of the Leibstandarte lay a 140-foot hill, the Wattenburg, to the east of the Aa canal and dominating the otherwise flat countryside. But shortly before the attack, there was a sudden order from the headquarters of the Führer; there was to be no movement at all across the canal towards Dunkirk. The reasons for this seemingly astonishing directive on the threshold of what seemed certain to be a great German victory have caused raging controversy since the war.

Broadly speaking, Hitler, prompted by von Rundstedt, Commander-in-Chief of the German forces in the west, and by Göring, who wanted a share of the glory for his Luftwaffe, became convinced that a reversal was looming and that the Panzer divisions should be halted until more infantry could be brought up.

Whatever the reasons, the order was too late to stop the SS-Verfügung Division which was already across the canal line at Watten. As for the Leibstandarte, Sepp Dietrich himself took the initiative – and, incidentally, proved not for the first time that the Leibstandarte was not above a spot of insubordination when it considered circumstances warranted it. The Führer's order was ignored; the attack over the canal at Watten went ahead.

Under heavy artillery fire and in an exposed position, the height was seized in triumph.

Implacable courage, total ruthlessness and at times

almost suicidal behaviour – these were qualities that Hitler and Himmler had demanded from their SS right from the very moment of its formation. Until the invasion of the west, however, opportunities for displaying them had been limited by the relative softness of the opposition. Neither, at this period of the war, had the frequently horrific cruelty of the Waffen-SS manifested itself to any great extent, but soon all that was to change dramatically.

First signs of that courage occurred with an engagement along the Lys River and its canals which the British were determined to hold. Into the attack sped the 3rd Panzer Division and the attached SS Regiment Deutschland – the latter forging well ahead and leaving the Panzers to battle with British resistance, a state of affairs which, as we have seen, had been paralleled in Poland and had the effect of reducing the Wehrmacht to something like apoplexy.

Soon Oberführer Felix Steiner, the Regimental Commander, was ordering the attack. In went his Third Battalion, supported by two batteries of SS artillery, creating total havoc among the British defenders. So far so good, but Steiner was robbed of SS Totenkopf Division which should have been reassuringly on his left. The problem was how to get across the Lys with the now wretchedly slim forces available. It looked as if Steiner had over-reached himself. Suddenly, as if to underline the point, a clutch of tanks emerged from a British-held village to the north and hurled itself at the 1st Battalion. Engineers were proving infuriatingly slow at slinging crossings across the Lys; even the lightest of vehicles could not avoid plunging into the water. Anti-tank guns were therefore conspicuous by their absence.

By all the rules of accepted warfare, this should have spelt the end of Steiner and his men. But this was the Waffen-SS and it fought like a cage-full of jackals. A private leapt forward on to the rear deck of a tank and attempted to force a grenade into its observation slit, but was mowed down by a following tank. Another man was crushed to pieces by the wave of the British armour as he advanced clutching grenades. The Germans stood firm and emptied their rifles, sometimes at a range of just fifteen feet. There followed an outburst of machine-gun and anti-tank rifles.

Neither did Steiner's heroes let up when SS Totenkopf Division, previously held down by engagements of its own, arrived to beat back the British armour before Steiner's bridgehead was blasted out of existence. The result was an important advantage for the Allies; most of their forces were able to withdraw behind the Lys.

Rewards for individual acts of heroism were comparatively rare within the Waffen-SS: to serve in the élite battalions was considered honour enough. But there were exceptions in this case. The Iron Cross First Class was awarded to three company commanders. Steiner made it clear that if casualties had not been so high there would have been more awards.

Bravery is something that must be conceded whole-heartedly in any account of the Lys incident. However the Waffen-SS was soon to have its name besmirched by a later incident of atrocious cowardice – SS Totenkopf Division was the first to show the other, darker side of what was so often a glittering coin.

The flat countryside surrounding the hamlet of Le Paradis in Pas-de-Calais is rich in potatoes and sugar-beet; corn and maize and mangolds grow also in this beguiling spot. It is a peaceful oasis and the scores of people who still make a pilgrimage there find it particularly hard to believe that violence and cruelty and slaughter once came to this gentle, proud land.

In 1940, Le Paradis consisted of a few houses, a café and a shop with, a hundred yards to the south, a cross-roads near the Rue du Paradis. An *estaminet* stood on the corner with the rest of the village widely scattered beyond.

It was to this area that British troops, the 1st Royal Scots, the 2nd Royal Norfolks and the 1st/8th Lancashire Fusiliers, were forced in the face of the relentless advance of SS Totenkopf Division.

SS Regiment Deutschland had continued, throughout 27-28 May to fight along the Lys, while Totenkopf had crossed the canal line at the point known as La Bassée Canal at Béthune. The canal looped into the city, but there was a bypass that cut straight across it. This meant that the Germans had to make two crossings in their advance, a manoeuvre which was to cost them dear.

Not that things were any better for the British. The British 2nd Division was bleeding itself dry to keep open the line of retreat to the Lys. Nazi intelligence sources had learnt that the British regiments opposing them had instructions to delay the German advance until the last possible moment.

On the southern bank of the canal, advance members of SS Totenkopf arrived and were massed for the next day. There were two infantry regiments and on their left was a Panzer division. The infantry regiments were motorised – reinforced with an SS artillery regiment for the attack. One infantry regiment was to occupy the villages of Le Cornet Malo and Le Paradis, while the other was to go to its aid as needed and support the flank.

Throughout, the Germans made numerous attempts to cross the canal, but the British held on tenaciously to the shattered bridges, being forced back eventually on Le Paradis.

Early in the morning of 26 May, Battalion Headquarters had been re-established at Duries Farm on the Rue du Paradis, 500 yards west of the crossroads; half an hour later, the Germans renewed the attack with heavy, devastatingly accurate mortar fire. Soon they were bayoneting their way into Le Cornet Malo. The

British contested every house and building to the death, refusing to evacuate even as much as a cowshed so long as there was breath left in the body of each and every soldier.

One British company lost all its officers. Two depleted companies were merged into a single unit and Le Cornet Malo was defended by just sixty men. The order that went out to them was clear: the position was to be held to the very last round.

It only postponed the inevitable. At one point, there had been a message of hope: a relieving force consisting of a French infantry brigade and an English tank regiment was on its way. But Duries Farm could report nothing. And no reinforcements came.

Le Cornet Malo fell and the Germans pushed on to Le Paradis. The German infantry deployed its battalions on the left, right and centre. This was the opposition facing the battered remnants of the Royal Norfolk Regiment.

From their spy holes in the farm buildings, the British defenders had a good view of the open fields and some scattered houses along the Rue du Paradis. Meanwhile in the 15-feet square 6-feet high cellar, the Signals Section of Battalion Headquarters was trying desperately to keep in touch with the outside world.

The farmhouse was shaken constantly by the mortar shelling; the cellar became steadily more unbearable with the reek of explosives. Then came the clump of two particularly heavy explosives and dust showered from the cellar ceiling. When it cleared, the dull, quiet voice of a signaller was heard reporting: 'The line to C Company is dead, sir.'

The final link with their comrades was being severed for the Royal Norfolks . . .

Soon the commanding officer was issuing the instruction that he dreaded above all others. All equipment was to be destroyed. Wireless sets, telephones, typewriters, signalling gear – all were ground to pulp and ignited.

The farmhouse, which was by now on fire, had to be abandoned.

Their refuge now was a crude little cowhouse to which the men had dashed amid the whine of German bullets. Here they could hold out for an hour at the very most. In a daze the dirty, dog-tired unshaven British troops, who but a few months before had marched with spit-and-polish pride across their parade grounds, watched as a grubby white towel was fastened on to the rifle of a platoon sergeant major.

The towel was thrust gingerly through the door. The firing ceased. Encouraged, the sergeant, accompanied by about half-a-dozen men, left the cowhouse. The silence was shattered by a renewed burst of fire. Bullets raked the surrender party. Unprepared for this sort of treachery, the men crowding round the door inside the cowhouse were not able to step back quickly enough to allow what remained of the surrender party to regain safety. Plainly, the commanding officer reasoned, nothing but total surrender would satisfy the Germans who even now could be heard whooping with triumph outside.

Blinking and stumbling and taking in briefly the superior number of Germans and the burning, blackening surroundings, the British came out, hands above their heads. A rasping voice rapped out the command: 'Halt!' Then came an order, spoken in English, to keep their hands on their heads.

At first it seemed that treatment was going to be reasonable. The prisoners were allowed to keep some personal belongings, including photographs, but then one private made a bad mistake.

A sudden question was rapped out: 'Have you a knife?' Without thinking, the private said: 'No.' Then came a sharp tug at the belt and a heavy blow to the back of the head; the army knife suspended from his belt had been spotted. Next, came a pole-axe blow and a short sharp dig with a rifle. One prisoner had his cigarettes snatched away. 'Do you want a smoke?' said the German with suspicious friendliness. The man leant forward to take the packet. As he did so, a rifle was swung and smashed straight into his face. Yet another private, who was losing blood and whose wounds badly needed dressing, sat down – only to leap up in agony as a heavy boot crushed into his backside.

Then came some appalling luck for these particular prisoners, which was all part of a chaotic and bloody war. A separate group of wounded prisoners, standing apart from the rest, were the centre of furious argument among a knot of Germans. Eventually these prisoners were marched away to the other side of the road where there was another German unit – one which was, as it turned out, to treat its captives humanely.

The rest had fallen into the hands of the 4th Company, 2nd Totenkopf Infantry Regiment, under the command of 28-year-old Obersturmführer Fritz Knoechlein.

A product of the Brunswick cadet school, Knoechlein was one of those individuals who had quite literally been made by the SS. A casualty of the economic chaos which had hit Germany after World War I, Knoechlein had never known confidence, respect or steady employment. He had seen what the indignity of poverty in the Weimar Republic had done to his father. He himself had eked out a precarious living as errand boy, insurance salesman and clerk.

Nazi Germany seemed to offer an exciting prospect; service to the Führer would be an adventure. In 1934 he had joined one of the first Verfügung units. After training at the cadet school he became Platoon Commander to SS Deutschland. The very year of the incident at Le Paradis he had been transferred as Company Commander to the depot which was located near the concentration camp at Dachau.

He embarked upon his new job with enthusiasm.

Now there was a short, nerve-shattering lull for the prisoners. Some of the Germans moved off, but the guards continued to watch the British carefully. Then at last came the order to march and the prisoners found themselves marshalled along the Rue du Paradis. Immediately before them, on the left of the road, they spotted a red brick farm but were directed away from this through a gate off the road into a meadow. In front of it, nearest the gate, was a shallow pit, another farm building behind it.

The prisoners were marched in front of this building, but it is doubtful whether at this point they had taken in their surroundings. All eyes were on a couple of German heavy machine-guns set up in the meadow.

When the ninety-nine prisoners were all in the meadow, there came the dreadful command: 'Fire!' Then the slaughter began and the men fell, cursing, screaming. From left to right and back again, the machine-guns raked the defenceless knot of prisoners.

One private shouted: 'I am not going to die like this,' and, as if with a strange sense of fatalism, turned and faced the fire yet again and for the last time.

The survivors testified that when the firing ceased, the screams of agony went on and on. That, in a sense, was the most diabolical aspect of that day's work.

For there were survivors at Le Paradis. By a fantastic stroke of fortune, Private Albert Pooley of the 2nd Battalion of the Royal Norfolks and with him Private William O'Callaghan emerged alive. Along with the rest, they had been paraded for slaughter. Along with the rest, they had been sprayed with bullets at close range. And, along with the rest, they had heard the *coup de grâce* administered by the Germans to the dying.

Pooley later recalled that as he lay in the field, feigning death: 'My arm was over my head and I could just look along the pile of bodies. I saw a German soldier step down into the hole with bayonet fixed. It was a terrible suspense. A bayonet is not a nice finish. Then a whistle blew and I heard an order. The man clambered out before he reached me.'

The two men – Pooley badly wounded, O'Callaghan

72

less so – managed to stagger slowly and agonisingly out of the field of the dead which was now being churned into a quagmire by pelting rain.

They were later sheltered by villagers at Le Paradis, but both men feared that reprisals could be visited on the French. Eventually, they surrendered to the Germans, but kept quiet the fact that they were survivors from the massacre.

One of those villagers, Madame Castel, was threatened by an officer of SS Totenkopf. She and others in the area would, she was informed, be shot if they did not reveal the whereabouts of British soldiers. Throughout the uncomfortable interview at which this sturdy French peasant woman had been forced to kneel down, Madame Castel studied the SS man carefully, taking note of the twitch in his face and eyes.

That twitch helped eventually to identify Fritz Knoechlein. It was Madame Castel, the courageous French peasant, who on 12 October 1948 stepped into the witness-box of a Hamburg military court and pointed to Knoechlein hissing: 'That is him, that is the man!'

Fritz Knoechlein went to the gallows on 28 January 1949, found guilty of 'committing a war crime in that he in the vicinity of Paradis, Pas-de-Calais, France, on or about 27 May 1940, in violation of the laws and usages of war, was concerned in the killing of about ninety prisoners of war, members of the 2nd Battalion, the Royal Norfolk Regiment, and other British units'. Establishing that guilt had taken nearly three years of probes, searchings and questionings by war crimes investigators before the men who died at Le Paradis were avenged.

Even to some of his fellow members of the SS, Knoechlein was regarded as detestable, particularly when it was learnt that even after the massacre he had run about like a madman, desperately looking for more British soldiers to shoot, justifying his action by asserting that the prisoners had gone on shooting after surrender.

From General Erich Hoepner's staff office had come demands for an enquiry. Hoepner had not been the only man to be suspicious about the events at Le Paradis. SS Colonel Gunter d'Alquen, a journalist and accredited war correspondent for the Wehrmacht, had seen the bodies and was told that the execution of the British had been carried out because they had been using dum-dum bullets.

Inevitably tongues wagged. 'Papa' Eicke was certainly not prepared for there to be any sort of investigation. He managed to stall awkward questions until his troops were comfortably out of the neighbourhood and on their way to take over from the Leibstandarte at Boulogne.

There was no court-martial for Fritz Knoechlein. Eicke went racing to his mentor, Heinrich Himmler, who promptly decreed that what had happened at Le Paradis was henceforth to be designated 'a state secret'. Nemesis was to be delayed a long time for Knoechlein. As late as 1944 he was commanding a regiment of volunteer SS in Norway and, as an SS Obersturmbannführer, received the Knight's Cross.

Near the northern end of the front, Leibstandarte SS Adolf Hitler was, under Sepp Dietrich, in ebullient mood. The pace of their advance had produced a mood of euphoria; everyone was spoiling for the next clash. The feeling was transmitted down the lines.

The order had come to resume the thrust to the Dunkirk perimeter and the objective of the Leibstandarte was the small French town of Wormhoudt, some twelve miles from Dunkirk. For the second time in just over a generation places in the area knew the sad slaughter of war: Ypres, Menin, Poperinghe.

At 14.00 on 27 May, Wormhoudt shuddered from the sticks of bombs as the Luftwaffe buzzed and roared overhead. In the streets the all too familiar scene was

74

repeated: the fires and the flying debris and the terrified populace.

As the dust settled, it became apparent that the town had suffered badly. Hardly a building had escaped damage; civilian casualities had been high. And the German troops were still to come.

Dietrich ordered the attack to begin on 28 May at 05.00 hours. Three battalions were on the left, the middle and in reserve, while tanks of 10th Panzer were in support. The actual taking of the town was entrusted to 2nd Battalion. Sepp Dietrich was in sparkling form. The proverbial candy for a baby would not be in it. The Leibstandarte could have Wormhoudt for lunch.

It was by no means to prove as easy as that. Intelligence sources had confirmed that the Germans were overwhelmingly superior to the British, but in fact enemy positions were being held with infuriating obstinacy. Dietrich's mood changed abruptly: what the hell was going on at the forward command posts? What ridiculous set of circumstances threatened the whole battle tradition of his beloved Leibstandarte?

The corpulent Bavarian and ex-butcher was basically a simple soul who disliked and feared mysteries. The brutal frontal attack, and the sledgehammer kill, followed by a tankard or two of beer: that was the Dietrich style.

Some jealous souls said that this style was more suited to the job of nightclub bouncer than professional soldier. Many spoke of a want of elementary intelligence. One of his Obergruppenführers, Wilhelm Bittrech, later recalled: 'I once spent an hour and a half trying to explain a situation to Sepp Dietrich with the aid of a map. It was quite useless. He understood nothing at all.'

Dietrich's contempt for authority – even for authority that could prove dangerous – was absolute. In their closely detailed history, *Hitler's Elite: Leibstandarte SS 1933-45,* James Lucas and Matthew Cooper cite Dietrich roundly turning upon, of all people, Himmler during a heated discussion and telling him: 'My position as guard commander will no more allow your interference on security matters than it will upon the morality of my men. They are mine and we are Hitler's. Now go back to your office and let us get on with the job.'

This was the man who, on what was to prove an ill-fated forty-eighth birthday, eased his generous, beer-inflated bulk into a staff car and went to find out in the company of an adjutant why his 2nd Battalion was not pushing ahead with the vigour expected of it.

The car set out from the small town of Esquelbecq, about one and a half miles from Wormhoudt. It travelled fast across the flat and open countryside – too fast, as it happened.

The shell from the British anti-tank gun struck the side of the car like a giant fist, killing the driver. Within seconds the flames were shooting upwards. Cursing every Bavarian oath in the book, Dietrich rolled over and away, momentarily blinded as his face hit the thick, oozing mud of a welcome ditch. His adjutant crept into a nearby conduit.

Dietrich reasoned that if he lay still and kept his head down, he would be safe. One movement and the watchful British would have him. But being motionless had its perils. All was quiet along that straight bit of road. Then Dietrich heard the sizzling and smelt the burning. Waste oil from the car was coming straight for him. It was a sheet of flame which he knew that at all costs he must beat off. There was one particularly uncomfortable moment when he had to coat his entire body with mud to avoid certain burning.

Dietrich and his adjutant lay in their bolt-holes for five hours – all due to the incompetence of the dead driver who had strayed as near as fifty yards from a particularly strong British position. Attempts by some of the Leibstandarte to recover the couple proved fruitless under fire.

Not daring to think of the fate of Sepp Dietrich, the

rest of the SS troops pressed on with the advance, but they too came up against opposition, notably from the Cheshire Regiment. To make matters worse, the commanding officer of the 2nd Battalion, Sturmbannführer Schutzeck, had been seriously wounded during the attack on Wormhoudt.

Dietrich and his adjutant were rescued eventually and the advance continued. Attack was severe and unrelenting: tanks, infantry, artillery, bombing. The 2nd Warwickshire Regiment had the job of defending the town and it managed to throw back the initial attack – but all that changed with the arrival of the Leibstandarte.

In the house-to-house fighting, SS records were to reveal, eleven officers and 320 men were captured. Those British who were left attempted withdrawal, but they were pursued by the Germans and taken prisoner.

Some eighty members of the Royal Warwickshire Regiment, the Cheshire Regiment and the Royal Artillery were among a group of prisoners who at Esquelbecq were taken by No 7 Company, 2nd Battalion Leibstandarte.

As at Le Paradis on the previous day, the captured men were marched into a field, but the pattern of slaughter this time was to be different.

Instead of lining up in the open, the men were marched into a barn situated near a row of trees. Some of the survivors admitted later that they had been innocent enough to impute charitable motives to the men of the Leibstandarte. It had come on to rain and presumably the barn was to act as some form of protection or, at the very least, a reception centre for the prisoners.

There were signs, however, of something decidedly more sinister. One end of the barn was guarded by no less than eight Germans. Another four faced its entire length, covering a small doorway. These guards were made up from the 2nd Battalion Leibstandarte, together with a special escort from the Signals Section of No 8 Company.

The only British officer among the prisoners, Captain

Lynn-Allen, refused to be intimidated by the SS and protested unflinchingly about the brutality of some of the guards.

He told one of them: 'I wish to complain that there are wounded men inside and there is not enough room for them to lie down.'

The guard answered in American-accented English: 'Yellow Englishman, there will be plenty of room where you are going.'

Lynn-Allen ignored the threat, stared the German out and said calmly: 'I am not satisfied.'

The effect was terrifying. The German's look of studied insolence gave way to blind anger. His face red with rage, he reached down for a stick-grenade protruding from his boot and, with a swift over-arm motion, lobbed it straight into the prisoners.

Lynn-Allen, grabbing Private Bert Evans, who had stood next to him throughout the exchanges with the SS man, sprinted sharply for the door as fragments of the grenade scattered in all directions. Together, they ran along the tree-lined edge of the meadow, making for a welcoming clump of trees. There was a small pond of stagnant water and, taking a swift decision, Lynn-Allen hauled his companion with him into the pond.

They ducked into the cold, churning mud, lying down as deeply as they could in the water – but it was not deep enough and that is where the German found them. He levelled his revolver and fired twice. Lynn-Allen was killed instantly.

Then it was the turn of Bert Evans, and the revolver fired again. The bullets struck a tree, ricocheted and hit the private in the neck. As he fell forward, he heard the German give a grunt of satisfaction and move away.

Every muscle in Evans's body was tensed for another sprint, but caution and reason won and he remained in the pond, from time-to-time groping fruitlessly for the body of Lynn-Allen.

From the barn he could now hear a succession of shots

and screams and, as he later admitted, he broke down and wept. It was later revealed that when yet another succession of grenades were lobbed at the prisoners, two NCOs threw themselves on them to protect their helpless men and died instantly. Death did not come swiftly to all: the screams which Albert Evans heard came frequently from men enduring the agony of shrapnel buried in flesh. One man was blown clean outside the barn after the explosion, but he left his legs behind.

When the last grenade had been lobbed, there came a sharp order: 'Five men are to march outside.' These were escorted to a point some short distance from the barn. An armed guard was mustered as a firing squad; the prisoners died under the dull, short stutter of bullets. Then came the call for five more . . .

After they too had died, anger and loathing erupted in the barn. The request for a third group of five prisoners was stubbornly refused. For a moment the SS were nonplussed, but a sudden renewal of the rain jerked them out of their indecision and they stormed the barn, trampling on the dead and the wounded as they opened their automatic weapons on those prisoners that remained.

The eventual departure of the murder band and the triumphant race of the Leibstandarte towards Paris meant inevitably that the massacred at Wormhoudt became lumped into the normal roster of war casualties.

Of the fifteen survivors, some were rescued by the Red Cross, some were tended in local villages. As at Le Paradis, many gave themselves up to prevent reprisals against the local population.

At the scene of the atrocity had been left behind the grotesque mess and litter of war: guns, pouches, bren carriers, steel helmets and the dead.

In 1941 bodies which had been buried hastily a year before were taken up by local labourers under German supervision and re-interred in Esquelbecq, Wormhoudt and elsewhere. The graves are now tended by the

Commonwealth War Graves Commission.

Many of the stones carry the phrase 'buried nearby' because the men of the Waffen-SS had removed identity discs from each prisoner. Precise identity of the corpses was not always possible.

Unlike the men of Le Paradis, those who died like cattle herded into a shed were not avenged. After the end of hostilities, war crimes investigators received depositions on 'the murder of 80 or 90 British prisoners of war by members of the German Armed Forces at Wormhoudt (France) on 28 May 1940'. Several German witnesses whose testimony would have proved valuable were long since dead – killed on the Russian front – and none of the British survivors were able positively to identify any of the men who did survive as having been involved. There were graphic individual accounts of what happened but none of these added up to conclusive proof to convict the killers.

Few Germans were prepared to reveal what they knew of the behaviour of their comrades – a state of affairs which throws further light on the clannish qualities of the élite Leibstandarte. Investigators were convinced, but could not prove, that Sepp Dietrich had extracted from his men an SS oath of silence which none dared to break, even when the war was over.

Some men of the Leibstandarte were to be punished for murder. But that was for another atrocity.

Operation Dynamo, the evacuation of the British Expeditionary Force from Dunkirk was all but completed by the first few days of June; in all, a third of a million men were evacuated from the exposed beaches. Dunkirk, still defended stubbornly by forty thousand French soldiers, held out until the morning of 4 June. The Leibstandarte harried the departing forces for as long as it could, but this was regarded by then as a waste of time. France still remained unconquered and there was work to do.

The Leibstandarte was ordered into reserve, then pulled back to near Cambrai to be fitted out for the forthcoming offensive against the French armies south of the Somme-Aisne line, a blueprint for which had existed as early as 1937. There it linked up with Verfügung Division while Totenkopf Division was soon being ordered to the Channel coast south of Dunkirk. It was to have its headquarters at Boulogne and then make the quick thrust into France.

The Germans, as it turned out, were to hurl themselves across France like a tidal wave. The speed of the advance, once the Somme river line had been broken through, surprised even the Führer.

All three Army Groups were to be used in a three-prong offensive. Army Group B was to attack on 5 June along a front embracing the Channel coast and the Aisne, north of Rheims. Army Group A was to inch forward on 9 June between the Aisne and the Franco-German border. Army Group C had the task of assaulting the Maginot Line and the Upper Rhine front about a month later.

It was indeed an impressive line-up, but the fate of the French was sealed before a single shot had been fired. It was a sad question of mathematics, not military skill: the Germans had 140 divisions and the French a mere sixty-five.

In the headlong pursuit of the badly mauled French forces, all the Waffen-SS formations were well to the front. Battle losses, however, had been heavy and there was an urgent call for reinforcements: 270 for the Leibstandarte, 2,020 for the Verfügung Division and 1,140 for the Totenkopf Division.

It was a source of pride to the Waffen-SS that officers shared each and every danger with their men. Indeed, it seemed almost to be a matter of honour to be profligate with lives – a spirit of self-sacrifice which may well have satisfied Himmler's romantic notion of self-sacrifice on the altar of the Nordic ideal, but which placed heavy demands on manpower.

In addition, high casualty rates did severe harm to the calibre of command: the SS Junkerschülen had to be plundered for cadets destined to be yanked from the parade grounds as inadequately trained replacements. Still, the two SS divisions did receive the heavy artillery battalions they desperately needed. And the unblooded Polizei Division, left to kick its heels and stare balefully at the Maginot Line, was at last given something to do. But the Polizei remained the poor relation of the Waffen-SS and the role assigned to it, fighting in the difficult terrain of the Argonne, south of the Ardennes and north of the Meuse, denied it any chance to shine. The quality of the French defenders, belonging to the Maginot Line garrison, was high.

The final phase of Hitler's campaign in the west was not to give the Waffen-SS its greatest role in the war; that was to come in the east and above all in Russia. Such glory as there was belonged to the Verfügung Division, the Totenkopf Division and, even more so, the Leibstandarte. All three of the SS formations swept in triumph through central France in the wake of Kleist's Panzer divisions.

The Aisne, Soissons, Villers-Cotterêts: then the helter-skelter race for the Marne was on. The river was reached on 12 June, and 2nd Battalion forced a crossing near St Avige. After that, there was a brief rest, broken in sudden exuberance by the Leibstandarte when the news reached them of the fall of Paris. At their billet in the village of Etrepilly the SS rejoiced by giving the bells of the little church an elated celebratory ring.

Paris was entered by General von Kuechler's 18th Army on 14 June. It was undefended and the swastika was promptly hoisted on the Eiffel Tower. Two days later Marshal Pétain asked the Germans for an armistice.

While the conquerors basked in the summer sunshine

of that first year of the Paris occupation, the fighting went on. Hitler was afraid of a new front being formed south of Paris and acted swiftly to quell any opposition. It was the same in the east with Army Group C being ordered promptly to launch an assault across the Maginot Line and the Rhine front.

When Kleist's Panzer Group was advancing through Champagne towards Dijon in Burgundy, the Waffen-SS behaved strictly according to the rule book. The SS was content with a policing role.

But if the hour of glory belonged primarily to the Wehrmacht, Sepp Dietrich was not prepared to hide his light under a bushel. There was only one place for his Leibstandarte and that was in front. Wherever possible the burly Bavarian shoved his legions as far forward as he dared, refusing to recognise any authority but his own.

The role in France was all but over; the battle honours for the Leibstandarte were not. During the advance and under Kleist's orders, it made for the river Allier near Moulins. This was to be an operation which provided a classic example of the war conditions under which the Leibstandarte was happiest. The French blew up a bridge under the advancing formations. Promptly the officers re-routed their men to a railway bridge which threatened to become a blazing inferno. Over it they tumbled and on went the lightning-fast drive for Vichy. The roads were choked with French troops but it was not the Leibstandarte's way to pause. The contents of automatic weapons were emptied from moving vehicles into the obstructive French. The advance never slowed. Armoured cars were catapulted at barricades. Occupied towns were quite simply by-passed; SS infantry then saw that they and their inhabitants would cause no further trouble.

By 25 June 1940, which was the day that the ceasefire came into effect, the Verfügung and Totenkopf Divisions were well south on the Spanish frontier. The Polizei Division, part of Army Group A, had fought in the Argonne Forest and captured the town of Les Islettes.

For the Leibstandarte there was a slight disappointment. It had been intended originally that Hitler's élite should march in a victory parade through Paris. Instead, prosaically, the regiment found itself in garrison at Metz.

This was not a rest-cure. Some of the tired, battle-stained veterans of France must have resented being sent back to school. Training, which some might fondly have supposed to be behind them, started all over again. It was a re-toughening process for the Leibstandarte; in the process it found itself with a new reconnaissance battalion.

Sepp Dietrich's superb fighting machine had not slowed down. It was merely flexing its muscles.

5

The Waffen-SS units fought in the early campaigns in the war in the Netherlands and in France with a brand of courage and tenacity of which any country could be proud. Exceptional physical fitness, iron discipline, superb training – these were qualities which the men of such regiments as the Leibstandarte had undeniably exhibited in abundance.

But there were to be no thanks – and certainly none from the Army. The Wehrmacht establishment continued its opposition because, to many of the professional soldiers, the lack of military tradition of the new force was one of the most distasteful things about it. This surely was the reason, many argued, why inexperienced hotheads had been allowed to threaten the outcome of whole campaigns.

Accounts from the front often deliberately left out Waffen-SS achievements. As might be expected, no one was more incensed at this than Himmler who had remained very much in the background during the battle of France.

The owlish figure with the pince-nez was conspicuous by his absence. This was due not to lack of interest but lack of health. Himmler had suffered from strained nerves and agonising stomach cramps for years, and had put himself in the hands of an Estonian masseur named Felix Kersten who was able to relieve the pains.

When Himmler was at last able to visit his Waffen-SS he went, understandably enough, to see the Leibstandarte at Metz, and was full of grumbles about the scurvy way he considered it had been treated. Although he rarely showed violent emotion, the Reichsführer-SS did allow himself to fulminate: '. . . There is the complaint from the Wehrmacht that we have heard ever since 1933. Every SS man is a potential NCO but it is a pity that their commanders are so bad. After the war in Poland they said that the SS had huge casualties because they were not trained for the job. Now that we have very few losses they suppose that we have not fought.'

There were all the signs of another clash. Normally Himmler would have been delighted to take on the Army he hated, but this was a luxury quite out of place during a war. Once squabbles of this kind blew up, it was difficult to know where they would end.

Himmler had another, more pressing reason for avoiding any confrontation. His own prestige – of which he was overwhelmingly conscious – was at stake. Only a few months previously, his Führer had been lavish with praise. Hitler had spoken to the Reichstag about the campaign in the west and had gone out of his way to say things which Himmler had longed to hear.

The Führer had declared: 'Within the framework of these armies fought the valiant divisions and regiments of the Waffen-SS. As a result of this war the German Armoured Corps has inscribed for itself a place in the history of the world; the men of the Waffen-SS have a share in this honour'.

Hitler then went ahead to present no less than six Knight's Crosses to SS officers. One went to Sepp Dietrich of the Leibstandarte. Two were awarded to regimental commanders of the SS Verfügung Division; Felix Steiner of SS Regiment Deutschland, and George Keppler of SS Regiment Der Führer. The rest went to lower-ranking SS officers.

The Army gritted its teeth and kept quiet. It remained sorely tried, however, because Hitler had not yet finished. He authorised the establishment of a new Waffen-SS Division, the fourth to be created since September 1939.

But how to counter inevitable obstruction by the Army? In the past it had shown itself less than friendly to Hitler's wishes, and there was no reason to suppose that it had changed.

Even Himmler had to admit that he had become to a certain extent the prisoner of his own ideology. It had been all very well before the war, strutting about and talking of only the purest Aryan strain being acceptable to the SS, but the need for recruits would plainly become more pressing. And where were they to come from?

True, there were the young conscripts whom the Army had allowed to volunteer for the SS, but these were needed as replacements for the field divisions. The Totenkopf had other sinister roles allotted to it – forming, for example, the basis of additional, un-authorised field units, and to provide Himmler with his own personal armed police. Once again, the Reichsführer SS called on the persuasive talents of the Swabian saw-mill owner's son, SS-Brigadeführer Gottlob Berger.

There was, Berger argued, a solution that had been proposed before but should now be put into operation and expanded quickly. The Wehrmacht's conquests of Denmark, Norway, Holland and Belgium – Himmler had racial scruples about the French – had reunited the Nordic ideal.

Here was manpower in abundance; the SS recruiting agencies had only to stretch out their hands.

It was a most agreeable day for Himmler when Keitel, chief of the OKW, notified the Army High Command that 'the Führer and Supreme Commander of the Wehrmacht has ordered . . . the establishment within the framework of the Army, of a new SS Division . . . which shall make use of the manpower becoming available from those countries inhabited by people of related stock (Norway, Denmark, Holland)'.

To this day collaboration remains an emotive word and can still touch the raw conscience of a nation; the blunt truth is that there was no shortage of collaboration in World War II.

Nazi-style parties proliferated in the occupied territories. In Norway the puppet traitor Vidkun Quisling formed the Nasjonal Samling party in 1933 and embraced Fascism with enthusiasm. In Holland, Dutch Nazi leader Anton Mussert was in 1942 named by the Reich Commissioner as leader of the Nationaal-Socialistche Beweging. The collaborator in Belgium was Leon Degrelle, founder of the Fascist movement Rex.

The youth sections of these parties proved rich territory for Gottlob Berger's recruiting officers – sufficient in fact to raise two regiments: Nordland, composed of Danes and Norwegians; and Westland which was made up of Dutch and Flemish-speaking Belgians.

Heinrich Himmler's citadel of bureaucracy, the ever-growing SS-Führunghauptamt (SS Main Operational Office), the headquarters organisation of the Waffen-SS, ordered that the two regiments, together with the already existing Germania, should be lumped together as a single Division. The commander of the Division was a familiar figure: Felix Steiner, SS Standartenführer of Deutschland. He sent his men promptly into training, to be ready for the kill in Russia the following April.

A positive frenzy of reorganisation had gripped the Waffen-SS. Verfügung Division was given another of the Totenkopf regiments in exchange for Germania and retitled Das Reich. Under that name, it was to stand for everything that was most detested in the Waffen-SS. Another two Totenkopf regiments were brigaded as Kampfgruppe Nord (later to be converted to a Division.) No less than another five Totenkopf regiments were left and two cavalry regiments, out of which were formed two SS brigades under the direct control of Himmler – *not* the Army.

Himmler also announced the abolition of the terms 'SS-Verfügungstruppe' and 'SS-Totenkopfverbände'; from now on all armed units of the SS would be included in the Waffen-SS.

It was a massive assumption of power, but Himmler was far from finished. He next issued a directive listing all organisations that were from then on to be part of the Waffen-SS. In addition to units, departments, installations and training schools, the concentration camps were also included, along with their staff and guard detachments.

By the end of the war it was estimated that some 30,000 to 35,000 Waffen-SS personnel were employed in the camps, many of them former members of Totenkopf. Wounded Waffen-SS soldiers were sometimes assigned to these units, while some of the able-bodied Totenkopf were sent to the front as replacements. Post-war apologists for the Waffen-SS have frequently denied that this happened. But none of them have been able to explain away the Waffen-SS uniforms worn by the guards – or the Waffen-SS paybooks frequently carried in those uniforms.

In 1941 recruitment for the war in the east was the priority. In the spring the Waffen-SS stood at four Divisions (Das Reich, Totenkopf, Polizei and the new Viking), two brigades (the Leibstandarte, Nord) and one infantry regiment.

It was ready for a task that Himmler saw as the culmination of everything he had dreamed and fought for: the pure Nordic strain, the last word in Aryan purity, was to take on the 'vile, sub-human hordes' who dwelt in the east.

In constant talks with the Führer, Himmler had stressed that it was not enough to send more soldiers against the Russians. This was to be a holy war to the death; only his Waffen-SS had the right ideological conviction to make it all possible.

There was to be brief disappointment. The motorised Waffen-SS units were drafted east, along with the bulk of the German Army, to take up positions on the frontiers of the Soviet Union. Then anti-Nazi activity in the Balkans, combined with the farce of Mussolini's invasion of Greece, imposed a heavy switch south. Operation Barbarossa, the invasion of Russia, had to be postponed for three weeks.

It was the second readjustment to which the SS was subjected: only weeks before, SS Division Reich, SS Polizei Division, SS Totenkopf Division and the Leibstandarte SS Adolf Hitler had been looking forward to the invasion of England. But Operation Sealion was one particular project with which Hitler never proceeded.

On 28 October 1940, Adolf Hitler alighted from his special train in Florence to be greeted by a radiant Benito Mussolini. The Duce could not contain his news one instant. He gasped: 'Führer! We are on the march! Victorious Italian troops crossed the Greco-Albanian frontier at dawn today.'

The news did not come altogether as a surprise to Hitler. Mussolini had written to the German dictator some days earlier and had informed him broadly of his plans. The Duce had been careful, however, to antedate the letter so that it was not received until it was too late for any objections to be raised.

But objections there were. To attack Greek mountain troops at that time of the year was regarded as nothing short of a major blunder. Why on earth had Mussolini done it?

The Italian leader had been put out by Hitler's dazzlingly successful conquests. He had stormed: 'The Führer is always presenting me with victories. This time I am going to pay him back in his own coin.'

Hitler had tried to talk Mussolini out of such a perilous adventure, one which would set the Balkans in an uproar and could very well lead to a threat from the east. Hitler had wanted to deal with that sphere of influence in his own time.

All the forebodings turned out to be accurate. Within three weeks, Mussolini's campaign lay in ruins. Hitler, whose manner to his axis partner remained uncharacteristically restrained in the circumstances, directed the Army to prepare a plan for a German attack in the east.

The proposed invasion of Greece was code-named 'Operation Marita'. Sixteen German divisions were moved to southern Rumania. For the Leibstandarte, the period of refresher training and pep talks was over. It was moved from Metz to Bulgaria where the 12th Army, in which it was to serve, was to strike towards Skoplje in southern Yugoslavia.

Originally the Greek mainland only was to be seized, but British troops had landed in Greece early in March, and now there was a decision to occupy the entire peninsula and the island of Crete.

There were other pinpricks. The way to the Greek border had seemed clear; after all, had not Yugoslavia joined with Germany, Italy and Japan to sign the Tripartite Pact? Then a group of Yugoslav officers carried out a coup against their government – and threatened the Führer's plans. Hitler's rage was terrible to behold. Yugoslavia must be crushed with a 'merciless harshness' at the same time that Operation Marita was launched against the Greeks.

Mussolini, whose miserable showing in Greece had now reduced him to a mere puppet of Nazi Germany, received a letter from Hitler informing him that the German attack on Yugoslavia would begin within twenty-four hours. All Italian forces should be subject to the strategic orders of Germany. Mussolini agreed; he had no choice in the matter.

The Germans attacked on 6 April 1941. They were ruthless but completely successful; eleven days later Yugoslavia surrendered. The honeymoon period for the Germans in World War II had some time to run.

For the Leibstandarte, this particular theatre of war was to provide at least one novel experience. The Germans found themselves up against Australians and New Zealanders who exhibited the sort of aggression that Sepp Dietrich's comrades were to recognise and respect.

The scene of the clash was the Klidi Pass, gateway to Greece, which the Leibstandarte was ordered to open up. It was not just that the troops were of a different calibre to those the Germans had previously encountered. Here was bitter cold and relentless driving snow, with the British and Imperial forces dug in firmly on the surrounding crests of the mountains of northern Greece. Both sides – the Australians had just come from Egypt – cursed the weather and neither side gave any quarter in the full days of fighting.

For the Leibstandarte, victory was particularly impressive; fighting in the Netherlands and France had not been across countryside that was mountainous. Here in Greece, engagements were across violently uneven terrain caught in winter's iron grip.

The bill for the Leibstandarte was remarkably lenient. The Regiment lost fifty-three dead, 153 wounded and three missing.

In the mid-1950s one of the most frequently toasted members of the HIAG – Hilfsorganisation auf Gegenseitigkeit der Waffen-SS: the Waffen-SS Old Comrades Association – was ex-policeman, ex-miner Kurt ('Panzer') Meyer, ex-Oberführer of the Leibstandarte, a Waffen-SS

91

veteran who became one of Germany's best known soldiers and who first sprang into prominence when, as SS-Sturmbannführer and Commander of the Reconnaissance Detachment, he broke through the Klissura Pass in Greece at the head of his unit.

The determined onslaught of the Leibstandarte – the men almost literally stormed through the pass – illustrated graphically not just the courage of the Waffen-SS but the special quality of its leadership. The close rapport between officers and men was deplored by Army veterans who claimed that it prejudiced discipline. By and large, though, it proved the opposite.

In his memoirs, *Grenadiere,* Meyer relates how he and a small group inched along the road through the pass, while two of his companies scaled the cliffs to take the defenders in the flank.

Then it was as if the road had been torn apart; giant craters opened up from the series of deafening explosions which had ripped into the uneasy silence. There were roars and shudders as pieces of the road were catapulted into the valley which fell away from them in a sheer drop.

The Greeks had set off their main demolition charges and the men gasped amid the dirt, the smoke and the confusion. They were momentarily paralysed, a dangerous prey to the sudden stutter of machine-gun fire.

Meyer wrote:

'We glue ourselves behind rocks and dare not move. A feeling of nausea tightens my throat. I yell to (Untersturmführer) Emil Wawrzinek to get the attack moving. But the good Emil just looks at me as if he has doubts about my sanity. Machine-gun fire smacks against the rock in front of us . . . How can I get Wawrzinek to take that first leap?

'In my distress I feel the smooth roundness of an egg hand-grenade in my hand. I shout at the group. Everybody looks thunderstruck at me as I brandish the hand-grenade, pull the pin, and roll it precisely behind the last man. Never again did I witness such a concerted leap forward as at that second.

'As if bitten by tarantulas, we dive around the rock spur and into a fresh crater. The spell is broken. The hand-grenade has cured our lameness. We grin at each other and head forward for the next cover'.

Ascending the mountain slopes under a concentrated barrage of shells, Meyer's men had to struggle on without the shield of armour; worse, the artillery had intense difficulty in finding level ground from which to fire accurately. Mortars and support weapons were to be luxuries for those who found themselves on even ground; for others it was to be a case of personal weapons only.

The crews of the battery of 88 mm guns found themselves working in the most hazardous conditions imaginable. It was not just a case of blasting the enemy and rendering it inoperable; each round was likely to send the crew crashing over the precipice.

Kurt Meyer's achievement, including taking the key town of Kastoria and another eleven thousand prisoners, was to gain for him the Knight's Cross; few so far in World War II had been so dearly earned.

Nothing could stop the Nazi tanks rolling into Athens and the swastika flag being hoisted over the Acropolis. Sepp Dietrich accepted the surrender of the Greek forces. The Greeks had been able to humiliate the Italians, but found Field Marshal Wilhelm List's 12th Army of fifteen divisions a decidely different proposition.

It was all, perhaps, a mere hiccup for the plans of Hitler, but for the Waffen-SS there had been value. The greener troops had received an introduction to the realities of warfare that was far tougher than the theatres of France and the Netherlands.

Not for the last time, the Leibstandarte seized most of the glory, but there was also a feeling of some satisfaction and achievement among the men of SS Das Reich

Division, who covered the distance from Vesoul in eastern France to Temesvar in south-western Rumania for the Yugoslav invasion in less than six weeks. When other armies slept, the Waffen-SS kept going.

It was Das Reich, part of General Georg-Hans Reinhardt's 41 Panzerkorps, which flattened the Yugoslav army, virtually dazed into submission already by the wave upon wave of Luftwaffe attack. Into heavily shattered Belgrade rolled the men of Das Reich; four days later the Yugoslav army had capitulated.

But Greece had been the ultimate target and the Germans had grabbed it. During the entire Balkan campaign, Germany had lost 2,559 dead, 5,820 wounded and 3,169 missing.

This time, in Athens, the Leibstandarte got its victory parade. Then it was north for the refitting and the waiting for the war's most momentous summer.

6

In stark military terms, there was a classic simplicity about Adolf Hitler's line-up for the invasion of Russia. The Führer, as supreme war lord, envisaged an advance into the Soviet Union in three distinct directions. Army Group North would mastermind the thrust towards Leningrad; Army Group Centre would make for Moscow; the Ukraine would be in the hands of Army Group South.

The resources of the Reich were indeed formidable: seven Armies, four Panzer groups, three air fleets. That amounted to three million men, 600,000 vehicles, 750,000 horses, 3,500 armoured combat vehicles, 7,184 artillery pieces and 2,100 aircraft.

But the campaign in Russia cannot be thought of in terms of logistics, of strategy and tactics. This was a war of ideologies, a head-on conflict between the Bolshevism of Stalin in his 24-year-old Soviet Union, and the highly inflammatory racial doctrines of the Nazi Germany which Hitler had brought into being a mere six years before he went to war.

In a sense, the war in Russia was to seem more logical to the SS man than to the conventional soldier. This phase of the war, went Himmler's argument, was the logical reason for existence: every phase of training had been but a preparation for this hour.

Himmler spoke long and often on the subject of Russia.

Here is the transported Reichsführer-SS speaking to reinforcements for Kampfgruppe Nord in the very first month of Operation Barbarossa, code-name for the Russian invasion.

'To you SS men I need not say much. For years – over a decade – we old National Socialists have struggled in Germany with Bolshevism, with Communism. One thing we can be certain of today: what we predicted in our political battle was not exaggerated by one single word and sentence. On the contrary, it was too mild and too weak because we did not, at that time, yet have the insight we have today. It is a great heavenly blessing that, for the first time in a thousand years, fate has given us this Führer. It is a stroke of fate that the Führer, in his turn, decided at the right moment to upset Russia's plans, and thus prevent a Russian attack. This is an ideological battle and a struggle of races. Here in this struggle stands National Socialism: an ideology based on the value of our Germanic Nordic blood.

'Here stands the world as we conceived it: beautiful, decent, socially equal, that, perhaps, in a few instances is still burdened by shortcomings, but, as a whole, a happy beautiful world full of culture; this is what our Germany is like.'

Speaking of Russia, Heinrich Himmler on the threshold of becoming the most powerful agent of terror in the twentieth century, went on:

'On the other side stands a population of 180 million, a mixture of races, whose very names are unpronounceable, and whose physique is such that one can shoot them down without pity or compassion. These animals, that torture and ill-treat every prisoner from our side, every wounded man that they come across and do not treat them the way decent soldiers would, you will see for yourself. These people have been welded by the Jews into one religion, one ideology, that is called Bolshevism for the task: now we have Russia, half of Asia, a part of Europe, now we will overwhelm Germany and the whole world.

'When you, my men, fight in the east, you are carrying on the same struggle, against the same sub-humanity, the same inferior races, that at one time appeared under the name of Huns, another time – one thousand years ago at the time of King Henry and Otto I – under the name of Magyars, another time under the name of Tartars, and still another time under the name of Genghis Khan and the Mongols.

'Today they appear as Russians under the political banners of Bolshevism.'

In a later speech Himmler dispensed with the rhetoric and put his plans for Russia with brutal directness: 'We must make sure that in the clearing of territories in the Ukraine no human, no animal, not an acre of agricultural land, not a line of railway remains, that no house is left standing, that no mining installation can be used, that there are no wells that are not poisoned. The opposition must find a totally destroyed and burnt-out land'.

And again: 'What happens to a Russian or a Czech does not interest me in the slightest. Whether these nations live in prosperity or starve to death interests me only insofar as we need them as slaves for our *Kultur*. Whether ten thousand Russian females fall down dead from exhaustion while digging an anti-tank ditch interests me only insofar as the anti-tank ditch for Germany is finished. We Germans, who are the only people in the world who have a decent attitude towards animals, will also assume a decent attitude towards those human animals, but it is a crime against our own blood to worry about them or give them ideals.'

Lost in the midst of his idiosyncratic, cranky view of history, the Reichsführer-SS in his terrifying ignorance gave no thought to what, in the long run, would matter most of all: the likely fighting ability of the new enemy. For this time there would be no docile, already demoralised foe. Ideology, fuelled by the mechanics of terror every bit as efficient and ruthless as those of the SS, would make the troops of the Red Army formidable opponents.

At first there was some excuse for Nazi euphoria. After all, had not the Germans fought four successful campaigns in under two years? Three million fighting Germans with magnificent technology could surely be guaranteed to make this a short war. The four and a half million Russians, so Intelligence sources suggested, were deficient in speed, decision and organisation. On the other hand, the commanders were as lavish with manpower as the Germans, even in the most seemingly hopeless of engagements, and there were prescribed penalties for failure: the hangman and the firing squad.

On the morning of 22 June 1941, German radio audiences awoke to the voice not of Adolf Hitler but of Propaganda Minister Joseph Goebbels, who intoned the proclamation from his master: 'Weighed down with

97

heavy cares, condemned to months of silence, I can at last speak freely, German people! At this moment, a march is taking place that, for its extent, compares with the greatest that the world has ever seen. I have decided again today to place the fate and future of the Reich and our people in the hands of our soldiers. May God aid us, especially in this fight! '

Four hours earlier, Russian frontier guards had stared in horror at a dawn sky suddenly fractured with the brilliance of six thousand flashes from the German guns. Punch-drunk with sleep and fumbling for their tunic buttons, the guards stumbled from their barracks, gasping and choking through the smoke. To the sound and sight of the guns was now added something almost as sinister – the squeal and the clatter and the thud of tanks.

This was the first act in a drama which had originally had the prosaic title of Directive No 21. Its code-name was something far more dramatic. This was Operation Barbarossa, Hitler's crusade for the very soul of civilisation.

To the men of the Wehrmacht and their sinister shadows in the Waffen-SS had also gone the injunction: 'the Führer-Chancellor of the Reich and with him the German nation are certain that you will do your duty and that you will pursue the struggle relentlessly until the enemy is destroyed.'

And Hitler added the meaningful rider: 'The SS, picked troops of the very finest quality, will always be sent to the most exposed positions and will show the German nation that it can count on them.'

The intentions were that the Waffen-SS was to be given a strictly subsiduary role in Barbarossa; indeed its total strength at the start of the campaign amounted to 160,405 men. There was the Leibstandarte which had been redesignated a Division, and SS Division Viking with Army Group South; SS Division Reich with Army Group Centre; SS Totenkopf Division and SS Polizei Division (in reserve) with Army Group North. Far north of the main front, in Finland, was SS Kampfgruppe Nord and SS Infantry Regiment 9 with von Falkenhorst's Norwegian Army Command.

To this strength had to be included other functionaries now attached to the Waffen-SS and gathered into the Reichsführer's net. All the fevered years of pleading, scheming, outwitting and ultimately overruling the fastidious distaste of the Army establishment towards the armed SS had paid off in full measure. Now within the Waffen-SS were Reserve Units, the Inspectorate of Concentration Camps, the Guard Battalions and those who manned the garrison posts.

All were to see action very early in the war on Russia and most were to fight with a dedication, ruthlessness and exquisite cruelty that was often matched by the Red Army itself. The Waffen-SS was by no means to dominate the war in the east, but its excesses were such that the Russian campaign has gone down in history, justly or not, as 'the war of the SS'.

Save for the Polizei Division, which did not give an account of itself until early August, all formations under Army command went straight into the holocaust.

The extent of the front, even illustrated on the map, is breathtaking and almost unfathomable. Here was not a question of hundreds of miles with objectives limited to towns, villages and ultimately the sea. Rather here was, at one time, a span of no less than two thousand miles.

It stretched from the bleak, icy wastes of northern Finland, through the wide steppes of central Russia, to the high mountains and sub-tropical airs of the Caucasus.

Field Marshal Gerd von Rundstedt, Commander of Army Group South, had previously been singled out by Hitler for a pep talk. The Soviet military machine, asserted the Führer with supreme self-confidence, was a creaking, inefficient structure that had been bled dry by the Stalin purges of the 1930s and was so riddled with insecurity and constipated with ideology that it was utterly incapable of fighting effectively. Hitler had blandly announced: 'You have only to kick in the door and the whole rotten structure will come crashing down.' Full of abstract philosophical theories, Army commanders staggered out of the war-lord's presence; only later, on the field of battle, did it all seem strangely irrelevant.

By June the forty-six divisions which made up Army Group South had closed up to the border with the Soviet Union. It was composed of 6th, 11th and 17th Armies, bolstered by 1st Panzer Group.

Its task was to cut off and destroy the Russian forces west of the Dnieper river. The Panzer Group, placed on the left flank, was to slice through below Kovel. Then would come the giant pincer embrace. The Russian armies of the south-west front would be gripped by all the awesome might of German armour. Then would follow total destruction.

Put thus succinctly, it sounded like a relatively easy assignment, but took no account of the vast distances involved. Army Group South held a line from the southern edge of the Pripet Marshes to the Black Sea and its first mammoth bound was from the frontier to the Dnieper – a distance of three hundred miles. Then it would be on to the first prize, Rostov, which was yet another seven hundred miles.

And the conditions were truly appalling. More than one SS man was to reflect ruefully how pleasant had been that little rest-cure in the Balkans. For in this part of Russia the land was primitive indeed; communications scarcely existed and a downfall of rain could turn pitted, cratered roads into swamps which could hold an entire tank column in their sticky embrace.

The Soviet High Command saw the front in the south as the most decisive area to defend, and assembled the greatest concentration of its forces there.

German miltary intelligence spoke of sixty-nine rifle, eleven cavalry and twenty-eight armoured divisions. Its commander was the dedicated, fanatical Stalinist Semen

Budenny, who had survived the sweeping purges of the army in 1937-38, to be created one of five Marshals of the Soviet Union. His massive resources were to be deployed over flat land eminently suitable for the advance of tanks, with the river lines of the Prut, San, Bug and Dnieper providing the main obstacles. The strongest defence line was the Dnieper – three-quarters of a mile wide at Kiev. Along the old 1939 frontier coursed the man-made defensive system known as 'the Stalin line'.

On 22 June the Leibstandarte, posted to the Lublin area in Poland, streaked down the road to Ostorwiecz, making for the Vistula and ultimately the wide steppe lands of Galicia and the western Ukraine. The enemy it faced could not in any sense be compared to the Poles, the French or the defenders of the Netherlands. At this stage, the Russians were fighting a losing war and, so determined were they in retreat to leave nothing behind for the enemy, that they coldly slaughtered their own people in a particularly terrible interpretation of the policy of 'scorched earth'.

This sharp realisation of the calibre of their enemy came as a severe shock at first to even the hardened, arrogant young fighters of the Waffen-SS. After two terrifying days of battle, the forces of SS Viking had wrenched Dubno from the Russians and got their first taste of the deadly potential of the T34 tank.

By 30 July the divisions of von Stülpnagel had rolled on and seized the town of Lvov. A vivid description of the scene in the aftermath of a tank battle survives in the diary of young Peter Neumann, ex-member of 27th Troop of Hitler Jugend, who served with Viking.

'We didn't even have to bother about prisoners. Each new district that we enter is already deserted. The Russians carry away their dead and wounded and even spent shell-cases and cartridges. They leave nothing behind, not a sign that they have been there. Except death and destruction.

'At Lvov we saw a frightful scene. Before leaving, the Russians burnt and pillaged everything, took everything away. Not being able to move their prisoners eastwards they simply massacred them.

'In the NKVD prison where the Russian and Polish political prisoners were housed, there remained only about a hundred survivors. The other prisoners must have been machine-gunned in the courtyards of the jail, because the bodies were all heaped up, at times to an impressive height.

'The population of Lvov didn't escape the massacre, either. It seems that the Reds were thrown into disorder by our advance and went quite mad. They fled on foot, in carts and lorries, in complete chaos, firing like lunatics at everything in sight. They never stopped firing from the moving lorries, aiming their MGs at houses as they went by.

'It was the political Commissars who ordered the Red troops to shoot all the prisoners, men and women alike. These people had all been arrested during the last few weeks on the most ridiculous pretexts: persistent lateness at work, unintentional bad work construed as sabotage, or non-execution of requestioning orders.

'The smell of filth and decay in the streets was indescribable. The Army "crematorium" lorries were soon found to be inadequate, and enormous piles of wood have been built outside the town on which the corpses are being burnt.

'Before the bodies were taken away, many people tried to identify the remains of friends or relatives. Handkerchiefs pressed to their mouths, they rummaged among the dead, turning over the bodies from which rose clouds of flies.'

A new sort of enemy, indeed! They were a people not prepared to lie down and die, who did not cower before the SS firing squads. That air of invincibility which had seemed inseparable from any true description of the

German fighting man was being slowly but surely ripped away. Those whom Heinrich Himmler had designated as 'sub-human' turned and fought.

And the Russian fought with seeming indifference as to whether he won or lost. Tactics were evidently elaborate trappings of war to be planned by text-book generals pouring over maps in the comfort of head-quarters. In the battles of west Ukraine, where heavy rains soaked the battlefields, the Russian infantry often hurled itself at the enemy from open lorries, standing up and firing straight into the German columns. When a shell destroyed a lorry, those who survived sprang over the side and charged on foot, scorning any cover.

The forces of the Leibstandarte were still displaying all the old optimism and ruthlessness which had sub-jugated the sadly weakened western front, but a year earlier and a whole world away. The much vaunted Stalin Line, a combination of concrete, field-works and natural obstacles, had been smashed through at Miropol – what was to stop this truly magnificent advance was Zhitomir.

But before that lay Romanovka – and a sharp surprise for the Leibstandarte.

Meanwhile, at home in Germany, the busy Propaganda Ministry of Goebbels was whipping up support for the men wearing the armband inscribed with the name of the Führer. A typical morale-booster was a radio feature called 'The SS in the War'. It was monitored by the British and a transcript has survived. It came direct from a parade of 1st Battalion, Leibstandarte SS Adolf Hitler.

Over marching music and shouted commands, the commentator enthused:

'These are the men of the Leibstandarte, soldiers of the Führer, trained and educated in the spirit of the SS during the years of peace; seasoned and proven in the best soldierly tradition on all the battlefields of this war. The Leibstandarte and the other divisions of the Waffen-SS form part of the great structure of the armed forces. They are fighting at the front to safeguard the honour, greatness and freedom of the Reich against the external enemy. They have come from the ranks of the SS, the ranks of those men whose task it was and still is to protect the Führer and safeguard the Reich internally. Only the best German and Germanic men are worthy of or equal to this lofty task. The aim of the SS Head Office, in its capacity as Chapter of the Order, is the political soldier of the Germanic Order. Therefore the basic law of the SS is the law of race and selection.'

The scene then shifts to a medical examination in a Waffen-SS recruitment centre.

'The men – tall and fair – are standing here in a long file; these men have volunteered for service in some division of the Waffen-SS, in the Leibstandarte, the Reich Division, the Viking Division, or the Totenkopf Division.

'Every SS man who does his duty in the homeland today has been, or will be again within a short time, a soldier in the ranks of the Waffen-SS or the armed forces, and he performs his duty as a soldier in the knowledge that if he is killed on active service the great SS community of comrades in the homeland will stand by his dependants and will give them more than financial security. The welfare department of the Waffen-SS and the comrades in the units of the SS vie with each other in their care for the dependants of their dead.'

Then the commentator quotes the Reichsführer-SS: 'Every war lets the best blood, yet the unfortunately necessary death of the best man, regrettable though it is, is not the worst. Far worse is the lack of those children during the war who were not begotten by the living and after the war not begotten by the dead. Therefore the victory of the arms also demands the victory of the cradle.'

Many hundred miles away from the stirring rhetoric, the martial music and the reverential intoning of the homily of Heinrich Himmler, hard, bitter fighting was raging at Romanovka in the densely wooded region north of the Northern Highway. Not only was the enemy suddenly superior, but he had quality tanks – more specifically *the* tank – the T34 with its hardened armour and sloping angles.

Here was something that could not be kicked, whipped, bullied or machine-gunned. This magnificent piece of armour was immune except to the 88 mm flax gun. The Soviet assaults came in continuous waves against the thin SS formations. The Northern Highway was the corps supply line which the Germans had to hold and the Russians needed to cut.

The attacks came hourly and the men of the Leibstandarte noticed that the troops seemed to be of an altogether higher calibre, at least in terms of violent courage, than the Germans had encountered previously. Charges were made with the bayonet and engagements were hand-to-hand. In country of deep forest, Germans and Russians hacked and stabbed at one another, while mortars burst their lethal shrapnel.

Although the Russians had a considerable advantage with their armour, they lacked men experienced enough to use it properly. The crews grew tired and careless, frequently blundering into ambushes. There were frequent breakdowns; there was a division which followed its corps commander into a swamp – to the humiliating loss of every tank.

Even so, the Russians had one supreme advantage: sheer force of numbers. The battered Leibstandarte man, weighed down by sacks of grenades, cursed the endless indomitable Russians who seemed to face him at every turn.

At Zhitomir, SS Viking celebrated its success in reducing the town to ruins. Its men were given instructions to search every ruined home and building for, in addition to People's Commissars, all of the town's officials, whether civilian or military. When these officials were rounded up, they were shot.

Typical of these 'punishment operations' is this example from an official SS report which survived as evidence at the Nuremberg Trials.

'In the neighbourhood north of Zhitomir twelve villages were screened and a total of fifteen functionaries liquidated. In the course of an investigation of the village of Techernjachov and in a search for Communist functionaries, thirty-one Jews who were active Communists and also acted partly as political commissars were executed.

'In the course of an action carried out in Rudjna and Trojanov twenty-six Jewish Communists and saboteurs were seized and shot. In the centre of the big square a gallows was erected for two Jewish murderers who were hanged there. Around the place of execution was a crowd of several thousand people. The Wehrmacht was also represented in large numbers. In addition, four hundred Jews . . . were made to witness the execution. Before the execution took place, the loudspeaker van announced in German and Ukrainian the deeds of horror committed by the two men, Keiper and his assistant, and the proposed penalty. In addition, two big posters, which were fixed on the gallows, indicated once more the crimes committed. The pronouncing of the sentence was repeatedly interrupted by calls of approval and applause. The indigenous population accepted, with particularly great satisfaction, this measure of retaliation for Jewish horrors committed over a period of ten years.

'Afterwards, 402 Jews from Zhitomir were shot. The

execution of the two Jewish murderers as well as the shooting of the 402 Jews was carried out in an exemplary manner.

'Following an urgent call for help from the Commandant in Radomyschl, a detachment and platoon of Waffen-SS went there, where they found the conditions to be untenable. The newly-appointed mayor was unmasked as an informer of the NKVD and a member of the Communist Party since 1925. It was also proved that up to the last day he was in touch with Communist bands. His deputy was also a Bolshevik . . . Jews were also arrested who openly had opposed the German forces and had refused to work for the labour organisation. In this action, 113 persons were shot.'

The Leibstandarte was after bigger fish and the columns raced on, taking satisfied note that the Luftwaffe's Dorniers and Junkers screamed reassuringly overhead.

The men of SS Viking, free of their grisly mopping-up at Zhitomir and looking for a fresh conquest, romped towards Bielaya-Tserkov, one of the strong-points of the enfeebled Stalin Line.

Russian positions in the Kiev sector and along the Dnieper were seemingly being obliterated. Bielaya-Tserkov was encircled from north to south and crushed in a pincer.

Not surprisingly, the most worried man on the Russian front was Marshal Budenny. A former sergeant-major and an old crony of Stalin, Budenny had been one of the founders of the Red Army Cavalry after the revolution. Not many of his colleagues had a high opinion of Budenny's capabilities, but were wise enough to keep their views to themselves.

Budenny was a toady who soon realised that susceptibility to flattery was Stalin's greatest weakness. While one of Budenny's closest friends, and co-Cavalry founder, Yugorov, had perished in one of the giant purges,

Budenny, the womanising, tipsy braggart with handlebar moustaches, mahogany butt revolvers and boundless confidence, survived. Not only did he dodge the firing squads, which was no mean feat, but he had gained the unstinted admiration of "the boss", Joseph Stalin. Still, Budenny knew that all this could change overnight if he did not produce the expected victories.

To add to the troubles of the Russians, Hitler had a sudden change of mind and the forces which had been heading for the Ukrainian capital of Kiev suddenly switched the lightning-fast advance to the region of Uman, further south-east, where the Soviets were engaging 11th and 17th Armies.

The threat came from the Leibstandarte and SS Viking, spearheaded by the Panzers. The SS divisions detached themselves from the mêlée and, after a series of running battles, flung a ring of steel around the area of Uman. Trapped within it were the 6th, 12th and part of the 18th Red Army.

Red-eyed, punch-drunk through lack of sleep, the men of the Leibstandarte patrolled the captured areas like zombies, shaking themselves into fresh action when the seemingly cowed Russians appeared capable of breaking the SS ranks and storming the town.

Such successes by the SS seemed satisfactory enough, but German conduct of the campaign so far was not faultless. Men of the Leibstandarte and Reich cursed the buzzing of Messerschmitts: liaison with the Luftwaffe was poor and the pilots, who could not tell Russian from German tanks, seemed scantily trained in observation.

But the most serious threat to the occupying troops of Uman – and elsewhere in Russia – was the activities of another army. It had no uniforms. Its conscripts could be of any age. Men and women served with equal enthusiasm.

This was the citizen army that was willing to harass and destroy the enemy as best it could, even if it meant deliberately destroying its own homes and families in the process.

Russian patriotism was fierce and proud. But this alone did not account for the success of the citizen armies. Their resolve was stiffened by terror: terror of the Commissars who were quite capable of hanging laggards publicly in the village squares.

Peter Neumann of SS Viking learnt to be on his guard against the citizen soldier of Uman.

'One has to be very careful where one walks since the entire countryside is mined. Incautiously opening a door may set one of the infernal things off. In some places everything is a booby trap. The magnificent pistol lying on the floor conceals a wire connected to an explosive charge. In the harmless interior of a samovar, pounds of cordite are hidden, waiting to blow up. Jam-jars, vodka bottles, even a well, the rope of which one is tempted to pull in order to get a drop of fresh water – they are all death traps to be steered clear of.

'Sometimes it's easy to spot the wires leading to the acid on the percussion cap. The difficult thing is to dismantle the contraption without being despatched to a better world in the process.

'The simplest system is, from safe cover, to toss in three or four hand-grenades before entering any building. The explosion sets off the booby traps at the same time.'

This cat-and-mouse war ended abruptly at dawn when a mass infantry assault was launched against the exhausted men of the SS. But the pincer held; from Kasalin, back along the line on the way to Zhitomir, streaked the 1st Panzer, linking up with armoured elements of a Hungarian infantry division; together they clamped hard on the twenty-five Russian divisions. By 1 August 1941 the Russian defences at Novo Archangelsk were breached and the Uman pocket sealed.

More than 100,000 Russian soldiers poured into

captivity. The Leibstandarte took 2,200 officers and men and destroyed sixty-four tanks.

Lavish indeed was the praise for the Leibstandarte. Major-General Werner Kempf, commanding the Corps of which Leibstandarte was then part, proclaimed:

'Since 24/7, the Leibstandarte SS Adolf Hitler has taken the most glorious part in the encirclement of the enemy around Uman. Committed at the focus of the battle for the seizure of the key enemy position at Archangelsk, the Leibstandarte SS Adolf Hitler, with incomparable dash, took the city and the heights to the south. In the spirit of the most devoted brotherhood of arms, they intervened on their own initiative in the arduous struggle of the 16th Infantry Division (motorised) on their left flank and routed the enemy, destroying numerous tanks.

'Today, at the conclusion of the battle of annihilation around Uman, I want to recognise and express my personal thanks to the Leibstandarte SS Adolf Hitler for their exemplary effort and incomparable bravery.

'The battles around Archangelsk will be recorded indelibly and forever in the war history of the Leibstandarte SS Adolf Hitler.'

Reichsführer-SS Heinrich Himmler could not have asked for anything better. Here indeed was justification for the nurturing and building of an élite. Himmler doubtless reflected also that, only a year before, men such as Kempf would cheerfully have waived their pensions rather than toss even a morsel of praise in the direction of the Waffen-SS.

Times had indeed changed. The chicken-fancier and amateur herbalist had been proved triumphantly right: a new Army had been created which had every right to rival and at times outstrip the pretensions of the old.

Or had it? The Leibstandarte might be carving itself a place on the roll of honour in those early months of

110

Barbarossa, but the Waffen-SS was by no means distinguishing itself everywhere else. From the SS Divisions Leibstandarte, Das Reich, Totenkopf and Viking it was legitimate to expect that hand-picked personnel, good training, effective leadership and first-class armament would produce a very special brand of excellence.

Himmler, it will be recalled, had to make doubtless distressing compromises with his conscience over such matters as racial purity and physical perfection when it came to recruiting for the Waffen-SS at war. Where demands for troops proved heavy, it was bound to be only a matter of time before these imperfections showed.

Less than a month after the beginning of Barbarossa, along the northern section of the Finnish front, SS Kampfgruppe Nord, with a Finnish and a German Army division, assaulted the Russian stronghold at Salla. The result was a complete rout. Five SS battalions were badly mauled in two attacks. On the third attempt the Russians, as if losing patience with such patent amateurism, threw in everything they had in an attempt to dislodge the interlopers.

The result was better than anything that the Red Army could have hoped for. The Russian attack threw the SS into a state of panic. Many of the Waffen-SS cast aside their weapons and fled the battle, screaming in terror: 'The Russian tanks are coming!' Thirteen officers were killed and seventy-three other ranks, 232 were wounded and 147 missing.

The figures for those dead were not a source of much anxiety to Himmler. What worried the Reichsführer-SS was that some men had so demeaned themselves as to be taken prisoner. The code of the SS stipulated a fight to the death – either that or suicide.

Plainly, ideological indoctrination was no guarantee of success in combat. Himmler, even in his most private moments, must have been forced to admit that the trouble lay in the basic composition of Nord. It had come into being through a shotgun wedding of two former

Totenkopf regiments. Among them were doubtless fanatical Nazis of irreproachable credentials: racial paragons all. But there had also been men trained for police duties and utterly inexperienced when it came to combat. What could a thug, adept at directing concentration-camp guard detachments, know of the brutal realities of the battlefield? Reservists, many of them on the edge of middle age, were good in the SS for little beyond disciplining and bullying defenceless prisoners. A fatal weakness in the composition of the Waffen-SS had shown itself for the first time. It must indeed have been a bitter lesson for the Reichsführer-SS when he received a report on the conduct in battle of SS Kampfgruppe Nord.

If fatal flaws were already beginning to appear in the structure, Hitler did not notice them. At his East Prussian headquarters in Rastenburg, the Führer stared with grim satisfaction at the giant arrows on the map streaking south-east. There was not a break in the seemingly unstoppable progress of Army Group South towards the Sea of Azov.

But with the men of the Waffen-SS, and every bit as much for the tired, begrimed, bloodyminded Wehrmacht infantryman, there lurked a doubt. What *real* chance had they in this Godforsaken, inhospitable land, with its vast reaches and seemingly limitless manpower? A few million casualties meant nothing to Stalin; he could well afford them. Into the minds of some of the older officers there floated a saying remembered from World War I: *'Viele Hunde sind der Tod des Hasen' (Many hounds spell death to the hare).*

Where was the strategy of Blitzkrieg now? True, there were advances in the first weeks and months, but an advance had to presuppose a breakthrough leading to ultimate destruction. Too often the situation at all levels was total confusion that was not reflected in the maps.

Every thrust meant a return in kind, every blow a riposte, every pincer found itself outflanked by a Soviet arm. In a mood of petulance one bewildered Panzer commander had asked: 'Are the Russians outflanking us or are we outflanking them?'

Many of the short-term gains of the Leibstandarte came, it seemed to many observers, through Russian miscalculations rather than brilliant thinking by the Wehrmacht. For example, at the town of Sasselji, Russian troops thought they had found a point of retreat and blundered straight into the occupying Germans.

Victories like this brought only limited satisfaction. But this was a strange sort of war. At one moment, near Sasselji, the Leibstandarte was fighting in maize and sunflower fields; the next, at the large industrial city of Kherson, the conflict was street-to-street, house-to-house, room-to-room. Towards the end of August, 17th Army had crossed the Dnieper and there was an order for the advance on the forbidding, drought-ridden emptiness of the Nogai steppes.

Here indeed was a region that would test the staying power of even the most flexible élite formations: desert country where troops coughed and choked and stumbled through red-brown dust, which hung like a curse over the slowly moving columns. Dead tree trunks and telegraph poles were the only markers in this arid waste-land.

Then from Führer headquarters came a new directive: Army Group South was, as a main objective, to knife its way through to the Crimea which was to be captured at all costs.

This sudden acceleration rattled Stalin. The Soviet headquarters, STAVKA, gave instructions that propaganda was to be whipped up. The Russian press was fed with bloodthirsty stories of what the Fascist barbarians would do to the beautiful Crimea if allowed to occupy it. Meanwhile, the Soviets informed the Russian people, the struggle to throw the Nazis out of the Ukraine was meeting with some success. One magazine editorial trumpeted: 'The Dnieper flows red with German corpses.'

There were corpses all right, but many of them – a

horrifyingly high number – were not the result of the fortunes of war but of the deliberate policy of atrocities practised by both sides.

The usual humane conventions of warfare were brushed aside as outdated sentimentality. In their place, the Germans had perfected *Kommisarbefehl*: the order that all political commissars of the Red Army captured in battle were to be shot forthwith.

It could indeed be argued that the Germans were only repaying in kind. Field Marshal von Manstein, in his memoirs, related that on the very first days of the offensive 'our troops came across a German patrol which had been cut off by the enemy earlier on. All of its members were dead and horribly mutilated.'

The onset of winter was signalled by the appearance of fresh Siberian troops, and October opened with a grim five-day battle for Taganrog, reached by establishing a bridgehead across the Mius river.

During this engagement the Leibstandarte was left in no doubt about the sort of enemy they were facing. Six members of the SS Division were captured while on patrol. They were handed over to the Soviet secret police. Later, their bodies were stuffed down a well at Taganrog: they had been mutilated with indescribable barbarity.

It was later learnt that the six, who had already been at the tender mercies of Russian tortures, were led into a courtyard shortly before the arrival of the German forces. The Russian execution squads had then been let lose with axes, bayonets and rifle butts.

Sepp Dietrich's reprisals were swift and merciless. The order went out that all Russians captured within the next three days, irrespective of whether they had fought at Taganrog or not, were to be shot in reprisal; altogether four thousand men, many of them presumably innocent of any atrocity, were mown down on Dietrich's personal orders.

There was no shortage of men willing to carry out these

acts of revenge. If there were, then specialist extermination squads existed.

It has been argued by the apologists that such licensed murderers cannot, in all justice, be described as members of the Waffen-SS; they were a ragtag and bobtail of racial Germans and foreigners, co-opted for the purpose; no more frontline fighters than some of the police thugs swelling the Totenkopf.

But the distinction between the members of the extermination squads and the Waffen-SS became increasingly blurred as the war went on. Those who breached the iron discipline of the Waffen-SS frequently found themselves transferred for 'punishment duties' to the Einsatzgruppen (action groups), set up four weeks before Germany attacked the Soviet Union. Organisation was in the hands of the Reichssicherheitshauptamt (RSHA), the Reich Chief Security Office in Berlin and the high commands of the Wehrmacht and the Army. Altogether four Einsatzgruppen were set up, with the initials A, B, C and D. Each group was between 800 and 1,200 men in strength. Their officers came from the Gestapo, the SD and the SS. Their members were recruited from the same organisations as well as from the Ordnungspolizei (civil police) and, in the overwhelming majority, from the Waffen-SS.

For example, Einsatzgruppe A, under SS Brigadeführer Franz Stahlecker and SS Brigadeführer Heinz Jost, was made up as follows: 34.4 per cent members of the Waffen-SS; 3.5 per cent members of the Sicherheitsdienst (SD); 4.1 per cent from Kriminalpolizei; 9 per cent from the Gestapo; 8.8 per cent from Hilfspolizei (Auxiliary Police); 13.4 per cent from the Ordungspolizei; the rest were technical and office staff. In all, it has been estimated that up to 1,500 members of the Waffen-SS served with the Einsatzgruppen.

The task of the Einsatzgruppen was to combat partisans and members of the opposition, and to uproot and dispose of entire sections of the population, mostly in the

115

Soviet Union. Its first objective was the persecution of Communists, Jews and gypsies, but the activities of the groups did not stop there. Hitler saw his programme in ideological terms, or so he claimed in *Mein Kampf* when he wrote: 'Our task is not to Germanise the east in the old sense, to teach the people living there German language and German laws, but to make sure that in the east only people of truly German blood live.' It has been estimated that the Einsatzgruppen were responsible for the murder of at least two million Slavs.

The calibre of recruit has been described by George Keppler, Commander of 2nd SS Panzer Division Das Reich:

'They are late or fall asleep on duty. They are court-martialled but are told they can escape punishment by volunteering for Special Commandos. For fear of punishment and in the belief that their career is ruined anyway, these young men ask to be transferred to the Special Commandos.

'Well, these commandos, where they are first put through special training, are murder commandos. When the young men realise what they are being asked to do and refuse to take part in mass murder, they are told the orders are given them as a form of punishment. Either they can obey and take that punishment or they can disobey and be shot. In any case their career is over and done with. By such methods decent young men are frequently turned into criminals.'

An Einsatzgruppe would be attached to a specific Army Group and move with it, and frequently had the support of other Waffen-SS formations.

The following report, submitted as evidence at Nuremberg, shows the Einsatzgruppen in action:

'The head of a collective farm, in the vicinity of Bobruisk, was arrested because he had intentionally dis-

116

organised production by ordering the farmers to cease their work, and by giving instructions to hide the harvested shares in the forests. A total of 600 persons was arrested in Bobruisk and vicinity by a detachment of Einsatzkommando 8. Out of these, 407 persons were liquidated.

'The executed comprised, in addition to the above mentioned, Jews and elements who had shown open resistance against orders issued by German occupation authorities, or had openly incited to acts of sabotage . . . A large-scale anti-Jewish action was carried out in the village of Lachoisk. In the course of this action 920 Jews were executed with the support of a Kommando of the SS Division Reich. The village may now be described as "free of Jews".'

Fighting soldiers or members of an SS murder band – it was all the same when it came to facing the Russian winter; particularly the winter of 1941 when the men of the Leibstandarte prepared for their next objective, the assault on Rostov.

It was not just the snow, although before long there was to be plenty of that. Neither was it the exquisitely cruel sub-zero temperatures that made grown men cry and drove them to stripping clothes off their dead comrades. Already by November there had been rain – not sporadic heavy showers, but needle-sharp downpours that swept straight into the columns, halting the most determined advance.

Rain did not just chill to the bone and make its victims bath in mud. It brought with it disease and death: from bronchitis, dysentry and infections of the lungs. It severed communications and disrupted fuel supplies. The gauge of Russian railway tracks was different from Germany's; there was no way adequate supplies of food could be got through, no replacements for boots or for the socks that had rotted away in the filth and the wet.

All this before winter – the *Russian* winter – had really arrived . . .

None of these conditions of course stopped the Russian guerrilla bands. They continued their deadly assaults, harrying the columns. The first November days brought the snow and conditions worsened: conditions which had to be withstood on a staple diet of thick soup of ground buckwheat and millet. The mood of despair which settled even on the Leibstandarte caused some of the Russian prisoners mild astonishment. For by their standards this winter was a mild and gentle thing. They marvelled at any enemy whose commanders could send them into battle so ill equipped, without proper clothes and food.

On 17 November 3rd Panzer Corps, with the Leibstandarte under its command, opened the assault on Rostov. Originally it had been intended to attack from the north, but Russian opposition proved too strong. Now the approach was made from the coast, and at first the forces moved with all the old dash. After only two days of fighting, the Germans smashed through to the north of Rostov, but soon forces already defending that area found themselves in trouble.

Soviet 37th Army hurtled ahead – and the Germans were in a novel situation. Often in the past, Russian forces had been pressed untidily into battle. The result had been chaos. But not this time. SS Viking, helping to clear the northern suburbs of the town, was forced to give ground; soon a situation developed where a breakout was impossible. For eight days the Germans battled against the Russians and the inevitable citizen militia.

Field Marshal Rundstedt, Commander-in-Chief of Army Group South and the senior officer in the German Army, was in charge of forces which had been ground into total exhaustion by cold and disease. It was a humiliating moment for this tough, professional soldier who had fought under the Kaiser: he had to admit that to defend Rostov was impossible.

The sorely pressed German forces could not be

expected to be up to the job. The lesser evil would be to fall back to the better defended Mius river line, even if it meant abandoning Taganrog. Expecting Hitler to reject the plan, Rundstedt acted first and reported afterwards.

After the war, Rundstedt told Allied interrogators: '. . . An order came to me from the Führer: "Remain where you are and retreat no further." I immediately wired back: "It is madness to attempt to hold. In the first place the troops cannot do it, and in the second place if they do not retreat they will be destroyed. I repeat that this order be rescinded or that you find someone else." That same night the Führer's reply arrived: "I am acceding to your request. Please give up your command." '

Germany's most celebrated soldier then left the eastern front, never to return.

The Leibstandarte, whose Waffen-SS battle this was, had lost. Professionalism however dedicated, ideology however deeply inculcated, counted as nought without reinforcements, adequate clothing – and, the old problem, sheer lack of numbers.

The year 1941 was drawing to a close. It was but five months since Hitler had launched Barbarossa, less than a year since he had exclaimed in a moment of hysterical hyperbole: 'When Barbarossa commences, the world will hold its breath and make no comment!' At that time Hitler had been told – and had believed – that the enemy would have approximately 155 divisions, a figure which matched that of Germany.

And now? German Intelligence was producing new figures: ominous statistics which turned many a General pale. They were these: despite the fact that German armies stood before Leningrad and Moscow, despite the prisoners taken, the Soviet Union could muster two hundred infantry divisions, thirty-five cavalry divisions and forty armoured brigades. It was further estimated that there were sixty-three divisions elsewhere in the Soviet Union, together with six-and-a-half cavalry

119

divisions and eleven armoured divisions. It was also pointed out to Hitler that Stalin had recruiting methods which made those of Nazi Germany seem positively benign.

No longer was it solely the burnt-out forces of southern Russia that felt the blasts of cold. A chill was spreading slowly towards Berlin and into the hearts and minds of some of the Führer's High Command. To many the sensation seemed uncommonly like fear.

There were going to be a number of long, hard winters ahead for the German Army.

7

Back in mid-November 1941, Army Group Centre had lunged towards Moscow. Hitler vowed that by the time he was finished with the capital, there would be no embraces left in the Russian bear. But that adventure, code-named Operation Typhoon, had been launched too late and the pattern become all too familiar.

The heavy snows and the sub-zero temperatures had arrived, and with them the frost-bite that found its way only too easily into the skins of the insufficiently clothed, half-starved Germans. Telescopic sights of tanks became useless; fires had to be lit below the engines of the tanks; the oil became viscous.

The effect of Russian cold on the fighting man in the field cannot adequately be described by anyone who has not experienced it. When boiling soup was issued to the troops from the field kitchen, it had to be eaten in thirty seconds before it became lukewarm. Within sixty seconds it became a block of ice. Intestinal disorders and frost-bite were rampant . . . Some soldiers, driven quite literally mad, dosed themselves with schnapps and, half drunk, took their own lives with a hand-grenade pressed against the stomach.

The Russians, on the other hand, thrived: thrived to roll back the enemy from the gates of Moscow. It was a violent and unexpected counter-stroke by one hundred Russian divisions. There had been disappointment for the Führer too at Leningrad, which had been cut off from the rest of Russia by a ring of Panzers, all the while subjected to intensive bombardment from artillery and aircraft. Here, despite the cold and the hunger, the people of Leningrad – four thousand starved to death by Christmas – had held out gallantly.

The general air of gloom did not escape the Waffen-SS commanders as they assessed the cost of Barbarossa so far.

It was indeed a grim toll. Casualties amounted to 407 officers and 7,930 other ranks killed, 816 officers and 26,299 other ranks wounded, thirteen officers and 923 men missing, and four officers and 125 men killed in accidents.

Waffen-SS losses were, in proportion, much higher than those of the Army. By mid-November, SS Das Reich Division, had lost 60 per cent of its combat strength, including a staggering 40 per cent of its officers. It had spearheaded a major attack on Moscow, achieving one of the deepest penetrations of the offensive.

Although, as we have seen, SS Commanders such as Sepp Dietrich were not above disobeying orders, the outcome of insubordination never made life easier for those who were brave or foolhardy enough to try it. Withdrawal under hopeless conditions was not the way, generally speaking, of the Waffen-SS. The Leibstandarte, and Das Reich in particular, invariably obeyed Hitler's orders of 'no withdrawal'. The result in Russia was often nothing but increased losses.

What had been achieved in the first months of blood-letting in Russia? What had been the long-term advantages of all those tactical successes in the Ukraine? The answer was ironic: it had taken very heavy casualities for the Waffen-SS to achieve the admiration and even the respect of an Army which had regarded it originally as an unwholesome band of *arrivistes*. Himmler, for all his bureaucratic intrigues and racial claptrap, had been unable to improve the brand image of the armed SS legions; the men did it themselves on their own merits, but the cost had proved appalling.

The severe winter of the Rostov withdrawal inhibited widespread military action, but with the onset of spring spirits rose again and Army Group South found itself the decisive front, its task to destroy the enemy in front of the Don, to cross the Caucasus and seize its oil-producing centres.

In May the pincers of German armour sealed off the Russian bridge-head south of Kharkov. For the Leibstandarte it was time for a breather and then for a change of scene.

Hitler was worried about the French defences and his élite forces were scooped out of Russia for a spell of duty in the west. They left behind them an enemy which had been encircled and destroyed many times but still had the awesome resources to come back for yet more.

What could the German commanders really know of the Russian mind, of a fighting machine that was positively eager to sacrifice ten of its lives for a single German? Colonel Bernd von Kleist wrote with an awful prophetic truth: 'The German Army in fighting Russia is like an elephant attacking a host of ants. The elephant will kill thousands, perhaps even millions of ants, but in the end their numbers will overcome him and he will be eaten to the bone.'

The Alpine air at the Führer's Obersalzberg retreat was only pleasantly cold on that November day in 1942. The icy blast of the real world outside, however, hit the relaxing generals like a sledge-hammer: a tough Russian armoured force broke clean through the Rumanian 3rd Army just north-west of Stalingrad. The Russians were driving in great strength from the north and south of the city to cut it off and to force the German 6th Army either to retreat or be surrounded.

Hitler, after flying into a series of tantrums at the very mention of withdrawal, personally ordered the 6th Army to stand fast. The fighting, bitter and bloody, continued with Hitler reiterating: 'Surrender is forbidden. The 6th Army will hold their positions to the last man and the last round and by their heroic endurance will make an unforgettable contribution towards the establishment of a defensive front and the salvation of the western world.'

It was futile obstinacy on the part of the German war-lord; 6th Army was finished utterly and passed into Russian captivity.

Stalingrad was a blackened mass; the Army which had attempted to capture it was dazed and broken, its pitiful remnants huddled in blood-caked blankets against the ice and snow with their sickening temperatures.

The Waffen-SS inherited the repercussions of the immolation of Stalingrad. The Red Army was now far freer from opposition – freer to sweep westward and streak to the Dnieper. In the south the Germans ran the risk of being pinned against the Black Sea and virtually annihilated. The threatened rout had to be stopped, and quickly.

Like an actor who plans his entrances at the highest pitch of drama, Sepp Dietrich gleefully seized the chance to occupy the centre of the stage yet again.

A rock-hard battle group with Dietrich in command was catapulted into action. First, skies above were darkened by wave upon wave of screaming Stukas. Then came the three-pronged armoured assault which was a pool of talents of all the outstanding SS legions.

Out on the right arm was the Reconnaissance Battalion of the Leibstandarte. Placed in the centre came the Der Führer Regiment of Das Reich, and with it the Leibstandarte Panzers. Over on the left was Fritz Witt's 1st SS Panzer Grenadier. It all added up to a tough array of military muscle. Every sinew was to be strained in a desperate bid to hold the line. This time, spirits did not plunge with the unspeakable winter temperatures; morale soared high even in the snowdrifts which clogged the movement of the solid mass of lumbering armour.

The Russians, flushed with the victory of Stalingrad and lashed into tireless movement by their high command were in no mood to slacken the tempo of the offensive. The fighting was as vicious as anything that the SS had yet encountered, and Dietrich's battle-plan had to be recast constantly in the face of decimation of his units.

Village after village, where the SS had comfortably settled in and embarked on its reign of terror, was snatched from the Germans. But retaliation never ceased; even the wounded hobbled back into the hell.

The Leibstandarte's Grenadier Battalion was in the hands of one of the legendary figures of the Waffen-SS: 31-year-old Joachim (he liked to be known as 'Jochen') Peiper, former Adjutant to Himmler, came speeding to the relief of 320th Infantry Division. It had been surrounded and saddled with a pitifully large number of wounded; its Commander knew precisely what would happen to these men if they were abandoned to the enemy. But for how long could the 320th hold out against the ceaseless batterings of the Russians?

Peiper was determined to slice into the enemy and push his hard-pressed division as far into Russian territory as he could. A protective screen was formed around the beleaguered division. Slowly, painfully, Peiper edged his men forward, beating off infantry and tank assaults, and saw them safely across the river ice.

Such an action was typical, not just of the Leibstandarte, but of all the Waffen-SS force which, now the Army was willing to agree, had something very close to heroic stature. No assignment was beneath the dignity of the company commanders of field rank: they led their men in hand-to-hand fighting for even the smallest village. An 'avowedly political force', the Waffen-SS were behaving uncommonly like the Wehrmacht soldiers at their best.

The German-held town of Kharkov, seat of the heavy industry of the Ukraine, loomed ahead. Here it was vital for Stalin to break the back of the German southern front. The Soviets had relished their recent victories. At Rostov the Red Flag flew triumphantly, while at Stalingrad the dead of the Wehrmacht lay rotting. Another reversal would be unthinkable. The advance must continue inexorably.

The German commanders saw the spectre of another Stalingrad, particularly when a terribly familiar order came from the headquarters of the Führer: not so much as an inch of ground must be relinquished. In his long discourses with toadying subordinates who did not dare question even his simplest decisions, Hitler rambled obsessively about holding the Donets Basin. 'It is the Ruhr of the Soviet Union,' insisted the war lord. 'If it is lost, I can see no point in continuing this war.'

Stalin, equally obsessive, was for hurling through the Donets with every resource he possessed. Then there would be nothing to stop the Soviet Armies reaching the Dnieper; the forces of Field Marshal von Manstein, Commander-in-Chief of Army Group Don, would be cut off from their rearward communications.

To Manstein only one course spelt sense: the line must be shortened drastically and more troops released to stem the tide. The alternative? Nothing less than a Super-Stalingrad.

Beneath an outwardly calm exterior, Manstein fretted, and the long nights were rendered sleepless by the ghost of the 6th Army at Stalingrad and its nightmarish death ride.

Manstein embarked eventually on an act of sheer courage which would have been beyond the moral capability of a lesser man: he flew to Hitler's headquarter's determined to thrash out his argument for withdrawal.

For hours the conference dragged on. Conversation with the war-lord was apt to be a one-sided affair with the unfortunate guest having to submit to an endless history lecture, all couched in such a way as to demonstrate the indisputable miltary genius of the speaker.

But Manstein was made of stronger stuff and he had a few historical precedents of his own. And for good measure he quoted a line of Frederick the Great: 'He that would defend everything ends by defending nothing.'

The result was an awkward silence and a sullen glare from Hitler who did not take kindly to anyone stealing the maxims of his idol. But, for all his obsessions, the terrible experience of Stalingrad had shattered the seeming infallibility of the man who had brought the German Army a string of remarkable victories. How could he lose ground with a minimum loss of dignity? Some withdrawal was plainly necessary; the Führer agreed finally to Manstein's forces pulling back to the eastern Donets region as far as the Mius river.

As he left Hitler, the blanket of depression which had weighed down the Field Marshal was suddenly pulled away. Perhaps now there was a chance after all. The withdrawal would be painful, of course, but at least any losses would be preferable to total annihilation.

And so the German forces pulled back from the Donets to the much shortened Mius position and a solid line was established. To the middle Donets went the formations of the 1st Panzer Army, commanded by General von Mackensen. They would protect the northern wing of the Army Group. From the lower Don went the 4th Army, making for the area between the Donets and the Dnieper bend on the western wing of the forces known as Army Group Don.

They were dogged, not just by the Red Army, but by that equally cruel adversary, the Russian winter. Drivers, almost pole-axed by fatigue, struggled along roads long submerged by the mountains of snow. The columns were spread out over enormous distances and the divisional commanders, touring their regiments, lashed them ever forward. If the troops were complaining of weariness, the physical resources of the engineers, coping with the endless breakdowns and the inevitable accidents, were strained to cracking point. For them there could be no question of sleep; the impetus to carry on came from their officers, who reminded them of their sure fate should the Russians win the day.

It was no empty threat, for the Germans were attempting to stem the advance of an army possessing an eightfold superiority in numbers and weapons.

To Stalin and his senior staff, any sign of German withdrawal spelt the realisation of a dream: the blasting into oblivion of the Nazi's entire southern wing along six hundred miles. Three Armies would be wiped off the face of the earth. It would be a blow so terrible that not even Hitler would recover from it.

Sections of the German Army presented a pitiable spectacle: casualties had reduced some companies to little more than twenty to sixty men. In the endless dark Russian nights they were expected to hold sectors up to a mile and a half wide. And these scattered pockets of resistance began to dwindle as the Russians harassed them unmercifully and picked them off one by one.

Army Detachment Lanz, together with Italian and Hungarian reinforcements, was fighting defensively east and south of Kharkov. Kharkov! Would Hitler really relent and rid himself of the senseless, suicidal defence of a town where already the partisan fighters were grouping, and where a victory would be pointless?

Hitler would not relent. The spectre of a second Stalingrad came back to haunt the sleepless hours of Manstein. No matter that Kharkov was already strategically outmanoeuvred by vast Soviet armies. No matter that the enemy was already racing ahead to the *south* where, in the very name of common sense, the chief priorities lay. Here the Russians could be intercepted and smashed, that thrust for the Dnieper halted now and forever.

All arguments were brushed aside; Hitler issued an order that allowed for no ambiguity whatsoever. Army Detachment Lanz, which at that time did not come under Manstein's command, received the order that Kharkov must be held. The task of defending the town was given to the newly-raised SS Panzer Corps under Paul Hausser, that Commander of the former Verfügungstruppe who had commanded the first of Himmler's Junkerschülen. The Corps contained what looked like a highly effective amalgam of the cream of Waffen-SS talent: the two crack divisions of Das Reich and Leibstandarte SS Adolf Hitler.

Manstein had one more try to talk the Führer out of an enterprise which had all the hallmarks of failure – and criminal failure at that. Quite apart from the fact that such a campaign amounted to military nonsense, it was also a bad psychological blunder. The Waffen-SS had been taught to regard itself as an élite which would at all times be treated like one. What was it to make now of its Supreme Commander who seemed prepared to see first-rate fighting formations destroyed in an enterprise doomed from the outset?

On 13 February, Adolf Hitler repeated that Kharkov must be held. Lanz was told to get the message to Hausser. For a moment Adolf Hitler allowed himself to relax. The Waffen-SS had been given its orders, and did not the Waffen-SS implement its instructions without question and without regard to cost?

In most cases, certainly. But there had to be an exception to prove any rule, and the exception in February 1943 at Kharkov was Paul Hausser.

The doom of the place was heralded by the roar and the thunder of the Soviet tanks, bent on a sole objective: total encirclement. Artillery fire rattled along the supply routes. Hausser had already made up his mind on his course of action. He had no wish, as a Waffen-SS man, to betray his Führer, for that is how any deviation from orders would surely be regarded. Yet lives would be needlessly thrown away. Hausser made yet another attempt to deflect Hitler: he appealed vehemently to Lanz to intercede and stop the defence that had no chance whatever of success. In a memo he sketched out succinctly the state of affairs facing SS Panzer Corps.

'Inside Kharkov mob firing at troops and vehicles. No forces available for mopping-up since everything in front line. City, including railway, stores and ammunition dumps, effectively dynamited at Army orders. City burning. Systematic withdrawal increasingly improbable each day. Assumptions underlying Kharkov's strategic importance no longer valid. Request renewed Führer decision whether Kharkov to be defended to the last man.'

Lanz later revealed that he agreed with Hausser, but dare not act. Later Hausser tried again: 'Decision on disengagement required by twelve noon. Signed Hausser.'

Again came a blank refusal, backed up after further exchanges by a repetition of the original order: 'Panzer Corps will hold to the last man its present position on the east front of Kharkov in accordance with Führer's order.'

And, as if to remove any lingering uncertainty, there came a communication personally from Hitler:

1. The eastern front of Kharkov must be held.
2. The considerable SS formations now arriving must be employed in freeing Kharkov's communications and in defeating the enemy forces pressing against Kharkov from the north-west.

Hausser was prepared to push his luck with Hitler to the limit, but he made up his mind that until Kharkov was directly threatened he would not disobey the order of his inflexible master. A detachment of tanks of Das Reich SS Panzer Grenadier Division flung itself at the invading Russians in the north-west and south-east of the city. Unexpectedly, the German thrust was successful and the Russians took a hammering which disconcerted its commanders.

But this was mere time-borrowing. Back came the Red Army – and with interest. Encirclement became more or less complete. There was only one remedy for Hausser: get out, stage a retreat and, if possible, return for a fresh crack later. Such a subtle approach, however, flew directly in the face of Hitler's express orders.

Hausser, that doughty old war-horse who had seen service in the old Imperial Army of the Kaiser, was not prepared to sacrifice his professional pride to the whims of anyone, Adolf Hitler included. Realism was called for, not the illusions of a man cocooned from the realities in the safety of his command post.

Casting all doubts and temptations of delay aside, Hausser dashed off the following communication: 'To avoid troops being encircled and to save material, orders will be given at 1300 to fight way through behind Udy sector on edge of city. Fighting through enemy lines in progress, also street-fighting in south-west and west of the city.'

Craven fear gripped Lanz at this flagrant piece of treason. What on earth would happen now? What form would the wrath of the Führer take? Lanz, by now whistling in the dark, riposted: 'Kharkov will be defended under all circumstances.'

Hausser tossed aside this communication as a piece of irrelevant babbling. The break-out to the south-west was on. The troops and the tanks turned their backs on Kharkov, sent on their way by the full fury of the Soviet bombardment.

Das Reich continued to fight, putting up a brave front amid what it saw as the shame of capitulation. But soon its detachments were forced out, the Russians firing at the backside of stragglers. In Kharkov itself, joyful partisans emerged from the smoke rubble and, as the very echoes of the departing tanks died away, raised the Red Flag.

The scene at the Nazi leader's headquarters can be imagined. Or, rather, it cannot by anyone who had not experienced the lash of Hitler's tongue, the demonic fury which turned the Führer white and, for a while, made him incapable of rational decision or effective command. That rage, always terrible to behold, was not to lessen – but not because Hausser had disobeyed his orders. Hitler had been found to be, quite simply, wrong. It was soon becoming increasingly clear that the decision to withdraw was not only correct but, in the light of future events, decidedly advantageous.

As it was, Hausser had left withdrawal to almost the last minute: the escape corridor was less than a mile wide. Red patrols had pushed into the suburb of Ossnova, and Jochen Peiper was despatched in a fruitless attempt to head them off.

The rest of the Germans, in what looked like singularly ignominious retreat, made for Krasnograd in the south. Like wounded animals that still have some vicious strength left, the Leibstandarte and Das Reich and Der Führer kicked out all the way.

At Krasnograd, Hausser intended to lure the pursuing Russians into a trap, simply by standing firm and then flinging his own forces directly in the face of Stalin's battalions. Strength was improved by the arrival of Totenkopf which had earlier linked up with the three Panzer divisions of 48th Panzer Corps.

The two armoured corps, one Army and one SS, as the components of 4th Panzer Army, now launched a concerted attack with effective air support northward towards Pavlograd and Losuvaya. Retreat had now been turned into an advance and once again morale soared among the SS formations. On 25 February, 4th Panzer Army clashed with a Russian army group led by General

M. M. Popov and wiped it out. Now it was the turn of the Russians to run, and they were pursued mercilessly.

There was evidence too that Stalin's forces were getting rattled and making bad mistakes. At one point the Russians found themselves trapped between the defensive lines of the 1st SS (Leibstandarte) Panzer Grenadier Division and the two attacking divisions of the SS Panzer Corps.

Hausser promptly exploited the weakness by wheeling the wing of the 3rd SS Totenkopf Panzer Grenadier Division, and by 3 March had encircled the Soviet force west of Bereka. The Russians found themselves at the mercy of the Waffen-SS: of Totenkopf, Das Reich and the Leibstandarte.

Tank corps and rifle divisons were decimated; forces were buzzed by ground-attack aircraft. The initiative, for the moment at least, seemed to have passed back to Hitler, although he was scarcely entitled to take credit for it.

Battle morale, although high among the SS, had been given a severe dent by the death of 'Papa' Eicke, killed when his light communications aircraft was shot down on a visit to a forward unit. In a laudatory obituary Hausser spoke of the former concentration camp guard as an inspiration to any division. There was mention of how he had inspired foreign volunteers within the Waffen-SS.

It is, as we have seen, a somewhat incomplete picture. But, in justice, it must be said that a change had come over Eicke in Russia.

His promotion to SS Obergruppenführer had made him into something of a recluse. He had shut himself up in his billet for days at a time, cutting tactical signs out of situation maps and playing his own war games – all with some coyness lest senior, and probably disdainful, officers had noticed a sudden acquired taste for military affairs.

All the same, his record could not but condemn him. Eicke had originally been dismissed from the Army, openly despised the officer corps, had been a failure as a policeman and a distinct liability to the National Socialists who had been seeking a respectable identity in the eyes of the world.

But there was no time for memories, tender or otherwise, of 'Papa' Eicke. Hausser went on to visit the battle groups and he was able to report a rather brighter picture. He could speak with some confidence of the counter-attack about to be launched. The intention was that the Corps would concentrate behind the Mscha river at Krasnograd and launch a counter-offensive with the aim of recapturing Kharkov. The Russians seemed to be behaving like so many demented lemmings, hurtling forward obligingly towards the pocket being provided for them. In the last ten days of February a counter-attack looked possible.

Needless to say, it all depended on the Russian weather, which lowered like some sardonic spectre over the battle fronts. Spring might, at first sight, have seemed a blessing. But spring would inevitably mean a thaw and that, in its turn, would mean mud – a black, sticky mass which lay glutinously on roads and paths and which would hold up progress with all the same aggravation as the snow had done.

Once again speed was important. The Russians realised that the steam-roller must go on. Stalin was not given to prayer, but he came near to it during the weeks leading up to this new battle of Kharkov. It was desperately important that the snow should continue; snow was something the Russians understood.

The Soviet High Command, one eye on its barometer and the other on its maps, switched its units right into the path of Hausser's SS Panzer Corps in order to protect Kharkov.

And then came the thaw. Stalin redoubled his energies. The Russian 25th Guards Rifle Division flung itself against the German Panzers. For five solid days of fighting, Kharkov was held against capture from the south.

But Stalin had overreached himself through sheer impetuosity. The Germans stood to the west of Kharkov; the battle for one of the foremost cities of the Ukraine was beginning.

This particular prize, though, was not to be gained for six whole days. Hausser, the man who had sent the Führer into a frenzy by disobeying specific orders, was to be proved right. He was to recapture a city that would have been lost for ever if the strict orders of the war-lord had been followed.

Insubordination by a senior member of the Waffen-SS saved Kharkov, and Hitler stood condemned for what, if he had been obeyed, would undoubtedly have been another Stalingrad.

It had not been a mere head-on assault on the objective; that would have been to adopt the reckless tactics of the Russians. Everything was worked out by Hausser with mathematical precision. First the city was sealed; there was some time of comparatively leisurely waiting. When conditions seemed to be favourable and the assault detachments, the Leibstandarte and Totenkopf, were alerted, the orders rattled over the teleprinter.

'SS Panzer Corps will take Kharkov. Its eastern wing will cut the Kharkov-Chuguyev road. Strong forces will thrust into the city from the north-east. In the west the city is only to be sealed off.'

And that is how they went in. The sudden thaw was not quite the problem everyone had feared. By 9 March, Kharkov lay open. Two days later the Leibstandarte went in and, with it, the 2nd SS Panzer Grenadier Regiment elbowed its way towards Red Square, fighting partisan defenders tooth and nail. Units on the fringe of Kharkov were, meanwhile, not neglected, and the Waffen-SS was also employed in sweeping the opposition from around the city.

On the western edge, Das Reich Division came up against a firmly-bunched contingent of Russians and were bogged down in defensive fighting. For a time, it looked as if it would be a mere spectator at the feast and that was not Hausser's idea at all. The whole point of the exercise had been for the Waffen-SS to keep on the move. There, only too happy to force the acceleration, was a company of Der Führer which hurtled towards a row of houses in the city. The west was fruit for the picking.

But movement could be too fast. What happened if there was a terrible trap waiting, as there had been at Stalingrad? Das Reich was hauled out of the street-fighting and brought over to strengthen the eastern wing. Totenkopf Division helped to throw out the ragged scraps of Soviet resistance. Kharkov once again belonged to Adolf Hitler.

The incredible had happened. Hitler, it had been thought, was utterly discredited by his appalling miscalculation and cretinous obstinacy at Stalingrad. This, Stalin had believed, was a blow which surely spelt the end of Nazi Germany's avowed intention to blast Soviet Russia off the face of the earth. The hammer and sickle would break the swastika; Bolshevism would triumph and the Red Army would sweep across the Dnieper to the ultimate subjugation of a Germany which had voluntarily trampled on the already withered plant of democracy.

And the reality? A glance at the situation map, a look at the casualty figures, answered that. Where was the Soviet 6th Army? Where was Popov's Armoured Group? Where were the Soviet tanks? Corps and brigades were in flight and in confusion. Fifty-two divisions and brigades had been snatched from the front in a brilliant offensive.

It was a terrible indictment of Stalin. In any nation with even the trappings of democracy it would have spelt revolution. But this was not a war of the old kind in which two clever soldiers faced one another. Both Soviet Russia and Nazi Germany were iron dictatorships, ruled by terror, whose leaders were not easily removed.

Even so, Stalin knew that he must recover the initiative quickly. And in that he was to be helped by Hitler, whose ill-fortune was soon monumental.

But that, in the dizzy victory of Kharkov, was not even thought possible. To the north of subjugated Kharkov raced Peiper, reaching, in mid-March, Byelgorod on the Donets. A link-up was achieved with the Grossdeutschland Division.

The SS surveyed its casualties: in the three months of 1943 it had lost 365 officers and 11,154 other ranks in dead, wounded and missing. There was to be a lull – destined to be smashed by a disaster for Germany which, at that time, was to become the greatest tank battle in history.

8

The Leibstandarte's role in the recovery of Kharkov was greeted with jubilation by Hitler. Joseph Goebbels recorded in his diary: 'Late in the evening (15 March), the Führer called me to brief me on the overall situation. He was exceptionally happy about the way the SS Leibstandarte was led by Sepp Dietrich. This man personally performed real deeds of heroism and has proved himself a great strategist in conducting his operations.'

For Sepp Dietrich there was the Oak Leaves with Swords for his Knight's Cross. The publicity machine of the Propaganda Ministry could scarcely contain itself.

'In Poland and in France, in Greece and above all in the endless expanses of the east, the Leibstandarte has stood in battle, and the same men have committed themselves with arms for the National Socialist greater Germany, who even, before 1933, strove in the black Schutzstaffel for the victory of the National Socialist movement.

'That their Obergruppenführer, the soldier of the First World War, the fighter of 9 November 1923, the loyal companion of the Führer, the old SS leader and present General of the Waffen-SS, who exactly ten years ago set up the Leibstandarte and commanded it as a Regiment and now as a Division in the field was today decorated with Oak Leaves with Swords, is their greatest joy and greatest pride.'

The Leibstandarte snatched the major share of the awards presented to SS Panzer Corps for the Kharkov achievement. Hitler was plainly in a generous mood; the Leibstandarte benefited to the tune of fourteen Knight's Crosses and higher orders, against ten for Das Reich and five for Totenkopf.

Predictably, one individual who watched the bestowal of these trophies with perhaps more satisfaction than anyone was Heinrich Himmler. The Führer, so reasoned the Reichsführer-SS, was plainly in a mind to be receptive to any suggestions for improving the lot of his champion fighters. Might not this be the time to broach the subject of possible expansion?

Finesse was needed in negotiating with Hitler; he had to be left with the idea that any proposals accepted were his in the first place. Himmler cast around for an ally – and found it in Sepp Dietrich.

Dietrich and Himmler did not have a face-to-face pact, of course. Each had a character scarcely likely to attract the other. No, it was the mystique of Sepp Dietrich that Himmler now set out to exploit. The Reichsführer-SS was a cunning man; his approach to Hitler was clever and bland. The argument ran like this: 'If, my Führer, Dietrich is, as you say, unique, then an obvious way to multiply his effectiveness is to increase the number of men he commands.' When that particular argument was listened to with at least polite attention, Himmler then moved in to expand his case. He had in mind, he told Hitler, the formation of a new SS Division to consist largely of members of Hitler Jugend. He urged that discussions be opened immediately – in fact, they were already in progress – between the Reichjugendführer Arthur Axmann and the SS leadership.

The upshot was that, in combination with the Leibstandarte, the SS-Panzer Grenadier Division Hitler Jugend (later 12th SS-Panzer Division Hitler Jugend) was to constitute the 1st SS-Panzer-Korps-Leibstandarte under the command of Sepp Dietrich. The Leibstandarte would supply the officers and senior non-commissioned officers.

Further generosity towards Sepp Dietrich would plainly be politic. Himmler proposed that the hero be made SS-Oberstgruppenführer, a position which had not yet been filled by any SS man. But the Führer was not prepared to go quite as far as that. He had never been at all keen on offending the Army's susceptibilities beyond a certain point, and to risk further conflict would seem madness. The answer was to create an entirely new rank, then everyone would be satisfied. And thus it was that Sepp Dietrich, the one-time garage attendant and chauffeur to Hitler, became SS-Oberstgruppenführer and Panzer Generaloberst of the Waffen SS. Everyone, Himmler included, professed themselves delighted.

With this orgy of self-congratulation out of the way, it was necessary to get on with the war, which meant, as a very high priority, restoring the strength of the Leibstandarte, Das Reich and Totenkopf. This was duly done with Dietrich's men getting the lion's share.

Individual strengths looked marvellous on paper, but what of the quality of the new intake? Hausser – who, incidentally, was kept kicking his heels for four months before receiving his Oak Leaves – did not think very much of it. He was not in the least concerned with racial characteristics but with fighting potential. And now here he was faced with some very scratch material indeed, including some former Luftwaffe personnel who had never heard a shot fired on the ground.

By the time that the process of refitting was completed,

the Leibstandarte's strength stood at more than twenty-one thousand men. But with the talent available, to say nothing of previous gigantic losses, the uses to which they could be put were strictly limited. Gone were the days of grandiose schemes for engulfing whole countries; in future, defensive actions were by necessity to become more fashionable.

What was Hitler planning to do next? His deliberations were sharpened by a new anxiety. There was every likelihood that before very long the English and the Americans would land somewhere upon the continent of Europe. If that happened, there would have to be a major withdrawal in the east.

The Russians, on the other hand, were in a position to launch major offensives. Indeed, it was felt that Stalin, who had vowed to throw the Germans out of Russia, would really have little choice. The real question was not *if* the Soviet leader would attack, but *where*? The senior German commanders felt that they had the answer. South of Kharkov the front swung eastward in an abrupt curve to form a vast salient enclosing the Donets Basin. This was an area of valuable coal-mining, engineering and manufacturing centres. The Russians would have an enormous advantage if they could slice their way through. Ahead would lie a clear route to the Ukraine, which could then be purged of German forces.

It might be thought that the application of military experience and logic was what was needed to counter the Russian move, but any action contemplated had to be tempered by the reactions and prejudices of the Nazi war-lord. One option was to get in first and hit the Russians before they moved, the other was to wait for the whole might of Stalin's forces to roll forward and then meet them head-on.

The latter course was decided on by the senior commanders: a course of action which would mean waiting for the Soviet attack, giving ground before it, falling back to a prepared line of the lower Dnieper, and then catapulting a powerful armoured force from around Kharkov, which would take the Soviet advance in its flank when its supply lines were well stretched out. This would cut off the spearhead and encircle it, while also smothering the rear echelons.

It was all very well on paper and it might have worked with anyone else but Hitler. Inevitably, though, it clashed with the Führer's entire battle philosophy. There was the possibility of giving up ground already gained; the very mention of such an idea was likely to provoke from the Führer at best a scowl and at worst a succession of tantrums accompanied by the inevitable historical discourse. None of the senior men of the Wehrmacht, still rattled by Stalingrad and fearful for the future, had the stomach for that.

How could an offensive be worked out that would satisfy Hitler? Whatever the answer, the location for a major battle was a far-flung plain fractured by a succession of valleys, small copses, and a rather haphazard string of villages with some rivers and brooks. At one point the ground rose slightly to the north, which favoured the defender. Visibility was a problem because of the large cornfields which covered the landscape.

It was a peaceful place that normally slumbered away its days in total indifference to the outside world. Soon its calm was to be blasted and shattered by the roll and snarl of tanks, the crunch of gunfire, the roar of flame-throwers and the screams of the dying.

Here was to be fought the last major offensive that Hitler was able to launch in the east. No previous tank battle in history had been on quite so gigantic a scale.

For this was the Kursk salient . . .

The Kursk adventure was code-named Operation Citadel. At the Führer's headquarters on 1 July 1943 there met a vast assembly of senior commanders: Field

Marshal von Kluge, commanding Army Group Centre; Colonel-General Hoth, commanding Fourth Panzer Army; Colonel-General Model, commanding the 9th Army; General of Armoured Troops Kempf; General Nehring, commanding the 24th Panzer Corps; Colonel-General von Greim, commanding the 6th Air Fleet; and General Dessloch, representing the 4th Air Fleet.

One thing that struck all those present, was the extraordinarily mercurial temperament of Hitler. One moment he could be plunged into utter despair, the next be screaming for the blood of his enemy and his own incompetent commanders. Now, faced with a new challenge, his mood was positively jocular. In high good humour he welcomed the company and, rather with the air of a managing-director announcing a surprise bonus, stated: 'I have decided to fix the starting date of Citadel as 5 July.'

Just four days ahead! There was no real problem there; the forces could be assembled beyond doubt. The main worry was: could such a date in fact be too late? Might not the Russians even now be preparing an especially hostile reception?

Indeed, German intelligence suggested that even now the Russians had moved something like a quarter of their armoured forces into the area of the Kursk bulge; they too had realised that it was a likely place for attack. But might not such an offensive be nothing but a ghastly recipe for annihilation?

Hitler's good mood did not desert him. He told the generals: 'I grant you the risks. But, gentlemen, think of the prize! If we can destroy the Russian Army, Stalin will be dealt a terrible blow. More important, the people will be prepared to forget Stalingrad. We will have redressed the balance.'

The generals were won over. On the dawn of action-day the waiting soldiers received a personal message from their Führer: 'Soldiers of the Reich! This day you are to take part in an offensive of such importance that the whole future of the war may depend on its outcome. More than anything else, your victory will show the whole world that resistance to the power of the German Army is hopeless.'

Soon the leading sections of Tiger tanks were roaring ahead and away, knifing through the silver-grey tall grass which was a particular feature of the area. Earlier the Stukas had screamed above Byelgorod, supplementing the shatter of the artillery barrage.

Exact details of strength to this day present something of a problem to the historian: official German sources quoted twenty-seven divisions as German strength, but did not give details of how these were constituted. Soviet intelligence put forward a figure of thirty-three divisions for the Germans, while the number of men was said to stand at 900,000 with 10,000 guns, 2,700 tanks and assault guns and 2,400 aircraft. The Russians claimed to have 1,300,000 men, 20,000 guns, 3,600 tanks and assault guns and 2,400 aircraft. The Russian figures, many military experts still point out, should be treated with caution. They may well have been loaded later to enhance further the victory of the Red Army. But that, in all conscience, was to be spectacular enough.

Any detached observer who had been able to observe the German formations on the eve of the battle might well have experienced a thrill of horror at witnessing so formidable a force. There were seventeen divisions of Panzer. In the 9th Army there were three Panzer Corps and two Army Corps of supporting infantry. The southern pincer, Hoth's 4th Panzer Army, had a clout that was the most impressive of all, and the Waffen-SS had its due and was magnificently represented.

Spread out from west to east were 3rd Panzer, Gross Deutchland, 11th Panzer, SS Leibstandarte, SS Das Reich, SS Totenkopf, 6th Panzer, 19th Panzer and 7th Panzer. Here indeed was the cream of Nazi armed might covering thirty miles of front.

In terms of men, however, the total strength of the

142

German Army had declined to around three million men, and the ravages of battle were to send the figures lower still. Nevertheless, a formidable force was at Kursk to mass and launch two armed forces. The northern arm, which was the responsibility of Army Group Centre, would meet the southern arm of Army Group South, and within the pincer the Soviet Army would struggle and eventually be squeezed into oblivion. The 4th Panzer Army, massed west of Byelgorod, was to break through the Soviet positions on both sides of Konarovka and drive, via Oboyan, to the objective of Kursk.

And what of the awesome might of Soviet armour? How would that appear to the observer? Over the area flew one of the Luftwaffe's star pilots, Hans-Ulrich Rudel. He was able to see the full extent of the Soviet forces. There were the T34s, whose role was to prove decisive in the battle to come. There too were heavy armoured guns on their self-propelled carriages and with gigantic barrels that catapulted 15.2 cm shells. This sort of opposition had not been encountered before.

The chief purpose of the aerial assault in which Rudel participated was to break the solid barrier of steel which the Russians had erected on the Byelgorod-Kursk highway. And it succeeded. With exhilaration Rudel and the other pilots saw the Soviet barrier shudder and then break.

It was just the chance for which Der Führer had been waiting. Its capture of the village of Luchi I put Hausser's SS Panzer Corps twenty miles deep into the defence zone of the enemy. One minute it seemed as if any form of advance would have been impossible, but now it was as if a gigantic steel door had been blasted off its hinges.

In high spirits, Hausser forged ahead. Suddenly everything was as it should be. War was mobile and fluid again, all the stop-go frustrations seemed to be set at naught; General Chistyakov's 6th Guards Army plainly had not known what had hit it.

Beyond lay open spaces. For a time the Waffen-SS regiments had the luxury of being able to fan out and press ahead without anyone to stop them. Parts of the Leibstandarte and Totenkopf romped ahead.

Now a new hero of the hour emerged. No 6 Company, 1st SS Panzer Regiment was commanded by SS Obersturmführer Rudolf von Ribbentrop, son of Germany's Foreign Minister. Ribbentrop found himself ahead of his comrades and hacking through the resistance.

The next objective was Prokhorovka. Here the day was to belong to the Waffen-SS. Hand-picked members of Deutschland and companies of Der Führer wheeled east for the attack, with artillery and mortars in full support.

To STAVKA these advances came as a severe shock. A breakthrough to Oboyan was on the cards; stopping it had to be a priority.

General Vatutin had a swift conference with one of his colleagues, a fat Military Council member with the deceptively amiable grin of a teddy-bear. This was Nikita Khruschev. The signal despatched by the two men was a clear order couched in decidedly cool language. This masterpiece of understatement read: 'On no account must the Germans be allowed to break through.'

More than the Russian troops was at stake. Vatutin and Khruschev were realists. Stalin was in the habit of dismissing and despatching key military staff who allowed the initiative to be snatched from their hands. No excuses would be tolerated or even listened to.

Something of the extent of Khruschev's anxiety may be gathered from the fact that the very same evening he turned up personally at First Tank Army Headquarters. Those in command were given a severe pep talk. 'The next three days are going to be decisive in this war,' Khruschev told them. 'The Germans have to regain the face they lost at Stalingrad. Our job is to see the Fascists break their necks!'

For all their advances in the early stages, the Germans

still had not got through to Kursk. The Russians wasted no time; they were making the area into as much of a defensive fortress as the straggling terrain allowed. A deep, well-armed system of fortifications had been dug, and the protection of the minefields was prodigious.

While the Russians waited for Hitler, the Red Army sections which were not actually fighting were toughened by constant bouts of physical training and forced marches. Nor was ideology neglected. Lectures were given in which German brutality was detailed; wall news-papers and news-sheets kept the troops fully aware of how the war was progressing and the infamy of the enemy conducting it.

Among the Germans there were heroes to join Ribben-trop. There was tank-man Michael Wittmann who on the very first day of battle had wiped out eight of the thirty tanks he was to claim before Kursk passed into history.

The three Panzer divisions of the Waffen-SS within Hausser's SS Panzer Corps had three hundred tanks, including a fair number of Tigers. In the campaign also was Hausser's latest present from Hitler – the Ferdinand.

The German High Command had experienced con-siderable shock at the appearance of the tough, fast Russian T34. Rushed on to the drawing-board and into production was a weapon that might prove its equal. The result was a hulking tank-destroyer – known as Ferdinand after its constructor, Ferdinand Porsche. This all-conquering monster had armour plating 200 mm thick, but, because of its weight, it moved at a lumbering twelve miles an hour.

In front of Hausser the Soviet field positions had been developed into a highly elaborate, deeply echeloned forti-fication system. Two rifle divisions, both of them crack formations, made short work of what seemed a choice example of Russian impregnability, and they had received full support from artillery, riflemen, tank companies and mortar regiments. Meanwhile, just ahead lay the corps of General Katukov's 1st Tank Army.

One of the first to break and go forward was 10th Company under SS Hauptsturmführer Helmut Schreider. Then came Führer Panzer Grenadier Regiment. Not far behind were the battalions of Totenkopf, the Leibstandarte, and 167th Infantry Division.

But Russian manpower seemed limitless. George Karck, Commander of 9th Company, 2nd Panzer Grenadier Regiment of Leibstandarte, swore in the face of the advancing Russians who stonewalled any appreciable advance. There was never any standing still for the Leibstandarte; Karck was determined to make the day his. With a knot of men, he knocked out five Russian bunkers with demolition charges. Like demons the SS men clawed their way through the maze of trenches up to the high ground, and forced a passage through.

Behind them, drowning the crack of anti-tank rifles, roared the Tigers. Trenches and dug-outs got the full force of the shells and the columns rolled forward.

Army Detachment Kempf – three Infantry and three Panzer divisions – crossed the Don on the right of SS Panzer Corps, south-east of Byelgorod. Here the opposition was rock-hard and there was no freewheeling progress. But the Soviet defence had received a bloody nose; the SS formations had held up far better than STAVKA would have dreamed possible. The cost to the Leibstandarte on the first day of battle was 97 killed and 522 wounded.

Fighting on the next day was not just against the Russian tank armies and the flame-throwers and the constant counter-attacks. Once again, 'the other army', the citizen's militia, often as terrifying as anything encountered on the battlefield, put in a sudden appearance. SS forces and others had to wheel away frequently from the battle lines to deal with partisans. Red Army battalions were filled out with civilians, often without boots and relying on their fists, clawing at the eyes of troops who wheeled back momentarily like terrified mice who had wandered all innocently into a cattery. There were fearsome cadres of women too, some of them formed into veritable brigades, who screamed and clawed at the invaders. Casualties in this citizen army were heavy and the Germans slaughtered them without compunction. But they paid the price. The second day's casualty list was 84 killed and 384 wounded.

Of course, the activities of the citizen army were a mere irritant on the stage of this bloody theatre of war, and such damage as they wreaked probably did not even merit a coloured pin on the situation map. But there were other anxieties facing the Germans which were far more serious. Tank losses had been agonisingly high: the Panther had proved a particular disappointment and the Germans had lost forty of these.

What of the Ferdinand, the tank whose design Hitler had regarded as his own particular pet? Major operational problems had been revealed: there were weaknesses in the suspension and there had been constant breakdowns. Another pride of the Führer, the Goliath, had failed to make much impression on Soviet fortifications.

In the case of the Ferdinand, production had not proved speedy enough; their crews were largely inexperienced and various war diaries refer to them as unconscious with exhaustion, not even waking to the noise of maintenance and servicing personnel.

To restore the balance somewhat, Soviet T34 tanks found a doughty challenger in SS units fighting at Teterevino, north-west of the route to Kursk from the south, and Oboyan to the south of the salient. A number of T34s were knocked out and the way was open to Russian Brigade Headquarters, which were captured in triumph. But later further advance was checked.

Elsewhere, Hausser was having some success. He had been able to move his motorised battalions northwards across the Psel river along a line of contact between the Leibstandarte and Das Reich.

Along one bank, Soviet artillery kept up a murderous, sustained barrage of artillery and mortar fire but a battalion of Totenkopf stormed a village, formed a small bridgehead over the river, and held on grimly while the nightmare of Russian opposition continued unabated. Then the Leibstandarte and Das Reich pushed on towards Prokhorovka, which lay to the east of Oboyan.

This aggressive thrust took the Russians by surprise. Stalin decided swiftly that such a move was the crunch at the Kursk salient; if the Germans were allowed to extract any more advantages, then the consequences might prove catastrophic. The Leibstandarte and Das Reich had got uncomfortably near to the salient. The time had come to close with the Germans once and for all.

There are people to this day who maintain that on a still night it is possible to hear, borne on the wind, the ghosts of the Panzers of General Hoth taking their dreadful death ride. For on that summer's day in the Prokhorovka area slaughter came to the German Army – slaughter on a scale that recalled the very worst battles of World War I. Exponents of tank warfare had, many years before, maintained that future conflicts would consist of vast tank fleets sweeping across open country. And now it had come true.

There was no land and no sky, only a yawning nothingness created by clouds of dust and smoke. Out of that dreadful reek, shadowy juggernauts thundered into the fray. Across the open steppes the Russian tanks, the T34s and KVs, struck across the flank of the Panzers and the terror had begun.

The tanks charged at they knew not what, the guns spat furiously at anything which crossed their path, even destroying their own side in the process. It is unlikely that even the most brutalised and unfeeling former pupils of the SS academies had conceived anything as terrible as this. Many of the tank crews, their bowels turned to water, pined for the good old days when it was all fun and you got up to boy-scout antics like digging a tank trench while knowing that within a prescribed time the tanks would drive over you whether the hole was completed or not.

And some had been terrified by *that* . . .

The day before the battle began, reports had reached the Germans that members of the Waffen-SS were being shot by the Russians on capture. There was no question of a trial; the tell-tale SS runes were enough to marshal a firing squad. Now even that seemed an easy death . . .

From dawn it raged, the greatest tank battle in history. During its progress no one could have had the slightest idea which side was getting the worst of it. But at long last the firing stopped, and knocked-out tanks of Russia and Germany littered the steppes; the silver-grey grass was stained with oil and blood from both sides, and the sky was jet from the smoke of belching fires.

Some accounting could be done of the losses. For it is true that tired Germans had fought an eight-hour battle under the gigantic dust-cloud and the stifling heat. The Russians, on the other hand, had been fresh, their machines in tip-top condition with full ammunition. Two of the Russian brigades had been equipped with the new SU85, a self-propelled 85 mm gun mounted on the T34 chassis – the mobile answer to the Tigers and the new L70 gun of the Panther. The total number of Russian casualties has never been revealed, but the cost to the Red Army of victory has been put at 2,108 tanks, 190 guns, and 33,000 prisoners. The plight of Germany's Army Group South (20,700 men lost) and Army Group Centre (10,000 lost in two days) underlined the uncomfortable truth that Germany had lost the initiative in the east for ever. The hammer had become the anvil.

In Moscow impatient queues formed for the newspapers. All the headlines were exultant. The most memorable, splashed boldly across a front page, read: THE TIGERS ARE BURNING.

9

Top priority calls from Adolf Hitler on 13 July 1943 summoned Field Marshals von Manstein and von Kluge to the East Prussia headquarters. This time Hitler's mood was anything but jovial. His wrath could scarcely be contained, but it had nothing to do with the débâcle at Kursk. Three days before, he informed his listeners, British, American and Canadian troops had landed in Sicily from North Africa. Italian resistance had collapsed – in fact, not to put too fine a point on it, the legions of Mussolini had turned tail and run. Already, the Allies were pushing ahead down the coastal roads.

Such news was bad enough. Manstein and Kluge stood and gaped, only to hear Hitler add bluntly: 'I am obliged to suspend Citadel.' After storming and raving about 'the lousy way the Italians are running this war', the Führer went on to confess that his main fear was that Eisenhower might land on the Italian mainland or in the Balkans. If that happened, the whole southern flank would be threatened.

Certainly the conflict in Russia would continue. Hitler made that clear, but his listeners gained the impression that the Führer's heart was no longer in it. The new threat had obviously disturbed him. Subsequent events were to show this shift of interest by the war-lord, but meanwhile the war in the east dragged on, with the Leibstandarte, after a period of rest for refitting, once again entering the fray along the Mius river line as Russian attacks were intensified against the Bryansk-Orel

150

1. The regimental banner of the Leibstandarte carrying the legend
"Germany Awake".

2. Waffen-SS recruits line up at meal time. The diet, in which the puritanical
Himmler took special interest, was decidedly Spartan, consisting usually of
mineral water and porridge. These young men would already have done an
hour of physical training, and would follow their meal with a bout of
weapon training.

3. A pre-war changing-of-the-guard ceremony of the élite Leibstandarte-SS
Adolf Hitler.

4. Waffen-SS troops wore the ordinary field-grey uniform of the German army. However, they sported a white shield on the right side of the helmet with the SS runes in black. On the left side of the helmet there was a black swastika in a white circle on a red shield. About eight inches from the bottom of the left cuff of the tunic was a narrow black band edged in white bearing the name of the regiment – in this case, Germania – in white lettering.

5. A camp concert provides an evening of relaxation from the gruelling fatigues of the barrack squares of the Waffen-SS training.

6. Hitler reviews his steel-helmeted legions in the Luitpold arena at Nuremberg in September 1938. The Führer made his first public reference to the Sudeten Germans here in the presence of 120,000 uniformed Nazis.

7. Josef ('Sepp') Dietrich, the former butcher who rose to command the Leibstandarte-SS Adolf Hitler. In 1946, Dietrich was brought before an American military tribunal and accused of being responsible for the murder of unarmed prisoners of war at the height of the Battle of the Bulge, in December 1944. He served a total of eleven years as a war criminal and died in 1966.

8. Reichsführer-SS
Heinrich Himmler,
architect of the Waffen-SS
and at one time the second
most powerful man in the
Third Reich, is seen here
with Hitler watching
military manoeuvres.

9. SS-Obergruppenführer
und General der Waffen-SS
Theodor Eicke
(1882-1943). ''Papa''
Eicke, a former policeman,
was Himmler's supervisor
of concentration camps,
many of whose members
joined the Totenkopf
Division which Eicke
commanded from 1940.
Eicke was killed in action on
the Russian front in 1943
when his light
communications aircraft
was shot down on a visit to a
forward unit.

10. The Muslim formations were among the more bizarre members of the Waffen-SS. The 23rd-Waffen-Grenadier-Division der SS Kama, three of whose officers are seen here, consisted largely of Croatians. Members of the various mountain forces were allowed to keep the fez, which now incorporated the insignia of the Nazi eagle and swastika.

11. The Ferdinand was the tank in which Hitler had pinned his faith to win the battle of Kursk during the Russan offensive. Overall weight of this monster was between 65 and 72 tons and the front armour was 200mm (8 inches) thick.

12. This photograph, found on the body of a Nazi soldier, shows the early, confident days of the Nazi invasion of Russia. With the battles of Stalingrad and Kursk, reflecting the numerical and tactical superiority of the Russians, defeat and despair came to the élite legions of the Waffen-SS.

13. Moment of truth for the SS: In January 1945, an American soldier stands guard over a line up of prisoners captured by Lieutenant General Alexander M. Patch's men when the Nazis attacked the 7th US Army lines.

railway. But it was very small beer for an élite, even one which had taken such a deeply humiliating whipping at Kursk and might well have welcomed a rest. On 25 July 1943 came the news that Mussolini had been deposed in Italy and that the Allies posed a very special threat there. Only the Leibstandarte, the old faithful, was deemed good enough by Hitler for so vital a task, and in all speed it was transferred to the Mediterranean peninsula. Its role there was scarcely in the tradition of the old days, though: a mere appendage to an occupation army, grappling with bands of partisans in southern Italy and Slovenia.

The news of Mussolini's overthrow gave Hitler a severe jolt and was seen as a blow to the prestige of Italy's former partner, the Third Reich. The Duce, Hitler learnt, had been arrested by the new Italian government and spirited away from Rome. The Führer was determined that Mussolini's stature must be restored quickly. Besides, the dictator of Germany appears to have had genuine affection for Mussolini. He and the Duce, the Führer often said, had sprung from the soil and had been appointed by destiny to be the saviour of their peoples.

Hitler began laying plans to snatch the former dictator from his Italian captors before he could be turned over to the Allies. Some of Hitler's advisers thought him mad to bother with Mussolini at a time when the war in Russia was going so badly and the Allies had landed in Italy. They thought it would have made better sense to leave the Duce to his fate, but that was not Hitler's way. He decided to turn away from the main theatre of war for a brief bid to save the Duce. A daring, impudent plan was plainly needed, but *what*? Granted that such a plan would be carried out, who better for the job than the men of the Waffen-SS?

One of the problems was to discover where Mussolini was. At first the island of Ventotene was favoured, then it was thought that the probable location was another island, Maddalena, near the northern tip of Sardinia.

Plans were drawn up for an invasion – the island would be assailed by destroyers and parachute troops. But, before the attempt could be made, Mussolini was moved on. Finally 'the valuable object' (code name given for the Duce) was located at a hotel atop the Gran Sasso d'Italia, the highest range in the Abruzzi Appenines. The place had one major snag: it could only be reached by funicular railway. Obviously some other form of landing would be required. The Führer set to work on a scheme he felt sure would be successful. But it needed a master executioner. Hitler conferred with Himmler, who promised to come up with someone of sufficient ruthlessness and bravery.

The chosen candidate, blissfully unaware of what lay ahead, was lazing away the early afternoon at the Hotel Eden in Berlin after a pleasant lunch with an old friend and fellow Austrian. Otto Skorzeny, an SS officer nicknamed 'Scarface', was a colourful freebooter whom Himmler and Heydrich had earlier marked out as a likely prospect for single missions requiring considerable resource. An ideal troubleshooter, in fact.

Hitler, after being tipped off by Himmler, liked the sound of Skorzeny. The man was a ruffian, of course. But Hitler liked ruffians; they were infinitely preferable to those snobbish, sniff-necked Wehrmacht officers with whom he habitually had to deal. Skorzeny brought a whiff of the old street-fighting days of the SA; such a man could be depended upon.

A telephone rang at the Hotel Eden. The summons made even Skorzeny turn cold. *The Führer*? What the hell could he want? The instructions had been to drop everything and fly immediately to Rastenburg.

On arrival, Skorzeny was received by a Waffen-SS Hauptsturmführer and introduced to a group of assorted Wehrmacht and Luftwaffe officers, together with an SS Sturmbannführer. The party was ushered into Hitler's presence. For a war-lord with considerable problems on his hands, the Führer seemed remarkably relaxed. Indeed

152

Skorzeny was puzzled while Hitler chatted on about trivial matters. When on earth was the old man going to get to the point?

Hitler suddenly stemmed the flow and rapped out: 'Which of you knows Italy?'

Skorzeny was the only one to reply, conscious of his inadequacy, as he admitted to visiting Naples twice.

'What do you think of Italy?' was the next question.

That was a tougher test than might have appeared, and Hitler knew it. If Skorzeny had spoken what was really in his mind, the reply would have been unprintable. For as a sop to Mussolini in happier times, Hitler had waived claims to the southern Tyrol, which was taken from Austria and awarded to Italy at the Treaty of Versailles. The loss was a source of hurt pride to many Austrians.

Skorzeny made what was probably the best reply in the circumstances: 'I am Austrian, my Führer'.

A ghost of a smile flitted across Hitler's face. Then he stared at Skorzeny thoughtfully. He snapped: 'All right, Skorzeny, you stay. The rest of you are dismissed'.

And so Otto Skorzeny was given the first of a series of briefings on the mission to rescue the fallen dictator. Hitler became increasingly impressed with the grasp of detail shown by his fellow Austrian.

Himmler, however, was less sure. He was aghast to see Skorzeny light a cigarette. A man who smoked was plainly unhealthy and therefore unfit for specialist work. The Reichsführer-SS exploded on one occasion: 'Those eternal weeds! I can see that you're not at all the man we need for the job.'

This judgment was wrong. Skorzeny wasted no time, mobilising fifteen Waffen-SS men, all of them to be decked out in Luftwaffe uniform. This group, with others, swooping down in gliders, was to disarm Mussolini's guards, free him and hold the hotel against any counter-attack. The Duce would be flown out in a tiny Fieseler-Storch aircraft, the only type which would have the chance of succeeding in the dangerous terrain.

On 12 September 1943, Skorzeny's team marched across an airfield not far from Rome. Among them was an Italian general kidnapped as 'insurance'; Mussolini's guard of *carabinieri* might hesitate to fire on a fellow countryman used as a shield. But now, at the very last moment, came a snag that Skorzeny could scarcely have foreseen. Out of the skies, Allied aircraft came swooping, strafing the airfield.

Skorzeny's heart lurched as he took shelter. That was surely the end of the precious gliders on the airfield. But fortune was smiling on him that day; at the end of the raid, which lasted half an hour, the gliders were unharmed. The mission could go ahead.

At lunch time the strange group took off. The wretched Italian general was promptly sick. Skorzeny saw the leading gliders suddenly disappear into a cloud-bank; they were never seen again. Skorzeny's glider was now the lead plane and it was flying blind, the pilot relying solely on Skorzeny's knowledge of the area. Seven gliders had set out on the mission; even before the destination was reached that number had been reduced.

Skorzeny, watched apprehensively by the bilious Italian, seized a knife and hacked away at the canvas wall of the glider until he had carved a hole that he could see through. It was a crude but effective aid to navigation, certainly better than the scratched perspex window at the side of his head.

Skorzeny glanced down, recognising the valley of Aquila below. Above the wind, he bellowed the order: 'Helmets on.' The Waffen-SS men snapped into action, grabbing the helmets and seizing the crossbar inside the glider. There was a sudden lurch as the pilot of the towing plane slipped the towrope.

Skorzeny craned his neck for the landing-strip he knew was there. Then he spotted something which brought him out in a cold sweat – the strip was littered with boulders. They would all be slashed to pieces, but it was too late to change the landing place now. Skorzeny shouted: 'Crash landing!'

The glider pilot felt a tightening of the stomach as the parched yellow grass and boulders swept up to meet him at fifty miles an hour. He caught a sudden glimpse of the squat horseshoe shape of the hotel. With an almighty crash, more than two thousand pounds of glider and men hit the ground, but not before the pilot had jerked the craft upwards and flung out the brake-flaps so that the nose would be positioned to act as an extra brake.

Skorzeny tore his way out of the glider, making for the hotel. Above him was the deafening roar of the towing planes and a succession of crashes and thuds as the gliders ploughed their way into the perilous landing-strip.

'Scarface' Skorzeny and another Waffen-SS man hurled themselves at the first Italian who challenged them. Skorzeny realised that his first task must be to dismantle the radio. Into the hotel charged the party.

In a room near the entrance they found what they were looking for. Skorzeny's heavy boot kicked the stool from clean under the operator. At the same time, his hand reached for his machine pistol; down crashed the butt on the radio.

Skorzeny was determined to grab the maximum glory for himself. He would be the first to greet the Duce and rescue him! As he and his men continued their hurtling progress through the hotel, Skorzeny kept his eyes on the windows on the other side of the horseshoe.

Incredibly, he was rewarded. A bald, elderly man was staring out of a second-floor window. It was impossible to mistake that distinctive jaw. It was the Duce, all right. But, my God, the old man must not be seen staring out of the window at German troops. He would give the whole game away and probably get himself shot in the process.

Skorzeny decided to take a risk. He shouted: 'Get

away from the window.' The effect was instant and Mussolini disappeared.

Suddenly a mass of cursing, bewildered Italians appeared, unarmed and plainly unaware of what was going on. Skorzeny shoved them aside and darted up the stairs, pushing the terrified Italian general in front of him and yelling: 'Don't fire.' The helmeted Waffen-SS followed.

In one of the rooms they found a pale, unshaven man, dressed in a crumpled blue suit. Skorzeny went straight to him. With a bow and a click of the heels, he announced: 'Duce, I have been sent by my Führer to set you free!' Greatly moved, Mussolini replied in German: 'I knew that my friend Adolf Hitler would not leave me in the lurch.' And he embraced Skorzeny warmly.

Exactly four minutes had elapsed since the lead glider had struck the hillside. Not a shot had been fired.

But this was no time for resting on laurels. Skorzeny promptly told the pilot of the Storch aircraft that he would travel with the Duce. 'But you're all of two hundred pounds,' protested the pilot. 'The aircraft will never clear.'

Skorzeny replied impatiently: 'Supposing you have to make a forced landing somewhere and get killed. *He* is going to be alone for anyone to snatch. If that happens, the rest of us might as well put bullets in our heads.'

Three people in *that* aircraft and a primitive runway two hundred yards long! It looked as if they hadn't a hope of clearing it, but Skorzeny was adamant.

The pilot ran the engine at top speed and, with the fuselage now out of the hands of those standing on the runway, the Storch lurched forward. Skorzeny peered over a pallid Mussolini's shoulder. The blur of the runway was coming towards them at top speed. Then, only too distinct, was the ditch that loomed up before them.

The Storch struck the ditch hard and bounced. Good, thought Skorzeny, it has at least catapulted us clear of the ground. But the feeling of relief did not last.

All at once, the Storch started to drop like a stone to the valley below. The pilot edged the stick forward. The plane began to increase its speed. Would the slipstream raise the wings? My God, it was working. Skorzeny opened his eyes as the plane levelled out above the valley.

On the ground one of Skorzeny's team, in charge of Mussolini's luggage, had fallen down in a dead faint.

Skorzeny arrived back in triumph – to a Knight's Cross and (much more important in the long run) the warm congratulations of Heinrich Himmler. From now on the resourceful Austrian was to become a firm favourite of the Führer and he was to call on him again, just a year later, for a still more outrageous scheme.

As for Mussolini, although he was grateful for his rescue, he was by now broken and had no stomach to continue the struggle or to regain any power. At Hitler's prodding, the Duce did set up the Italian Social Republic, but it scarcely had any existence other than its name.

Mussolini never returned to Rome; he set himself up at isolated Rocca delle Caminate, near Gargnano, on the shores of Lake Garda. Here, at Hitler's insistence, he was closely guarded by a special detachment of the Leibstandarte. This scarcely prejudiced the war effort, since Hitler always kept certain members of his bodyguard for his own use, such as protecting him at Berchtesgaden or Rastenburg. Members of the Leibstandarte even waited at table.

Nevertheless, Sepp Dietrich's feelings can perhaps be imagined when he was detached from the reeling 1st SS Panzer Corps in Russia and ordered to escort the Duce's mistress, Clara Pettaci, to her besotted lover.

But Mussolini, even Hitler had to admit, was now a lost cause – not a true revolutionary like himself or Stalin. Italy was lost. The battle of Kursk was lost. Defeat was still a novel sensation for Hitler. He was to become increasingly familiar with it.

Much of the original identity and intended role of the Waffen-SS had undergone a drastic change in the wake of the defeats of Stalingrad and Kursk. The glamour that had attached to service in the crack formations of the Leibstandarte was no longer strong enough to bring forth the necessary number of recruits. The military value of the Waffen-SS lay primarily in the élite, largely German, SS Panzer divisions, direct successors of the pre-war Leibstandarte and Verfügungstruppe. But these were tied down in Russia. There was a desperate need to fill the gaps, but in the absence of volunteers where were the reinforcements to be found?

Himmler turned to the reservoir of highly dubious and untrained talent which could be directly recruited. Much unblooded manpower came from the work camps of the Reichsarbeitsdienst (Reich Labour Service), but attempts to insinuate these forces into the Waffen-SS unleashed a storm of protest throughout Germany.

Church leaders and parents, aware of the dark reputation of the SS, objected strongly to fledgling soldiers who were little more than boys being fattened up for the battle front. By this stage of the war Germany had become largely soured with ideology; the casualty lists from the Russian front had sewn the first doubts about ultimate victory for the Third Reich. Yet by the mid-summer of 1943 the first ten thousand youths for the 12th SS Division Hitler Jugend were in training at an SS camp near Beverloo in Belgium.

Hitler professed himself delighted with this turn of events. It might have been thought that with the invasion of Italy and the push of Russia towards the frontiers of the Reich already beginning, the Führer would have been highly dubious of taking into his battle-formations youths with an average age of only eighteen, as was the case with fresh intake into two new SS divisions, Hohenstaufen and Frundsberg. The Führer, however, commented: 'Germany's youth fights magnificently and with incredible bravery. The youngsters who come from Hitler Jugend are fanatical fighters. These young German lads, some only sixteen years old, fight more fanatically than their older comrades.'

Waffen-SS shotgun marriages became more frequent. The 5th SS Division Viking together with a promising leavening of recruits from the occupied European countries were for example merged to form the 11th SS Panzer Grenadier Division Nordland. As the months went on and the situation became gradually more desperate for Germany, a number of decidedly strange SS divisions came into existence. Gone were all the old standards of training; the time had long gone, too, when the 'Nordic ideal' could be upheld rigidly. Into the ranks of the Waffen-SS coursed policemen and Wehrmacht rankers, many of them regarded disdainfully as scum by the traditionalists within the Leibstandarte, Das Reich, and, ironically, even Totenkopf.

It appeared most impressive. Himmler, as self-deluding and vainglorious as ever, was able to point out that between 1943 and the war's end, the strength of the Waffen-SS had more than doubled and that the number of SS divisions rose from eighteen to thirty-eight. But even he must have realised that the definition of 'SS Division' had changed radically. Of the new intake, only Panzer Grenadier Division Horst Wessel could be considered an élite German formation by the original standards.

Of the numerous regiment-sized SS 'Divisions' scraped together in the last months of the war, only two or three, composed of training personnel from various SS combat schools, were to be of any real value. By the end of 1943 the barrel was being assiduously scraped.

The war in Russia ground on, and remorselessly the first signs of the accursed winter made themselves felt. Each night the thermometer inched a little lower and the ground turned harder. The Wehrmacht had never been able to come to terms with the abominable cold; still less did the wretched younger troops, wet behind the ears from the training barracks, who clawed at wooden out-houses and buildings to get wood for fires. Little did they realise what was to come: temperatures would plummet well below freezing level by the New Year.

In rapid advances the Red Army swept on and wrested Kharkov from the Germans. By the last quarter of 1943, Saporzhe, Melitopol and Kiev were all to go. The position of Army Group South was perilous indeed and it was against this sombre background that the Leibstandarte and other divisions were recalled to the east.

Advances at first were encouraging. The Leibstandarte gave every appearance of being glad to be back in Russia, and in a mood of belligerence they pressed forward and thrust towards the Trostyavitsa and Irsha rivers. Then came the welcoming reinforcements of Tigers which took part in a joint raid with a Panzer-Grenadier regiment of 1st Panzer Division. Together they smashed into a solid concentration of Red Army tanks at Shevshentka. But optimism was short-lived. Elsewhere along the front, fifty thousand Germans were trapped in the Cherkassy region to the south-east of Kiev. A request was sent to Hitler for permission to pull out. But the supreme war-lord was running true to form and would have none of it.

Elaborate plans were drawn up for a breakthrough. That would be followed by the hammering of the encircling Soviet divisions, thus allowing for Hitler to realise another of his obsessions: the capture of Kiev. The Führer utterly refused to think in terms of a defensive war; an advance must go on as soon as possible. Once again the weather knocked all elaborate plans sideways. There was a thaw and with it a warm wind that ushered in the curse of the *rasputitsa,* slime – a thick, oozing, knee-deep black morass.

The inhabitants of the Ukraine, after years of experience, knew how to cope with these conditions. They simply withdrew to huddle over their stoves. No such luxury was permitted the German Army.

The fighting had to be waged while the mud snatched greedily at boots and insinuated its way into the tracks of the armour.

By some miracle, 5th SS Panzer Grenadier Division managed to struggle through the black obscenity, but at the pitiful speed of no more than two or three miles an hour. The demands on the precious fuel were ruinous and, to make matters worse, the frost returned. Out came the blow-torches to free the tanks that were stuck like insects on fly-paper.

Half a dozen Russian armies were opposing Bavarians, Hessians, Franconians, Austrians, Saxons, men from the Saar-Palatine, together with Belgians, Dutchmen and Scandinavians from the Waffen-SS volunteer regiments.

There were all the makings of another Stalingrad. Relief was needed quickly. Here was a call for highly-experienced crack divisions, each of them able to stand up to a Soviet tank Corps. Luckily the cream was still available: 1st Panzer Division, 16th Panzer Division and 1st SS Leibstandarte Panzer Division.

Into action went 1st Panzer and the Leibstandarte. Their brief was to kick the supine forces into action and get the advance moving. SS tank man Wittmann became the undisputed hero of the hour, hurtling his Tigers into the solid wall of T34s. A vast hole was ripped into the Soviet Army, but still the Russians came and took even more punishment from one of Sepp Dietrich's most able disciples. Other Tigers wiped out more Soviet machines, and Wittmann could chalk up a triumphant total of 107 enemy machines destroyed.

Well into February the advance went on, and for a while the Russians quailed against its fury. Frantic attempts were made by the Germans to hold the line, but the *rasputitsa* was not to be gainsaid, and effects of its cruel sweaty hold were terrible in terms of knocked-out machines and immobilised columns; more and more vehicles dropped out on roads that were nothing but gigantic hills of mud. Red Infantry knifed between tank spearheads and follow-up Grenadier units.

Here was no advance, not even a drive; just a series of bitter small battles which tied the Germans down and lessened their numbers remorselessly.

The call was on for a break-out; there was literally no other alternative and even Hitler recognised it. Out went the order for withdrawal from the Cherkassy pocket. But the break-out plans were scratchy and ill-conceived. Only Das Reich held fast; the rest of the encircled troops were badly mauled as they struggled to get out.

There was in truth little consolation now for Adolf Hitler. All he could do was brood over OKW maps and console himself with contemplation of those eastern regions which were still vassal states of the Third Reich. Warm and secure in his cocoon of delusion, it is doubtful whether the Führer knew or cared about the pitiful state of his retreating forces, coping now with the snow. There were thirty-five thousand survivors from the pocket and these totally defeated columns trudged, with leaden hearts, back to their severely shattered lines. Only the Leibstandarte remained at its outpost, witnessing the long trudge of defeat. The High Command communiqué indeed talked of 'heroic determination, aggressive spirit and selfless comradeship,' but they had availed the German Army and the Waffen-SS little.

A continuous front was out of the question. Manstein plainly had to get out of the Dnieper bend once and for all, falling back at least as far as the line of the Ukrainian river Bug. His mobile reserves, though, were but a shadow. With the breaking of the German front a series of encirclements took place which could not be anything but ruinous. The largest of these pockets was in the Korsun-Shevchenkovski area of the lower Dnieper; here SS Viking and the remnants of seven other divisions were trapped. Manstein, marshalling his by now meagre Panzer resources, scythed a corridor through to those encircled, but after that there could only be retreat and the columns snaked south-east with the Russians snapping greedily at their heels.

It was indeed a ghastly retreat. At the river, eight metres broad and two metres deep, teams of artillery plunged into the waves and ice-floes. That was to prove perhaps a worse end for many than the guns of the Russians.

This was death by freezing; the uniforms turned to ice and became almost a second skin. Many panicked and attempted to throw their equipment over the river, losing it all. Many could not swim a stroke but plunged in just the same. Lucky ones somehow survived by clinging to hastily felled trees. Others died as the Russian guns raked their bodies.

But for some of the Waffen-SS there was to be consolation that Christmas. The dead, whether they were Russians killed in battle or victims of the execution squads, were to provide some choice trinkets for Himmler's more dedicated lieutenants.

Among the mountain of documents submitted as evidence at Nuremberg after the war was a sheaf of macabre documents, accompanied by a respectful covering letter.

Personal Staff Reichsführer-SS
Archives File No 332/10

The Chief of the SS Economic and Administrative Office Berlin, 6 November 1943.
To the SS-Obersturmbannführer Dr Brandt
Personal Staff, Reichsführer-SS,
Berlin.

My dear Brandt,

I intend to make a Yuletide gift to the units of the Waffen-SS as indicated on the attached list *from the watches, wrist-watches and fountain pens* as listed on the same.

Please ask the Reichsführer-SS whether he agrees,

whether the gift shall be made in his name, or by using the attached draft, as I thought.

Please return all enclosures.

Kindest regards

Heil Hitler!

Yours

POHL

SS-Obergruppenführer and General of the Waffen-SS.

On the battlefront, the writing was now on the wall for Manstein. After acrimonious meetings at which the Field Marshal stoutly defended himself, he was relieved of his command – the blow softened with the addition of Swords to his Knight's Cross. Hitler told him: 'All that counts now is to cling desperately to what we hold. The time for grand-style operations in the east, for which I am particularly qualified, is now over.'

Later Hitler proclaimed: 'If something breaks down, Manstein doesn't get things done. He can operate with divisions as long as they are in good shape. If the divisions are roughly handled, I have to take them away from him in a hurry. He can't handle such a situation.'

But it was doubtful now whether anyone could. The Red Army flung its massive forces into an all-out drive for the Vistula. Just two weeks after D-Day in the west, 118 Infantry and forty-three tank divisions slammed into Army Group Centre. The defences crumbled speedily and across White Russia towards the Polish border went the fleeing Germans. Guns, material, vehicles, wounded, were all abandoned.

Soon it was summer in Germany, but the warm weather brought little lifting of the spirits. In fact, from 20 July 1944 onwards the country was to be saturated by a wave of denunciation, imprisonment, farcical show trials and executions. For 20 July was the date when a group of Army officers, with the defeat of Germany looming, attempted to murder Adolf Hitler and overthrow the Government. The assassination bid failed. The price Hitler extracted was wholesale slaughter, notably of the conspirators, but also of anyone who had shown the remotest opposition to the Führer's genius as the brutal servants of the SS.

The details of the so-called July Plot have been related many times and do not have a place in the story of the armed SS. But this is not to acquit Himmler's legions of cruelties elsewhere in 1944 and earlier.

The quality of the Waffen-SS as a brave fighting machine, operating within a highly efficient straitjacket of discipline, has been amply demonstrated. Now is the time to look at the other side of the coin and to give a clue or two as to why, as a criminal organisation, the Waffen-SS stained the reputation that its survivors still strive to cherish: that here was a special fighting force spilling blood only in the age-old profession of arms.

10

To Hitler the destruction of Warsaw in September 1939 was but one military victory in what, he felt sure, would be a series of triumphs for the then scarcely blooded Wehrmacht. Warsaw was a spot on the map of very little consequence; enough that it had been knocked out of the war and was unlikely to give any further trouble. What happened there after military action was solely the concern of Heinrich Himmler who would doubtless decide how to deal with the enormous Jewish population.

The Reichsführer-SS set about his task with zest, and indeed there was plenty for him to do. Among the shattered buildings of Warsaw – over ten thousand had been destroyed by the Germans – dwelt some 360,000 Jews;

this population was the largest of any city in the country. For the work, Himmler had an effective lieutenant in Hans Frank, head of 'the Government General of Poland'.

From the start of the occupation, the Jews were paramount among those regarded as 'sub-human'. All public offices were instantly purged of all Jewish staff, who were forthwith assigned to 'limited labour duties' and forced to wear the Star of David.

In October 1940 they were herded into a closed 'Jewish residential Area'. This was the notorious Warsaw Ghetto, scene not only of slaughter by various factions of the SS and the Waffen-SS, but of fierce, courageous resistance by Polish Jews.

The next month the ghetto was sealed off behind a ten-foot wall which covered an area of two and a half miles in the city. Into it were herded a besieged and starving community of some 400,000 Polish Jews. As an extra humiliation, Jewish police were made to work alongside German guards and a rigid check was kept on anyone entering or leaving.

The area of the ghetto was to be systematically reduced in size over the years. Within, conditions were soon to become indescribable, overcrowding being only part of the story. Diseases of epidemic proportions raged unchecked. It is almost certainly impossible to compute which proportion of deaths was due to disease and which to deliberately induced starvation.

Food was supplied by the Germans for about a quarter of the population – and, quite firmly, no more. The death rate climbed remorselessly. At the start of 1941 death figures stood at 900 a month; by the summer the figure was more than 5,500.

As the iron clamp of the ghetto organisers screwed progressively tighter, so the number of escapes was cut to negligible proportions. On 15 October 1941 Hans Frank issued a general order: 'Jews who leave the quarter without permission are liable to the death penalty. The same penalty awaits any person who knowingly gives shelter to such Jews.' The next month, Oberleutnant Jarke, Police Commandant of Warsaw, gave orders that all Jews – including women and children – found outside the ghetto were to be shot. Throughout the spring of 1941-42 the SS execution squads worked round the clock.

In this atmosphere of terror, there was but one consolation to the besieged Jews. At least, their community was able to remain intact and share its suffering. That particular Jewish quality, a fierce sense of togetherness, had not yet been violated. But even this crumb of comfort was to be snatched away.

On the morning of 22 July 1942 a meeting was called of the Judenrat, the Ghetto Jewish Council which the Germans had set up to relay their orders to the people of the ghetto. SS Sturmbannführer Hermann Höfle, the Resettlement Commissar, had appalling news for his audience. He announced that 'all Jews living in Warsaw, regardless of age or sex' were to hold themselves in readiness for 'resettlement in the east'. It was an order against which there was no appeal.

For nine long weeks the trains rolled. Their destination was the concentration camp at Treblinka which had on its staff members of SS Totenkopf. Up to one hundred people were crammed into a single cattle-truck, at the rate of 5,000 to 6,000 per day. No one was exempt: not even hospital patients or small children. On arrival, the prisoners were marched to ten gas chambers and killed in batches of two hundred. Resistance meant the firing squad. Some 6,000 Jews were disposed of in this way. How many there were will never be known with absolute certainty, but a figure of not less than 450,000 has been estimated as having perished in Treblinka. When the gas chambers became exhausted or broke down through sheer over-use, the guards were sent to slaughter survivors with any weapon that came to hand.

The sheer numbers in the ghetto and the logistics of supplying enough cattle-trucks to move them made the process of slaughter annoyingly slow for the SS; by the New Year of 1943 there were still 60,000 Jews who had somehow been allowed to live.

Such a state of affairs annoyed the bureaucratic susceptibilities of Heinrich Himmler. The business of removing the 'bandits' and 'sub-humans' was obviously far too slow. The Reichsführer-SS decided to look at matters on the spot. On 9 January Himmler turned up at the Warsaw Ghetto. The statistics of survival enraged him, but even he had to acknowledge that there was a limit to the amount of deportations that could be carried out by Hans Frank and his colleagues. Himmler ordered a further 8,000 Jews to be removed within the next nine days, but he was not to get his way. By the time that the deadline had passed, a mere 6,500 had been accounted for.

The reason was resistance: fearsomely brave, ultimately futile resistance by the various Jewish organisations which had sprung up in the ghetto.

Much has been made of those Jews who with seeming resignation gave up the fight and tramped with their families towards the trains which would take them to Treblinka. But there were many Jews who did fiercely resist, backed by the key resistance unit of the ghetto, the Jewish Combat Organisation (Zydowska Organizacja Bojowa) or ZOB. By a system of highly organised cells, the ZOB had built up some form of intelligence contact with the world outside the ghetto – with, primarily, the Polish Home Army (Armia Krajowa), the main resistance organisation of occupied Poland.

Into the ghetto were smuggled weapons, grenades and explosives. The mere fact that the 'bandits' had the temerity to resist at all scared Berlin. Above all, it scared Heinrich Himmler who was not prepared to let anything stand in the way of his overriding objective: to clear the ghetto completely and kill everyone still in it. On 16 February 1943 he ordered the total obliteration of the Warsaw Ghetto.

Oberführer von Sammern-Frankenegg was put in charge. Sammern-Frankenegg was as keen as anyone to get rid of the Jews, but zeal was no substitute for action and the SS man made the mistake of bungling a scheme which the Reichsführer-SS had planned as the crowning point of his career.

For 20 April was Hitler's birthday; Himmler was determined that the Führer should be given an appropriate present. And what could be more appropriate than the final 'clearing out' of the Warsaw Ghetto? An added source of satisfaction to Himmler no doubt was the fact that he had fixed the 'clearing out' for 19 April – Holy Monday in the Jewish Calendar.

It was a project which had the sort of bureaucratic tidiness so beloved of Himmler; the dates would look marvellous on an official report. Unfortunately for the Reichsführer, the Jewish resistance group had other ideas.

A group of SS moved into the ghetto, only to be greeted by a vigorous counter-attack by the resistance groups. Casualties among the Germans were high; Sammern-Frankenegg was sacked on the spot by Himmler, who by now was beside himself.

From that moment the Warsaw Ghetto was doomed.

On 19 April a Nazi armoured motorcade swept through the rubble-strewn streets of Warsaw, its outriders paving the way for one particular limousine that headed straight for the ghetto. In the back seat, Waffen-SS Brigadeführer Jürgen Stroop enquired testily about the noise being made by the 'sub-humans' within. He was told that armed resistance was continuing.

It was precisely to combat armed resistance once and for all that Stroop had been relieved of a police command in Greece. The situation was worrying, not because Stroop was any less ruthless than the dismissed Sammern-Frankenegg, but because he simply did not have at his command the necessary forces to quell anything approaching a major insurrection. And now here he was being told that the prisoners within the ghetto had enough arms to launch a counter-attack against the Germans for weeks if necessary.

Stroop, at this time, could only call on a mixed force of some two thousand men, many untrained as soldiers and made up of bands of riff-raff from renegade Latvians and Lithuanians, as well as two training battalions of Waffen-SS. But Himmler would not be interested in excuses. His orders to Stroop had been clear enough. The Reichsführer-SS had said: 'The ghetto is partisan territory. Comb it out with ruthless tenacity.'

That the ghetto would collapse was never in doubt. But it held out for an incredible thirty-five days. On the morning of 19 April the new Waffen-SS commander struck, and he was very far from being niggardly with the punishment battalions he had assembled for the purpose.

Against a meagre armoury of pistols, rifles, machine-guns and home-made grenades of dubious efficiency, Stroop attacked with tanks, artillery and flame-throwers. By that time the ghetto had shrunk, but it was honey-combed throughout with sewers, vaults and cellars which the defenders had turned into command posts.

The fate of the Jews during each day of the operation to clear the ghetto is on record: thanks to the minutely-detailed official report which Stroop himself compiled.

The importance of scrupulous efficiency was something that Stroop had absorbed from his background. His father had also been a policeman and a rigid disciplinarian. Stroop was often to recall his first experience of physical chastisement when a child in Detmold. He had used his mother's best cushion on a slide in the backyard of his home and had been chastised severely. His mother beat her children for every act of disobedience. Stroop remembered too the hour-upon-hour of enforced history lessons about the great destiny of Germany, about the fierce independence of Detmold.

The town had been originally in the Principality of Lippe-Detmold, a territory fiercely proud of being an independent state within the German Empire. Stroop's father had taken his boy constantly to gaze at a huge statue in the wooded hills outside the town. This was of the German tribal prince, Herman, who in AD 9 had slaughtered a powerful Roman army. Thus had young Stroop absorbed a background of fierce nationalism allied with brutality: something of the same sort of brutality which had led him to beat his elder brother insensible when a favourite toy had been 'borrowed'. Jurgen Stroop had been raised in the best possible school for National Socialism.

Every phase of the ghetto extermination was notoriously recorded, including the role of the Waffen-SS.

In his table of units employed, deaths and casualties, Stroop made constant mention of his contingent of *Trawniki,* soldiers from the SS camp at Trawniki in the Lublin district, most of them Ukrainians. The figure 1/60, for instance, would be a reference to one officer and sixty men.

Thus on the first day of the operation the report tabulated:

Units Employed:	
SS-Panzer-Gren. Res. Battl.	6/400
SS-Cav. Res. Det.	10/450
Police	6/165
Security Service	2/48
Trawniki men	1/150

Wehrmacht:	
1 10-cm Howitzer	1/7
1 Flame thrower	1
Engineers	2/16
Medical detachments	1/1
3 2.28 cm AA guns	2/24

1 French tank of Waffen-SS
2 heavy armoured cars of the Waffen-SS

On the first day of the ghetto operation, Stroop reported:

'Closing of Ghetto commenced 0300 hours. At 0600 detailing of the Waffen-SS (strength: 16/850) to comb out the remainder of the Ghetto. Immediately after the units had formed up, concentrated attack by Jews and bandits. The tank used in this action and the two heavy armoured cars pelted with Molotov cocktails [incendiary bottles]. Tank twice set on fire.

'At first this enemy attack caused the retreat of the units. Losses in first attack: 12 men (6 SS men, 6 Trawniki men). About 0800 hours second attack by units, under command of the undersigned [i.e. Stroop]. In the face of less intensive counter-attack, this second assault succeeded in combing out the blocks of buildings according to plan.

'The enemy was forced to retire from roofs and other prepared positions above ground level into cellars, dugouts or sewers. During this combing-out we caught only about 200 Jews. Immediately afterwards raiding parties were directed to dug-outs known to us with the order to bring out the Jews and to destroy the dug-outs. About 380 Jews captured by this. It was noted that the Jews had taken to the sewers. Sewers were completely flooded to make staying there impossible. About 1730 hours we encountered very strong resistance from one block of buildings, including machine-gun fire. A special battle-group crushed the enemy and invaded the houses, but without capturing the enemy.

'Jews and criminals resisted from base to base and escaped at the last moment by flight across lofts or through underground passages. About 2030 hours the external cordon was reinforced. All units were withdrawn from the Ghetto and dismissed to their quarters. Reinforcement of the cordon by 250 Waffen-SS men. Continuation of operation on 20 April.'

On Day Two, Stroop was recording:

'The resistance centres ascertained in the uninhabited but not yet released part of the Ghetto were crushed by a battle-group of the Wehrmacht, including Engineers and flame-throwers. In this operation, one man was wounded, shot through the lungs. Nine raiding parties penetrated as far as the northern wall of the Ghetto. Nine dug-outs were found, their resisting inmates crushed and the dug-outs blown up. What losses the enemy suffered cannot be ascertained accurately. Altogether the nine raiding parties caught 505 Jews today; those among them who are able-bodied were earmarked for transfer to Poniatowo. At about 1500 hours, I succeeded in the immediate evacuation of the block of buildings occupied by the Army Accommodation Office, said to be occupied by 4,000 Jews.

'The German manager was asked to call on the Jewish workers to leave the block voluntarily. Only 28 Jews obeyed this request. Thereupon I decided to evacuate the block by force or to blow it up. The A.A Artillery – three 2-cm. guns used for this operation – lost 2 men killed. The 10-cm. howitzer, which also was used, dislodged the gangs from their strong fortifications and also inflicted losses on them, as far as we were able to ascertain. This action had to be broken off because of the fall of darkness. On 21st April 1943 we shall attack this resistance centre again; as far as possible it will remain sealed off during the night.

'In today's action we caught, apart from the Jews, considerable stores of incendiary bottles, hand-grenades, ammunition, uniforms, and equipment.

'Losses:
2 dead (Wehrmacht)
7 wounded (6 Waffen-SS, 1 Trawniki man).'

On Day 4:

'A battle-group once more invaded the block of buildings, which by now had largely burnt out or were still aflame, in order to catch those Jews who were still there.

'As shooting again started from one block, aimed at the men of the Waffen-SS, this block too was set on fire, with the result that a considerable number of bandits were scared from their hideouts and shot while trying to escape. In addition about 180 Jews from the surrounding courtyards were caught. The main body of the units continued the cleaning out of the as yet unsearched buildings of the Ghetto, starting from the line we had reached yesterday. This operation is still in progress. As on preceding days local resistance was broken and the dug-outs discovered were blown up. Unfortunately there is no way of preventing some of the bandits and Jews from staying in the sewers below the Ghetto where it is almost impossible to catch them, since the flooding has been stopped. The city administration is unable to prevent this. Neither the use of smoke candles nor the addition of creosote to the water had the desired effect. Co-operation with the Wehrmacht is splendid.'

After the first week of the assault on the ghetto, Stroop was recording:

'Armed resistance was repeatedly encountered; in one dug-out three pistols and some explosives were captured.

'Furthermore, considerable amounts of paper money, foreign currency, gold coins and jewellery were secured today. The Jews still have considerable property. While last night only a glow of fire could be seen above the former Ghetto, today one can observe a great sea of flames. Since we continue to discover great numbers of Jews during the combing-out accomplished regularly and according to plan, the operation will be continued on 26th April 1943. Start 1000 hours.

174

'Included today a total of 27,464 Jews have been captured.'

'Our losses:
3 members of the Waffen-SS and one member
of the Security Police wounded.
Total losses up to date:

Waffen-SS	27 wounded
Police	9 wounded
Security Police	4 wounded
Wehrmacht	1 wounded
Trawniki men	9 wounded
	50 wounded
Waffen-SS	2 dead
Wehrmacht	2 dead
Trawniki men	1 dead
	5 dead

The sheer courage of the Jews shines through the deadpan exactitude of Stroop's report:

'In most cases, the Jews offered armed resistance before they left the dug-outs. . . . At times, the Jews and bandits fired pistols with both hands. Since we discovered several times today that the Jewesses had pistols concealed in their bloomers, all Jews and bandits will be ordered from today to strip completely when being searched. We captured among other things one German rifle, model 98, two .08 pistols and other calibres, also home-made hand-grenades. The Jews can only be induced to leave their dug-outs after several smoke candles have been burnt. According to depositions made yesterday and today, the Jews were asked to erect air-raid shelters during the second half of 1942. Just at that time, under the camouflage of erecting air-raid shelters, they began to build the dug-outs which Jews are now inhabiting, in order to be able to use them during any anti-Jewish operation. Last night some of the scouting parties used in the Ghetto were shot at. One casualty (wounded). These scouting parties reported that groups of armed bandits were marching through the Ghetto.'

On Day 26, Stroop wrote:

'In order to force the bandits in the sewers to come to the surface, 183 sewer entrances were opened at 1500 hours and smoke candles were lowered into them at an ordered moment, whereupon the bandits, seeking escape from what they supposed to be gas, crowded together in the centre of the former Jewish residential area, and we were able to pull them out of the sewer entrances there.

'I shall come to a decision after tomorrow's operations regarding termination of the action.

'Today afternoon SS-Gruppenführer und Generalleutnant of the Waffen-SS von Herf was present during the operations.'

After twenty-eight days Stroop was able to complete his report and announce its total success.

'1. Of the total of 56,065 Jews caught, about 7,000 were destroyed in the former Jewish residential area itself during the large-scale operation; 6,929 Jews were destroyed by transporting them to T-2; the sum total of Jews destroyed is therefore 13,929. Beyond the number of 56,065, an estimated number of 5,000 to 6,000 Jews were destroyed by being blown up or by perishing in the flames.

'2. A total of 631 dug-outs were destroyed.

176

3. Booty:

7 Polish rifles, 1 Russian rifle, 7 German rifles, 59 pistols of various calibres.

Several hundred hand-grenades, including Polish and home-made ones.

A few hundred incendiary bottles.

Home-made explosive charges.

Infernal machines with fuses.

Large amounts of explosives, ammunition for arms of all calibres, including machine-gun ammunition.

'With regard to the captured arms one must take into consideration that in most cases we were not able to capture the arms themselves, since the Jews and bandits before they were captured threw them away into hide-outs and holes which we could not discover. The smoke which we had developed in the dug-outs also prevented our men from discovering and capturing the arms. Since we had to blow up the dug-outs at once, we were not in a position to search for the arms later on.

'The hand-grenades, explosive charges and incendiary bottles captured were used at once against the bandits.

'Furthermore we captured:

1,240 used uniform tunics (some decorated with medal ribbons – Iron Cross and East Medal).

600 pairs of used trousers.

Pieces of equipment and German steel helmets.

108 horses, 4 of them still in the former Ghetto hearses.

4.4 million Zloty. We captured moreover about 5 to 6 million Zloty not yet counted, a considerable amount of foreign currency, including 14,300 dollars in paper; 9,200 dollars in gold; large amounts of jewellery (rings, necklaces, watches, etc.).

'4. With the exception of 8 buildings (police lodgings, hospital and accommodation for the *Werkschutz*) the former Ghetto has been completely destroyed. Where blowing-up was not carried out, only partition walls are still standing. But the ruins still contain enormous amounts of bricks and scrap material which could be used.'

Thus did SS Brigadeführer u. Generalmajor der Polizei Jürgen Stroop implement the express orders of his Reichsführer-SS.

Himmler, although a supreme apostle of violence, did not care to carry it out himself. Indeed, he was positively squeamish when he was obliged to witness the obedience of his most extreme orders. For example, on 15 December 1941, when in the centre of Prague he witnessed the machine-gunning of one hundred citizens accused of 'attempting to subvert the regime', he slumped in a dead faint in his high-backed chair, the unremarkable face of the bourgeois clerk suddenly chalk-white, the rimless glasses askew, the lips drawn back. On one occasion, when witnessing a mass shooting, he broke down in hysteria and had to be led away.

But removed from distressing realities, he could talk about the most appalling atrocities with the detachment of a mortuary attendant commenting on the latest intake of corpses. Thus, on the affair of the Warsaw Ghetto, he was able to report with complete detachment. His pride however was something by which he set great store; his account reads as if he himself had destroyed every single Jew in the Ghetto:

'I decided to destroy the entire Jewish residential area by setting every block on fire, including the blocks of residential buildings near the armament works. One block after the other was systematically evacuated and sub-sequently destroyed by fire. The Jews then emerged from their hiding-places and dug-outs in almost every case. Not infrequently the Jews stayed in the burning buildings until, because of the heat and the fear of being burnt alive, they preferred to jump down from the upper stories after having thrown mattresses and other upholstered articles into the street. With their bones broken, they still tried to crawl across the street into blocks of buildings which had not yet been set on fire or were only partly in flames. Some of the Jews changed their hiding-places during the night, by moving into the ruins of burnt-out buildings, taking refuge there until they were found by our patrols. Their stay in the sewers also ceased to be pleasant after the first week.

'Frequently, we could hear from the street loud voices coming through the sewer shafts. Then the men of the Waffen-SS, the police or Wehrmacht engineers courageously climbed down the shafts to bring out the Jews already dead.'

The language of Stroop's report was factual and passionless; its presentation, to say the least, was striking. The document, which came into the hands of the 7th US Army in 1945, caused a sensation when it was produced at the Nuremberg Trials. The Chief Prosecutor, Supreme Justice Jackson, told the hushed court:

'I hold a report written with Teutonic devotion to detail, illustrated with photographs to authenticate its almost incredible text, and beautifully bound in leather with the loving care bestowed on a proud work. It is the original report of SS-Brigadier General Stroop, in charge of the destruction of the Warsaw Ghetto and its title-page carries the inscription "The Jewish Ghetto in Warsaw No Longer Exists". It is characteristic that one of the captions concerned shows the driving out of Jewish "bandits"; those whom the photograph shows being driven out are almost entirely women and little children.

'It contains a day-by-day account of the killings mainly carried out by the SS organisation . . .'

As for Jürgen Stroop, he was first tried by the Americans at Dachau and sentenced to death for shooting hostages in Greece. However, the Americans did not carry out the sentence and handed Stroop over for re-trial in Poland. Again he was sentenced, and hanged on

8 September 1951. Appropriately, the execution took place in Warsaw, the Ghetto of which he had all but destroyed.

And the Ghetto? For many years it remained a vast field of rubble, an area of desolation which somehow fitted what many people regarded as a cursed land. There are two memorials on its site now. One is a jagged, almost brutal slab of rock which positively breathes violence and destruction: a crude, roughly-hewn tribute to brave men and women. It is also dedicated to a number of the resistance movements. The other is a striking piece of sculpture which crams a jumble of figures into a narrow rectangle, recalling the cramped conditions of the ghetto whose dead it commemorates. Both memorials seem notable above all for their bitterness.

That the bitterness would long survive the war was surmised by Hans Frank, Governor General of Poland, who said before he was hanged at Nuremberg: 'A thousand years will pass and the guilt of Germany will not be erased.'

Part of that guilt will forever be attached to the name of the Waffen-SS. It stands condemned by Jürgen Stroop, one of its number.

11

The presence during the battles at the Warsaw Ghetto of Lithuanians and Estonians in the ranks of the Waffen-SS was another sharp reminder of Himmler's enthusiasm for incorporating other countries into the one true Nordic family. In the early days of the war, the SS had netted disciples in France, Belgium, Holland, Norway and Denmark. It had all been an act of deliberate policy. In September 1940 Himmler told the officers of the Leibstandarte: 'We must attract all the Nordic blood in the world to us, depriving our enemies of it, so that never again will Nordic or Germanic blood fight against us.'

The enthusiasm which Himmler expended on preaching the nutritious virtues of porridge was now equalled by his dedication to building up foreign Waffen-SS legions. It was a mission which perhaps satisfied some romantic yearning in his dangerously simple nature. After all, he had personally named one division 'Viking' and this had been seen by many as staking a personal claim to one of those lands in the northern twilight, a home of pagan gods whose beginnings could be traced in the ancient runes.

Carried away by an obsession which was rivalled only by his hatred of the ever-proliferating Jews, Himmler was even to speak in glowing terms of the day when millions of Germans living in America would be members of the SS.

Nordic trappings aside, though, one of the reasons why the foreign Waffen-SS legions grew so fast was shortage of manpower, due to the Army's niggardly release of native German volunteers from the manpower pool. This compelled the SS to look elsewhere for recruits for the new field divisions. Nevertheless, the SS recruiting machine appealed to a latent nationalism in the articulate youth among German minorities.

Here, at last, was a chance for able-bodied men to grab an identity for themselves of which they could be proud: to become full Germans again and not just be tolerated in what was, basically, a foreign land.

A German recruiting leaflet aimed at the Dutch and headed 'The Waffen-SS is Calling – You Too Should Protect Your Home Country' proclaimed:

'It would be absurd if you did not start fighting the

enemy before he brutally demands entrance at the garden gate. This is not possible in a local war, and least possible at a time when continents are in revolt. Imagine a border landscape covered with snow-drifts and, breaking from the east, packs of ravening wolves, which exterminate every kind of life.

'Does not this picture fit the present time as well?

'Who does not want to annihilate the ravening beasts who are breaking into the Fatherland? Do you mean simply to stand at the garden gate of your own home country? Then it will be too late. Happy the country that keeps the war far away from its boundaries and does not hesitate to make sacrifices in blood to save the Fatherland.'

The leaflet then went on to outline how the recruit to the Waffen-SS would be treated if he went to Germany for training:

'Will there be a difference between the relatives of Reich Germans and those of the other Germanic tribes? No! It is for this very reason that the volunteer goes to Germany gladly, because he knows that the Führer keeps his word and that his family is being cared for in the best possible way.

'He will not be driven into battle as cannon fodder . . . The blood of *all* the fighters of the Führer is too valuable to be risked at random. That is why the volunteer gets the best possible training in Germany which a soldier ever had and the best weapons ever forged.

'The first pool of all volunteers from the other Germanic countries is the SS Training Camp at Senneheim in Upper Alsace, where all those assemble who are brave and clever enough to make the leap into the future. In this training camp, which was established as a transitional stage, all Germanic racial tribes come into contact for the first time, so that by taking part in sports, not only the learning of the German language becomes child's play but also the volunteers become familiar with the ideals of National Socialism and of the Schutzstaffel, especially, however, with the ancient German virtues – loyalty and honour, obedience, toughness, fighting spirit, comradeship. The volunteer also knows what it is like to become a member of a fighting community who with unflinching loyalty stand behind the Führer and his ideology.

'Those who are weak and soft can go home again. Those, however, who recognise that they are to be called upon to become convinced defenders of the Germanic idea in their own home countries will be able to learn from the best source that "freedom and happiness" cannot be achieved by dreaming while sitting at a fireplace, nor can they be achieved by sleeping or praying to heaven.

'The Germanic man does not have to be taught the hero-ideal, it is burnt into his heart . . . Enthusiastically, the militant mind will be in the forefront of battle for victory.'

The document then quotes a Dutch volunteer in the Waffen-SS writing to his mother: 'Our great leader Adolf Hitler will construct a new Europe and will lead us towards freedom. Our gracious Lord will let Germany be victorious, and I am proud to have marched with the German comrades towards freedom.'

In addition, glowing promises were held out to the Waffen-SS recruit. Pay and fringe benefits were good; high pensions were promised and there was even to be the gift of land once the war was over. The recruiting offices knew how to put over this sort of salesmanship.

For Himmler, however, ideology reigned supreme. In April 1943 the Reichsführer-SS made a secret speech to the assembled officers of the three SS divisions of the Leibstandarte:

'The result, the end of this war, regardless of how

many months or even years it lasts, will be this: that the Reich, the German Reich of the German nation, will with just title find confirmation of its evolution, that we have an outlet and a way open to us in the east, and that then, centuries later, a politically German, a Germanic World Empire will be formed. That will be the result, the fruit of all the many, many sacrifices which have been made and which must still be made.'

For Hitler ideology was all very fine. The Führer desperately needed manpower, particularly after the launching of the war in Russia. Barbarossa had only been activated for a few days before Hitler was calling for the formation of national legions to wage 'the battle against Bolshevism.' Every one of the occupied nations of western Europe was to provide legions. Hitler recognised that there would be waverers – the puppet governments of the occupied countries would doubtless raise objections. In that case, ideologically friendly states such as Italy, Spain and Croatia could be called upon to fill the gap.

And, indeed, some of the occupied countries *did* object. The Danish authorities are said to have proclaimed that anyone from Denmark who served with the Germans would be condemned as a traitor and, at very worst, deprived of any pension rights. Himmler, enraged at the temerity of the Danes, forthwith announced that the SS would pay the pensions and that the bill would be forwarded to Denmark. The result was five hundred Danes to form the nucleus of Volunteer Brigade Denmark. By May 1942, Danes were serving with Totenkopf and, later, with 1st SS Infantry Brigade, fighting along the Russian front.

Himmler might have beatific thoughts about one great happy 'Germanic' family of Waffen-SS, but the reality often turned out very different from the glowing language of the recruiting leaflet. German commanders within the Waffen-SS did not care overmuch if their new recruits were ethnic Germans – many were simply regarded as foreigners who had been foisted on already established legions like so much cannon-fodder. There was trouble particularly among Flemish volunteers for the Waffen-SS, who were frequently beaten and sworn at and generally ill-treated as 'filthy people', 'a nation of idiots' and 'a race of gypsies'. Nevertheless, five thousand men in service for the Reich was not to be sneered at – and that was the Flemish strength Himmler and his recruiting agents were able to muster during 1941.

The highest number of volunteers from the west entering the Waffen-SS were to be found, ironically, when the war was already lost. Collaborators, freelance adventurers and every variety of amateur Quisling woke up suddenly to what would surely happen to them when the British, the Russians and the Americans were at last masters of Europe. There would be reprisals, imprisonment. There would be war-crimes trials and executions. The only hope was that somehow the enemy would be defeated. Would it not even be better to perish in the east, fighting the Russians in combat than to fall alive into the hands of fresh occupying powers? With fear the greatest impetus, those in the foreign legions, particularly in the west, fought fearsomely, notably in the closing weeks of the war when Berlin was defended by, among others, Danes and Norwegians of SS Division Nordland and French SS men from the Division Charlemagne.

Gottlob Berger was tireless. He had his eyes on recruitment for the Waffen-SS in the east; indeed, he had been hard at this aspect of recruitment as early as 1940 and had concentrated on an area which, although in the eastern crucible of 'barbarism', must have had considerable appeal for Heinrich Himmler.

This was Transylvania, home of vampirism, of Count Dracula, every bit as cruel as the shadowy germanic world which had formed part of the romantic droolings of the Reichsführer-SS.

In 1940, Berger had managed to lay hands on no less

than one thousand promising young Rumanians who would at some time be of use to the Reich. The canny Berger had managed to get this material smuggled into Germany disguised as industrial and agricultural workers.

Berger next cast covetous eyes at Yugoslavia and began formulating his plans long before German victory there. He saw Yugoslavia as a useful source not just for a few hundred volunteers, but for no less than an entire SS division. The clutch of ethnic Germans which he secured was sent to swell the ranks of SS Das Reich. Himmler thought that he could do better; he began the familiar wheedling approaches to Hitler.

Hitler endured the philosophical ramblings of Himmler with patience; his concern was more practical. By the end of 1941 the activities of partisans in Serbia and Croatia were proving a decided nuisance. The raising of another 'private army' suddenly had distinct attractions.

The Führer agreed to the formation of SS-Volunteer-Division Prinz Eugen, which was designated a mountain division, and from the very first was committed to one of the most ferocious campaigns of the war between the Germans and the Yugoslav partisans. Later, in Bosnia, the Kama Division was set up under the leadership of SS officers and recruited from nationals, and was part of the 5th Waffen-SS Gebirgskorps (Mountain Corps).

The Prinz Eugen was, however, indisputably the cream of the mountain contingents and, where brutality was concerned, the most dedicated. It stands condemned for a series of atrocities in Yugoslavia.

The most notable of these happened in March 1944 during a mopping up operation when troops of Prinz Eugen and parts of Teufelsdivision (Devil's Division), under the command of 2nd Panzer Army, fell upon numerous Croatian villages, burning some two thousand inhabitants alive and setting fire to their homes.

Acts of brutality against partisans became a speciality; the mountain contingents became virtual slaughter

186

brigades, razing towns and villages indiscriminately.

A testimony has survived from the Brigade Commander of 1st Mountain Brigade, Oberst Pericic, of 26 September 1943. It concerned the use of SS units around Popovaca in Bosnia.

'On 16 September 1943 an SS unit of eighty men marched out of Popovaca to Osekovo with a mission to obtain cattle. A short while after the arrival in Osekovo, this unit was attacked by partisans. Under pressure, the SS unit had to draw back to E Station. There it had four badly wounded and several lightly wounded personnel. The leader of the unit telephoned Popovaca that he had been forced to retreat and that he had killed everybody that he had seen in the course of the withdrawal because it was impossible to tell the local population from the partisans. He admitted that during this action he had personally killed one hundred people.'

The various 'mopping-up' operations carried out by Prinz Eugen became more frequent. A report of the Yugoslav State Commission on War Crimes of the Occupying Power and its Collaborators, read:

'On 28 March this Battalion overran the villages of Dorfer Otok, Cornji, Ruda and Dolac Delnji and carried out horrific barbarism, burning and plundering. These animals murdered in a single day in the above-named Dalmatian villages 834 people, including grown men, women and children and burnt 500 houses down and plundered everything there was to be plundered. The German soldiers drove men, women and children into one place and then opened fire on them with machine-guns. They threw bombs among them, robbed them of their possessions and afterwards burned the corpses . . .'

The Russian prosecutor at the Nuremberg Trials revealed revolting atrocities by members of the Waffen-SS from Trieste during the summer of 1944 on the Slovenian population of the coastal area.

187

'On that day they took two soldiers of the Yugoslavian Freedom Army and of the Slovenian partisan armies prisoner. They brought them to Razorie where they smashed in their faces with bayonets, prized out their eyes and then asked them if they could still see Comrade Tito. After that, they called the local peasants together and beheaded the victims . . . Afterwards, they laid the heads on a table. Photographs of this occurrence were found on the body of a dead German later.'

Historians of Nazism still argue furiously whether 'fringe' organisations such as the infamous Sonderkommandos (Special Commandos) Dirlewanger and Kaminski should be included in any account of legions using foreign manpower or, indeed, in any story of the Waffen-SS. Senior SS leaders such as Paul Hausser, Gottlob Berger and Erich von dem Bach-Zelewski were, predictably perhaps, emphatic that in no way were these units considered part of Himmler's armed formations. Yet contradictory evidence does exist – conveniently provided by Himmler himself.

The Dirlewanger units was founded during the summer of 1940 when the Reichsführer-SS was busy raising his ten new Totenkopf regiments. The problem was to find a job for a particularly embarrassing misfit named Oskar Dirlewanger.

In 1935 the 40-year-old Dirlewanger had been sentenced to two years imprisonment for offences involving a minor. Berger had used his influence to get Dirlewanger, on his release, a job in the Condor Legion, serving in Franco's Spain. In 1939, Dirlewanger was back in Germany and once again a problem to Berger. Nonetheless, a place was found for the Swabian pervert in the SS reserve and he ended up as an SS Obersturmführer in the Waffen-SS. He was soon training his first draft of German convicted poachers at the headquarters of the Totenkopf units.

It was normally the practice in the Waffen-SS, as in

the Wehrmacht, to send men convicted by courts martial to probation units, for frontline service, but the Dirlewanger Regiment was also a repository. In August 1944, Himmler made no attempt to conceal his enthusiasm both for Dirlewanger and his activities:

'Dirlewanger, a brave Swabian ten times wounded, is an original. Only four hundred of his original two thousand convicted poachers are still alive. The gaps have been filled with probation people for the Waffen-SS, since in the SS we have a terribly hard justice. They get years of imprisonment for even two days absence without leave, and it is good when justice is severe. For instance, in the entire battalion that surprised Tito in his headquarters there were only probation troops. All eight hundred of them were men who had to redeem their honour. After that affair I told Dirlewanger to choose men from the concentration camps and habitual criminals. The tone in the Regiment, I may say, is in many cases a medieval one, with cudgels and such things. If anyone expresses doubts about winning the war he is likely to fall dead from the table. It cannot be otherwise with such people.'

Where therefore stands the claim that the Dirlewanger Regiment was not associated with the SS? Here is Himmler regarding it as an essential part of Waffen-SS discipline. Even earlier, on 29 January 1942, Himmler had issued a directive which established the position of the SS Sonderkommando Dirlewanger as a volunteer formation of the Waffen-SS similar to the units made up of volunteers from the Germanic lands of western and northern Europe.

There was a limit to the number of convicted poachers that could be absorbed by Dirlewanger and soon the gates were being opened to a pot-pourri of antisocial elements. Native Russians and ethnic Germans from the Soviet Union also poured in. Himmler was delighted. Soon the Sonderkommando had leaped in status from

Unit to Battalion to Regiment and then to Brigade. The fact that the new band consisted very largely of criminals from his own organisation or its branches did not seem to perturb him. A court-martialled and disgraced member of the SD, for example, must have been a special sort of human being, but there was clearly room for his like in the Dirlewanger as there was for the dregs of the Wehrmacht and civil jails.

Undoubtedly the most notorious crimes committed by Dirlewanger were in Warsaw, where he was awarded the Knight's Cross. Seldom can Germany's most coveted decoration have been so degraded; it was rewarded for literally revolting cruelty. The burning alive of prisoners with petrol, the impaling of infants on bayonets, the hanging of women upside down from balconies – these were some of the more printable excesses of the bloody cut-throats vomited from the jails of the Reich and beyond. Dirlewanger's excesses in Poland – experiments with young girls which indulged a taste for both sadism and necrophilia – were so appalling that they led to his eventual removal from the country.

In 1945 Dirlewanger's men, together with many German civilians, were set upon by Russian troops and then bayoneted. The wily SS Oberführer, however, gave the Russians the slip for a little while, but was re-arrested, and later his death from unspecified causes was announced. Rumours that he had survived the war and was enjoying, in some splendour, the protection of Egypt, were set at naught in 1969 by the exhumation of his body. A coroner's report established that the corpse buried at Althausen, Oberschwaben, was definitely that of Dirlewanger.

The Kaminski formations, like those of Dirlewanger, were pressed into service to fight the thirty-five thousand partisans under General Bor-Komorowski, who in August 1944 erupted on to the streets of Warsaw to clash with the Germans. In vain Guderian had applied to Hitler to have Warsaw placed under the command of the Wehrmacht so that the Army might have the job of putting down the revolt. Himmler was having none of that nonsense; he had gathered for himself the job of Commander-in-Chief of the Reserve Army by then. It turned out to be a ludicrous appointment but Himmler was not going to shed an iota of power. The anti-partisan activities were put into the hands of SS Obergruppenführer von dem Bach-Zelewski, who had at his disposal some of the most brutal of the SS cadres. In addition to Dirlewanger and twelve police companies commanded by the White Russian, SS Brigadeführer Bronislav Kaminski.

The Kaminski Brigade was incorporated officially into the Waffen-SS on the order of Himmler – thus, at a stroke, he gave himself a private army of 6,500 Ukrainian Russians, many of whom had a notorious and deepseated hatred of Poles.

The behaviour of the Kaminski formations was so unspeakable that Guderian complained personally to Hitler and pressed urgently for their withdrawal. The fate of Kaminski remains obscure; it is thought that, since he knew far too much about SS activities, he probably perished in front of a firing-squad.

Such excesses, ultimately, proved counter-productive. As the dire reputation of Prinz Eugen, for example, began to spread, voluntary recruitment slumped. Spurred on by Hitler, who wanted as much manpower as he could muster for the Balkans, Himmler ordered Berger to employ stronger methods to get volunteers. In fact, Himmler was to go even further: since volunteers were not forthcoming, there must be conscription. Obligatory military service was introduced. Thus the original identity of the Waffen-SS, an élite unit of fighting men, was shamelessly abandoned; from now on sections of the Waffen-SS were to become little more than murder bands of thugs. Even the methods of conscripting involved a lie; unsuspecting individuals drafted into the foreign Waffen-SS were told that they were being trained for a reserve army or for a short period of sports training.

Many of these conscripts, by no means all of whom were thugs but romantic youths with a boy-scout liking for adventure, were to suffer cruelly for their misguided zeal. It soon became clear that Hitler had no interest whatever in the German minorities once it was obvious that the war was lost. Russian conquest could not be long delayed; when it came, the fate of those who had served with Hitler, for whatever motive, would be terrible indeed. And so it proved, with droves of bewildered prisoners from the Waffen-SS disappearing for ever to the labour camps of the Soviet Union.

Whatever judgment could be passed on Heinrich Himmler during the first four years of the war, it could not be denied that he had remained consistent in his racial beliefs. Those Waffen-SS foreign units hitherto raised had all been composed of peoples with some claim to upholding the 'German ideal'. Why was it then, that in 1943, he authorised the enlistment, for anti-partisan activities in Yugoslavia, of a Slav Division? It could be argued that the mere fact that conscripts were now permitted into the ranks of the Waffen-SS had long put at nought one of the most fundamental principles of selection relished by the Reichsführer-SS.

The reasons for the change went deep. The vision of absolute victory for Nazi Germany in this war was beginning to recede. It could not be doubted that Heinrich Himmler had accumulated more power than any other man in the Third Reich. But how long could he hold it? How long would it be before the Allies finally rolled up the map of Europe for good? Once that happened, where would be the immense power of Europe's premier bureaucrat?

Himmler had one overwhelming ambition left: To command his own Army! The more men he had within his grip, the more chance there was of this ambition being fulfilled. There was more than a little of the child in Heinrich Himmler. His box of tin soldiers, the contents of which were impressive when laid on the nursery carpet, had to be bigger and better than anyone else's. But even Himmler, obsessive though he was, could not be blind to the way the war was going.

Clearly there was not much time. The drain on manpower continued to be grim; there were not enough active forces left in the field. The momentous decision to recruit outside the *Volksdeutsche* was therefore forced on Himmler by a combination of sheer necessity and overwhelming personal ambition.

In moments of rare relaxation he confided to cronies that, once the war was over and he and his men had proved themselves in the field, he would willingly retire and mow the front lawn on Saturdays like any other dutiful family man.

Meanwhile, there was a new preoccupation. It was intended to raise a Muslim legion. Clearly such people would not be ideal, but Muslims had one quality Himmler admired: they had a deep and biting hatred of Christianity. The hatred of the Bosnians for the Christian Serbs was well known. For Himmler planned to recruit from the strange minority of Serbian Muslims living in the former Austrian protectorate of Bosnia-Herzegovina. Originally this mountain people had been Christian, but the Turks had converted them forcibly to Islam. Tito's forces, so ran ever-industrious Nazi propaganda, were the sworn enemies of Muslims. They were quite happy to take on Tito; nonetheless many of them must have been somewhat bewildered to find themselves stuffed into uniforms which permitted them to keep the fez but added the insignia of the Nazi eagle and swastika. The new contingents were hustled into two weeks' brisk training by the SS.

Himmler recognised that his new force, called the 13th Handschar Division (a handschar was a Turkish sword resembling a scimitar) would have to be treated with care. There could be no aggressive indoctrination about the master race or the supremacy of Nordic man. Such

193

clumsiness could ruin everything. There had to be subtlety. The resulting soldier was a very strange hybrid indeed. True, the men wore the fez with SS runes, but they were led into prayer by regimental imams and were often commanded by former officers of the disbanded Habsburg legions. All the privileges of the old Habsburg days were shrewdly revived.

The Reichsführer-SS confided to Goebbels with something approaching joviality: 'I have nothing against Islam, because it educates the men in this Division for me and promises them heaven if they fight and are killed in action. That's a highly practical and attractive religion for soldiers! '

Unfortunately for Himmler, such confidence turned out to be totally misplaced.

There is little that is even remotely amusing in the history of the Waffen-SS, but the fact remains that the attempt to enlist the Muslims in the crusade of National Socialism turned out to be disastrous to the point of farce. It was as if the New York police had suddenly taken leave of their senses and had decided to recruit from the ranks of the Keystone Cops. The Grand Mufti of Jerusalem, who had been enlisted as overseer of religious practices, turned out to be both incompetent and untrustworthy. Training by the SS in France left the Muslims unimpressed; they promptly mutinied.

When the Division was sent to France, its first action was a flat refusal to fight. Instead, it fell with dreadful glee on defenceless Christians and massacred scores of them. Himmler was later to admit that the only solid achievement of the SS training was to stop the Muslims from stealing from one another.

By late 1944 the Reichsführer-SS, highly embarrassed, was forced to disband the 13th Handschar, together with other Muslim divisions that he had misguidedly called into being. This was far from being the last blunder Himmler was to make in recruiting foreigners.

By now all the old 'safeguards' – the pure Aryan

strain, racial integrity back to three generations, and the rest – were forgotten. Now there was the sheer desire to keep the Waffen-SS, *any* Waffen-SS, firmly in the fighting line. Surely the Slavs must be capable of doing *something* for Germany? Like a drowning man clutching at driftwood, Himmler had earlier seized on the Ukrainians. In 1941 these proudly independent people had welcomed the vanguards of Barbarossa as liberators against the yoke of Stalin. Admittedly, the Germans had behaved rather less than liberators, but might there not be a slim hope that the Ukrainians could be persuaded that the Germans really were bent on crushing the Bolsheviks?

In fact there *were* volunteers, who formed the basis of the 14th Galician Division. It was promptly hurled at the Russians on the eastern front, but was hopelessly surrounded and decimated. The engagement started with fourteen thousand renegade Ukrainians. A mere three thousand survived.

Now came Hungarians, Caucasians, Bulgarians; all theoretically beneath racial contempt. Their achievements in battle are not recalled today at sentimental, beery reunions of ex-Waffen-SS.

The case of Russian Waffen-SS units is of rather more interest. In order to whip up any enthusiasm for fighting their own people, Russian prisoners rotting in German prisoner-of-war camps clearly needed a leader of their own. Himmler considered that he had found one in General Vlasov, a captured Deputy Commander who had somehow survived by vowing a hatred of Stalin. Vlasov was given the thankless task of trying to convert other Russian captives to the German cause. Russian troops fighting for Germany realised that if they were caught by their own people, the hangman's noose was the sure fate. On the other hand, the Nazis were working them to death in labour camps. Which evil was worse?

Vlasov had, from the middle of 1942, managed to marshal some supporters and Himmler added a few Russians of his own. It was not an impressive total.

Their fate and that of the turncoat Vlasov was bizarre. In May 1945 Vlasov, stationed outside Prague, was approached by desperate resistance leaders. The fate of the city hung in the balance.

It was clearly about to be blasted by the resident Waffen-SS garrison. That could be prevented if Vlasov would turn his own Russians against the very Germans that had recruited them. It is unlikely that the wretched Vlasov cared over much what happened to Prague, but he had more than a passing regard for his own skin. He reasoned that if he turned against the Germans, possibly this would save his life when the war was over.

A running skirmish with the Nazis was the outcome, but it did not stop the inevitable arrival of the Red Army. By now, Vlasov had changed his mind again and decided to make good his escape. He made for the American lines – only to be promptly turned back again. Captured by his own people, Vlasov was shipped to Moscow and hanged a year later.

Two other foreign SS contingents have a decidedly piquant curiosity value: the Indian and British contingents of the Waffen-SS.

The Third Reich had its fair share of grotesques, but possibly none quite so extraordinary as Subhas Chandra Bose. He had been a rival of Gandhi for the leadership of the Indian Independence Movement. In 1941 he had arrived in Germany seeking support for his cause.

The propaganda value of such a figure seemed to the Nazis to be considerable. It would be useful to have a formidable ally who would form the nucleus of an eventual 'Indian Army of Liberation'.

The Legion Indien started out with eight followers. It went on to recruit Indian prisoners captured by the Germans in North Africa and Italy, but its final strength was never beyond two thousand men – scarcely promising material which was turned over to the Waffen-SS to lick into shape.

There was a conspicuous lack of enthusiasm for the

task. The Indians' equipment was requisitioned promptly for the newly formed SS Panzer Grenadier Division Horst Wessel. From then on it was virtually ignored.

Indeed, the very mention of an Indian Waffen-SS legion was guaranteed to send Hitler into a blind rage. On one occasion he stormed:

'The Indian legion is a joke. There are Indians that can't kill a louse and would prefer to allow themselves to be devoured. They certainly aren't going to kill any Engishmen . . . I imagine that if one were to use the Indians to turn prayer-wheels or something like that they would be the most indefatigable soldiers in the world.

'But it would be ridiculous to commit them to a real blood struggle. The whole business is nonsense.'

The Indian legions never did fight.

The British contingent of the SS, which seems to have been as ludicrously ineffectual as the Indian, had the distinction of being the smallest of all the foreign contingents. The British Free Corps, which was listed as a formation of the Waffen-SS under the charge of SS Hauptsturmführer Johannes Roggenfeld of SS Viking, was largely the brain-child of a raffish adventurer named John Amery. He was a blight on a famous name; Amery's father had been First Lord of the Admiralty and Secretary of State for India and Burma.

Amery, a man of pronounced right-wing, pro-Nazi views, had previously flirted with the French Fascists. After the fall of France the Germans, sensing what a valuable propaganda figure he could be, welcomed Amery to Berlin where he broadcast for them. As one of the founders of the British Free Corps, originally called the British Legion of St George, Amery told would-be recruits that he represented an organisation with 1,500 recruits who had volunteered from prisoner-of-war and internment camps, together with a number of servicemen who had heard of the project in England and had made their way undercover to Germany.

The 1,500 recruits, however, existed only in Amery's imagination and it is believed that the members of the British Free Corps never exceeded fifty. Nevertheless they did exist, wearing at first the familiar field-grey uniform of the Waffen-SS minus the SS runes. Later they wore German uniforms which carried the personal insignia of the Corps: a Union Jack on the left sleeve. The words 'British Free Corps' in Gothic lettering formed the cuff legend, while the collar patches depicted three leopards. The Corps flag was predominantly black, but in the top left-hand corner there was a Union Jack. On the opposite corner, the initials BFC were picked out in gold.

Most of Amery's activities would seem to have been confined to haranguing largely unimpressed audiences in occupied France on the evils of Great Britain and its politicians who had dared to wage war on the great Adolf Hitler. Nevertheless, the fact that the son of a prominent British politician should have taken up so deliberately a pro-Nazi stance, written books in favour of Hitler, and proclaimed his views on German radio, was enough to seal his fate once the war was over.

Postwar Britain, with leisure at last to count its dead and contemplate the overall cost of a dreadful war, was in no mood for mercy, particularly as every day the newspapers were full of fresh revelations of concentration-camp atrocities committed by the SS that Amery had so admired. Anger hastened his path to the gallows.

He plainly realised that his case was hopeless. Even so, it came as a surprise to many when, in November 1945, at the No 1 Court in London's Old Bailey, he pleaded guilty to a charge of high treason. At the age of thirty-three, John Amery was hanged at Wandsworth prison.

When these days ex-servicemen get together at meetings of HIAG der Waffen-SS to recall the old days, it is of the Leibstandarte and Das Reich that they speak, not of the lower-grade echelons. If the foreign SS divisions are mentioned at all, these are likely to be Viking and Nordland, who fought consistently and well. The rest were too small, under-trained and under-equipped.

Barbarism and gratuitous brutality were at their most refined with the Prinz Eugen. But this is to give other Waffen-SS forces no cause for moral congratulation. The killings at Oradour-sur-Glâne and Malmédy and the atrocities against the Maquis and other resistance groups in France were the work of those contingents who, to this day, claim to be among the élite.

12

Adolf Hitler must have reflected often that, despite the mounting sea of his troubles, he could at least depend on the loyalty and the resilience of the Leibstandarte and of Sepp Dietrich, the most unswervingly loyal of the old guard.

There was certainly plenty of kick left in the battle-hardened veterans, the men who in the last phase of the war in Russia had fought like demons to avoid destruction in the Kamenz-Podolsk sector of the southern Ukraine. Relief had come from 2nd SS Panzer Corps, but the Leibstandarte by then was in the position of an amputee who had lost far more blood than was good for the patient.

The precious months before the war on two fronts became reality were gradually melting away. Yet a fresh challenge awaited the Leibstandarte, this time in Europe.

The Germans had been monitoring an unusually large number of coded messages to the French resistance, and there was a good deal of jamming of German radar stations between Cherbourg and Le Havre.

All signs were of a coming invasion. At eleven minutes past 1 am on 6 June 1944 the Allies had started their assault upon the Normandy coast. Awaiting them were Waffen-SS armoured Divisions: 1st SS Leibstandarte; 2nd SS Das Reich; 12th Hitler Jugend, and SS Panzer Grenadier Division Götz von Berlichingen, established that very year.

The Leibstandarte, lying in the area of Bruges in Belgium, was not the first to go into battle, but on D-Day-plus-one Hitler Jugend was in action against Allied forces in the area of the old university town of Caen. French and Canadian forces clashed with the Hitler Jugend at Rots, west of Caen on the route from Bayeaux. Many of the Allied troops had wandered into a trap; the Waffen-SS had remained silent in the village until the enemy was ensnared inside.

Once the fighting started, as one Frenchman commented, 'They fought like lions on both sides, so that the dead lay corpse on corpse'.

British commandos and SS men charged in hand-to-hand combat; many were found literally in a death embrace. German and Canadian tanks clashed and from the blackened turrets hung the charred corpses of the machine-gunners.

From Hitler had come the order that the Allies must be pushed back into the sea, and to help in the work he rushed into France SS Panzer Divisions Höhenstaufen and Frundsberg. The Leibstandarte was concentrated south of Caen, but its progress towards the town was slowed by the persistence of the air assault. The cornfields of the Normandy countryside were crushed that summer under attack and counter-attack.

On 18 July the British opened their major offensive, Operation Goodwood. Three armoured divisions would advance rapidly and seize the high ground south of Caen. British armour found itself flung back by determined

German artillery units; then the Panzers, exploiting the weakness, threw themselves hard at the British whose tank losses were beginning to look worrying. But somehow the Allied line held, and over the next few days more objectives were seized from the Germans. One of these was Tilly-la-Campagne, taken by British and Canadians, but here 1st SS Panzer Division counter-attacked and delayed the enemy, inflicting serious casualties. A small engagement, perhaps, but it was an indication that plenty of life was left in the élite divisions.

Elsewhere loomed disaster. Americans began to out-flank the German Armies south of the Cherbourg peninsula. Hitler decided on yet another fresh desperate gamble. Cherbourg must be gained, and at once. The United States 1st and 3rd Armies must be split in two and destroyed.

On hand for the job was 7th German Army. Its 2nd Panzer Division, a Panzer battalion from the Leibstandarte and one from 116th Panzer Division were assembled, the object being to mount an all-out assault from the area of Mortain westward through Avranches to the coast. After that, the scheme was to wheel north and north-west and, from the western wing, smash the American divisions. Hitler had left one factor out of his reckoning: the strength of Allied air power.

Countless times in the past, the Leibstandarte and the other SS units had blessed the whining Stukas of Göring's Luftwaffe as they screeched overhead and flattened defenceless towns and villages. Now the Germans were to get a taste of their own medicine. The Allied air assaults came in wave upon wave, blasting the German columns without mercy. Losses were disastrous and so, of course, were the delays.

It soon became obvious that Hitler's bid to throw the Allies back into the sea was doomed to failure. Hitler announced that he was convinced the enemy would become worn down with fatigue and then it could be held in a vice and bled to death.

While Hitler dreamed his dreams of somehow winning the war in the west, affairs for the German Army elsewhere steadily worsened. By the middle of July the German front in the east had been pierced along its entire length. At the end of the month the Red Army was in the Gulf of Riga in the north, in the suburbs of Warsaw in the centre, and on the line of the San river in the Ukraine. By then, the abortive attempt had been made on Hitler's life, when a bomb was placed beneath the table in the conference room of the battle headquarters at Rastenburg in east Prussia.

On the Russian front the Waffen-SS, not for the first or the last time, managed to delay disaster. The Russians found themselves thrown out of the suburbs of Warsaw and across the Vistula, due to a nick-of-time assault by Viking and SS Totenkopf. Two entire Soviet armies were held at bay by three German divisions. The respite allowed the Germans to quell the Warsaw Rising.

Matters were stabilised along the Vistula, but in France the Germans were in a sorry state. British and American forces were, north and south, moving towards one another in a pincer movement of the kind which, in happier days, had been the speciality of the German Armies. Now it was Hitler's forces which were likely to be crushed by two mighty juggernauts. His elaborate plans for a breakthrough were set at naught; his forces were threatened with complete encirclement. And all the signs were that the Allies were bringing up reinforcements all the while: artillery, signals battalions, grenadiers. The Leibstandarte had virtually nothing; ignominious withdrawal was their only course in the face of sure annihilation. In mid-August came the order to pull out of France.

Hitler's élite had known rain, snow and mud. Now there came a new hazard: fog. It wrapped itself like a thick overcoat around the German columns that moved sluggishly out of the path of the trap that had been sprung for them. Ahead lay the heavily-wooded countryside on the way to the Dives river. From there the path lay to the St Lambert-Chambois area and the blessed relief of rest and refitting behind the Seine.

At the same time as the Leibstandarte was completing this sad role in Normandy, the Russians were launching yet a new offensive. Rumania capitulated after three days and the Soviet Union was the master of the vital oilfields at Ploesti. With the whole country in its hands, the Red Army plunged into Bulgaria. Hitler was soon to lose Greece and most of Yugoslavia. The Führer's Christmas present was the seige of Budapest.

In the west, the 1st and 3rd Armies of the United States had edged south on the western side of the same Cherbourg Peninsula Hitler had fondly dreamed of capturing. Resistance from the SS Division Götz von Berlichingen was strong and bitter, but nothing could check the inexorable roll of the American advance.

Now another shadow fell across the Führer headquarters. The prospect of black defeat, the end of dreams of world conquest, the abandoning of the mission to annihilate the 'all-pervading bacillus' of Jewry: these things were bad enough, but now the avenging gods produced in Hitler a new terror.

The Führer's slowly gathering mental unbalance was viewed with mesmerised horror by those close to him. The ruthless and amazingly successful strategist, the World War I corporal who had clashed with the stiff-necked conservatism of the traditional militarists and been proved right many times was now cracking visibly.

When Hitler narrowly escaped the assassins' bomb on 20 July 1944, the cynical and always realistic Dr Goebbels who knew very well that the war was lost, confided to a trustworthy friend, his Secretary-of-State Werner Naumann: 'A bomb up the arse is just the thing the Führer needs. It might bring him to his senses.'

But Goebbels was wrong. It succeeded only in unseating the reason of the supreme war-lord.

In the grips of paranoia, he saw treachery everywhere.

When Field Marshal Kluge, Commander in the West, was unable to produce the victories Hitler demanded, it was no longer a case of his being dismissed for military shortcomings. No, Kluge had surely been indulging in treachery. What had he been doing for no less than twelve unaccounted hours on 14 August? Hitler felt sure he knew the answer.

Undoubtedly, the Führer reasoned, Kluge had been putting out peace-feelers to the Allies. Even the information that the unfortunate man had been cut off by enemy forces and had been unable to communicate with head-quarters, did little to mollify Hitler. Hausser was told to take over the command in the west.

In normal times, for a member of the Waffen-SS to have achieved such a position would have delighted all Himmler's armed legions and infuriated the Army. But these were far from being normal times; Hausser had no stomach for the job. Indeed, military command appealed to no one in these demoralising times, unless it was Himmler, who was still nursing his ambitions.

Hitler, let down, as he thought, by Kluge and now with an unwilling Hausser on his hands, received another blow. Even his old friend Sepp Dietrich had expressed doubt on the wisdom of the whole Cherbourg adventure. But Dietrich had his pride; the doyen of veteran Nazis was not going to give up, even in the face of his master's familiar but misguided insistence on no withdrawal. The Waffen-SS continued, as far as it could, to obey the commands of Adolf Hitler to the letter.

But the hour now seemed to belong to Hitler Jugend. The short existence of SS Panzer Division Hitler Jugend had a terrifying effect on those who served in it. Young boys were shunted into manhood without ever having scaled the bitter-sweet bridge of adolescence; innocent young faces with classroom pallor had become hardened and brutalised. At a time when they should have been enjoying the controlled violence of the boxing ring, these boys had become magnificently-tuned killers, their training salted with hate. Long before the mature days of the Waffen-SS, members of Hitler Jugend had been crammed with Nazi propaganda as part of the school curriculum, stuffed full with all the rag-bag prejudices of the Third Reich. They knew all about the evils of the Treaty of Versailles, the theory of the Master Race, the poisonous influence of the Jews. On German Heroes Memorial Day in 1939, Admiral Erich Raeder proclaimed that the younger generation had planted in them 'the great tradition of death for a holy cause, knowing that with their blood they will lead the way towards the freedom of their dreams'.

Now it was SS Panzer Division Hitler Jugend who kept open the jaws of the pincers which had threatened to smash the beleaguered Germans. Those who did escape streamed across the Seine in headlong retreat.

Hitler's teenage battalions paid dearly for their fanatical devotion to duty. The losses were appalling. In the case of 12th SS Panzer, 80 per cent of the combat troops who had gone into action were killed. The other figures were no less appalling: 80 per cent of the tanks were no more, 70 per cent of armoured vehicles were destroyed, and the Division was left with only half of its original motor-vehicle strength.

There had been cases of parents, less-than-ardent Nazis, who, on hearing that their children had joined Hitler Jugend, had refused to have anything to do with them again. Under the stress of battle such rifts became dreadfully final.

In the wake of their headlong retreat through France, Waffen-SS forces, now robbed of conflicts and battles in the old epic sense, found their enemies were almost solely partisans: the Free French Forces of the Interior, known as the Maquis, one of the numerous undercover organisations which had steadily refused to recognise the

French government of Vichy but enjoyed the blessing of the Allies.

As in Russia, resistance was carried out in France by inhabitants of towns and villages; children, in particular, were used for carrying messages between one Maquis cell and another. The existence of the French 'citizen army' was used frequently by the Germans as the reason for their reprisals against civilians. In many cases, however, atrocities were committed out of spite, as the last kick on the journey home to defeat.

With the invasion of Normandy, Maquis operations had intensified. To prevent German reserves being rushed from the south and south-west to reinforce the hard-pressed Wehrmacht in the north, the Maquis made persistent attacks on road and rail communications.

It was a ruthless war; when it came to attack, the methods of German and Maquis bands were often indistinguishable.

The woods on each side of the valley in south-west France on that slumbrous summer day looked peaceful enough as the light military vehicle, with the sleepy SS Sturmbannführer in the back, wandered at a leisurely pace.

Even his fellow Waffen-SS did not bother to scan the valley, and they lounged comfortably on sacks of provisions, helping themselves from time to time from the broken sack of artichokes which had spilled its contents on the floor. At the wheel a Waffen-SS Rottenführer had allowed his eyes to stray from the road as he lit a cigarette.

At that point there was a sudden clearing among the trees high on the hill, and in it there stood a man who raised his right hand. A hundred yards further along the road another man did the same thing. He was plainly visible to anyone standing on another part of the hill which followed a bend in the road. The truck took the corner and the attention of the startled driver was wrenched from his lighted match and back to the way ahead. There was an almighty roar as some twenty newly-cut pine-tree logs crashed down in the path of the lorry. The driver pulled hard on the wheel and then, in a sweat of fear, jammed his foot against the brake.

Then the firing started, bullets raking the vehicle and cutting straight into the Waffen-SS men who had no time to reach for their weapons. Three of them were killed. The other two were dragged from the vehicle, gagged, and led blindfolded up a path to the nearby Maquis.

The firing-squad was ready and waiting. No one bothered with any proclamations. The Germans were made to stand over the newly-dug graves. Then the guns spoke. The bodies tumbled into their final resting places. Execution squads of the SS had done exactly the same thing to Russians, Poles and, later, French resistance fighters. It was an eye for an eye.

Later that evening other SS detachments found the remains of the burnt-out truck and eventually the bodies in the graves. Naturally enough, there was no Maquis.

But there was something else nearby: a pretty, light-yellow farmhouse whose white-tiled roof shone in the summer sun. Its only inhabitants were a farmer and his paralysed mother. Contingents of Waffen-SS surrounded the house, set it alight and hauled out the farmer. He was promptly hanged from the nearest tree. His mother, helpless in her bed, was left to burn alive.

Opposition from the Maquis, to say nothing of the worsening military situation, strained the resources of the Waffen-SS formations to the uttermost, and the reserves it needed to stiffen its ranks were now coming from elsewhere in the SS, notably the Gestapo and SD. The SD, incidentally, could give as good an account of itself when it came to terror as the Waffen-SS. It was the SD which had carried out the wholesale slaughter of the village of Lidici near Prague in May 1942, following the assassination of Reinhard Heydrich, Deputy Reich Protector of Bohemia and Moravia, by British-trained Czech agents. The blurring of differences between the various branches of the SS was to accelerate in the last two years of the war; nonetheless, an abundance of purely Waffen-SS atrocity remains to be recorded.

The countryside around Limoges had remained mercifully remote from the horrors of the war in France. It was a tranquil, green land where peasants carried on mixed farming in fields which lay within small copses and between gently flowing streams.

To the north-west of Limoges was the village of Oradour-sur-Glâne, situated on the north bank of the little river Glâne which was not far from the main Limoges-La Rochefoucauld-Angoulême road.

Oradour itself lay on a hillside. A couple of houses stood next to the river, and the church was on a slight rise nearby. It was a solid, prosperous, unpretentious community where no German had yet set foot. The inhabitants carried on their peaceful lives and were quite content to let the war pass them by. If there was any resistance in the area, it was extremely small. The only shots ever heard were those of a few keen hunters who potted with small-bore firearms. Cattle and crops were tended year after year; children were seen off each morning to the local school; the barber opposite the church did brisk business. The only noticeable privation of war was a shortage of tobacco, but the wine flowed freely in the knot of friendly little inns.

It was here, just before two o'clock on Saturday 10 June 1944, that the Germans came.

They consisted of the 3rd Company of the 1st Battalion of Der Führer, attached to Armoured Division Das Reich. The Division was on its way from Normandy. It was lunchtime at Oradour and none of the inhabitants was in any particular hurry to finish the week-end meal.

Suddenly the calm was shattered by shooting, shouted commands and the rumble of trucks. There was little time to take in the menacing knot of soldiers wearing steel helmets and dressed in the well-known green and yellow camouflaged denims worn by so many Waffen-SS units.

For a time there was an uneasy lull, while the customers at one inn eyed uneasily the SS men who had been posted at the doors. But it was not long before the town crier was reading out an order from the Germans. It directed that every man, woman and child must parade at once in the town square for identity purposes. A detachment of SS was then despatched to every house with the order to bring out the inhabitants. Some, realising what was in the wind, fled to the fields, pursued by the SS men who riddled them with machine-gun bullets. The inhabitants of isolated farms and nearby villages were also rounded up.

Easiest of all for the SS to find were the children. There were a great many of them at Oradour. There were several schools in the town, an elementary one for boys and another for girls. There was also a primary school and another which consisted mostly of refugees from Lorraine.

On the day that the Germans arrived, a medical inspection had been planned and some 190 pupils had been assembled.

With misleading reasonableness, the detachment commander explained that the children had been assembled for their own safety. There was fighting in the area and the young inhabitants would be at special risk. They would therefore be taken to the church with their teachers and some parents.

And they were. For two hours some four hundred people, many women with small babies, cowered in fear, wondering what was to happen to them. One who lived to tell the tale was Madame Marguerite Rouffanche, a native of Limoges. That day she lost her husband, a son, two daughters and a small grandson of seven months.

Later she described what happened:

'About 4 pm a number of soldiers, all about twenty years of age, entered the church with a kind of packing-case which they carried up the centre aisle and placed at the head of the nave near the choir. From this case there hung what looked like lengths of cord which were left trailing on the ground. These cords were lit and the soldiers moved away. When the fire reached the packing-case, the latter exploded and produced clouds of thick, black, suffocating smoke.

'The women and children, gasping for breath and screaming with terror, fled to other parts of the church where it was still possible to breathe. It was then that the door of the vestry was broken open by the sheer weight of a mass of panic-stricken people. I followed in and sat down on a step resignedly to await my fate.

'The Germans, realising that this part of the church was overrun, brutally mowed down all others who tried to reach it. My daughter was killed at my side by a shot fired from the outside. I owe my life to having the presence of mind to close my eyes and feign death.

'A volley rang out in the church. Then straw, faggots and chairs were thrown on top of the bodies which were lying strewn all over the stone floor. Having escaped the slaughter and received no wounds, I took advantage of a cloud of smoke to hide behind the high altar.

'In this part of the church were three windows. I went towards the centre one which was the largest, and with the help of the small step-ladder used for lighting the candles, I tried to reach it. I did not know how I managed to do so, but somehow extra strength was given me. The glass was broken and I jumped through the frame. The drop was over three metres.

'I looked up and saw that I had been followed by a woman whom I knew and who was holding out her baby to me from the open window. She let herself drop beside

210

me. The Germans, whose attention had been attracted to us by the child's screams, then machine-gunned us. My friend and her baby were killed and their bodies were subsequently discovered where they had fallen.

'I then proceeded to the vicarage garden, being wounded on the way. There, hidden among rows of green peas, I anxiously waited for someone to come to my aid, I lay there wounded until 5 pm the following day when at last I was discovered.'

This account, terrible and graphic though it was, missed out one macabre detail. The body of the mother who had tried to save herself and her child by climbing through the window was found on the slope beneath the church. The child, however, could not be found – at least not at once. Later someone opened the door of the lavatory which stood outside the priest's house. Stuffed down in the hole beneath the seat was the child, its skull crushed so that brain matter had oozed out. The walls of the privy were stained with blood.

Everywhere was panic and confusion, shooting, raging flames, guttural commands. Accounts overall of what happened were inevitably confused, but there were individual testimonies.

When the children walked away in orderly procession from the square of the church, one held back. He was seven-year-old Roger Godfrin from Lorraine. Roger was not taken in by the claim that his schoolmates were being rounded up for their own protection.

'I was very, very frightened. I called to both my sisters that we should run for it. But they only cried and wanted to find our mother. They screamed like all the others and were completely beside themselves. So I had to look after myself. I got out of the schoolyard over a hedge, where I lost one of my shoes.

'An SS man fired some shots at me: I fell down and pretended to be dead. Someone came and kicked me in the back right over the kidneys. I just lay there without moving.

'Then things went quiet, and I ran as fast as I could. All the while I thought about what my mother had always told us: 'If the Germans come you must hide.'

'Suddenly, I saw two Germans shoot Monsieur Poutaraud near a fence. One of them saw me and shot at me.

'Outside the town there were some troops in a small tank who caught sight of me. They began to chase me, but I jumped down into a brook and hid under the bank. When everything was quiet I ran into the woods and later a farmhouse in a little village.'

Roger was the only child from Oradour to be alive when evening came.

Those who escaped massacre in the church were herded into a village barn. Of the men only six survived. At the time of the massacre Yvon Roby was eighteen-years-old and was living with his parents at Basse-Forêt in the Commune of Oradour-sur-Glâne.

'The group locked in the barn with me included Brissaud the blacksmith, Compain the confectioner, and Morlières the hairdresser.

'We had hardly arrived when the Germans made us move two carts which were in the way; then, having forced us inside, four soldiers posted at the door covered us with their tommy-guns to prevent us escaping. They talked and laughed among themselves as they inspected their firearms. All of a sudden, five minutes after we entered the barn, the soldiers, apparently in response to a signal, opened fire on us.

'The first to fall were protected from the bursts of fire which followed by the bodies of the others who fell on top of them. I lay flat on my stomach with my head beneath my arms. Meanwhile, the bullets ricocheted off the wall nearest me. The dust and grit hampered my

212

breathing. Some of the wounded were screaming and others were calling for their wives and children.

'Suddenly, the firing stopped and the brutes, walking over our bodies, finished off with their revolvers at point-blank range those who still showed signs of life.

'I waited in terror for my turn to come. I was already wounded in the left elbow. Around me, the screams died down and the shots became less frequent. At last, silence reigned, a heavy depressing silence only broken from time to time by smothered groans.

'The soldiers then covered us with anything they could find which would burn: straw, hay, faggots, wheel-spokes and ladders.

'However, not all those around me were dead, and the uninjured began whispering to those who were wounded but still alive. I turned my head slightly and next to me saw one of my friends lying on his side covered with blood and still in his death throes. Would my fate be the same?

'I heard footsteps; the Germans had returned. They then set fire to the straw which covered us and the flames quickly spread through the barn. I tried to get away but the weight of the bodies on top of me hampered my movements. Furthermore, my wound prevented me using my left arm. After desperate efforts I finally managed to get clear. I raised myself gently, expecting to receive a bullet, but the murderers had left the barn.

'The air was becoming stifling. I suddenly noticed a hole in the wall some way up from the ground. I managed to squeeze through it and took refuge in an adjoining loft.

'Four of my friends had gone there before me, Broussaudier, Darthout, Hebras and Borie. I crawled under a heap of straw and dried beans.

'Borie and Hebras hid behind a pile of sticks. Brous-saudier was huddled up in a corner. Darthout, with four bullet-wounds in his legs, asked me to make room for him beside me. We lay close together side-by-side and

213

waited anxiously, listening intently to every sound.

'Alas, our ordeal was not over. Suddenly, a German entered, stopped in front of our pile of straw and set fire to it. I held my breath. We avoided making the slightest sound or movement, but the flames began to scorch my feet. I raised myself on top of Darthout, who did not move, and I risked taking a quick look; the SS man had gone. At this moment, Broussaudier came across the loft. He had discovered another means of escape. I followed close behind him, and, pursued by the flames, found myself outside, near a rabbit hutch, which Broussaudier had just entered.

'I went in after him and without losing a moment, scraped a hole in the ground in which I lay crouching. Then I covered myself with rubbish which was lying all around me. There we remained for three hours until the fire at last reached the rabbit hutch and the smoke got into our throats. I held my hands over my head to keep off the sparks which were falling from the roof and burning my hair.

'Yet a third time we managed to escape from the flames. I noticed a narrow gap between two walls. We managed to crawl up to it, still crouching, and breathe a little fresh air, but it was impossible to remain in such a position for long. We got up, therefore, and cautiously made our way towards the square. We had to make quite certain that there were no German soldiers left on guard there. Broussaudier went on ahead as scout. There was no one in sight. We reached the square. Dare we cross it?

'One glance to right and left and we made off as quickly as we could in the direction of the cemetery. At last we gained the shelter of a coppice. We embraced each other, so great was our joy at having regained our freedom.

'We then separated. I had to spend the night in a field of rye and on the following morning at about eleven o'clock finally reached my home in Basse-Forêt.'

214

Later, witnesses were to recall other horrors of that day: individual nightmarish snapshots of memory that were to stay with them always.

When the adults had been rounded up, the local baker had stepped forward and asked if he might go back to his shop; he had left some pastry in the oven.

One of the Das Reich men chuckled: 'Don't worry, we'll take care of that.' That oven was to prove particularly attractive for the Germans: they placed an eight-month old infant inside.

The full extent of the horror only became apparent when the Germans had gone, and the next day those who had survived wandered around the blackened ruins of the town, discovering horror upon horror.

Like a grotesque scarecrow the body of Poutaraud, the motor mechanic, dangled between the strands of a wire fence. He had been shot in the back, but his killer had not been content to leave matters there. A horse, peacefully grazing, was tethered to one lifeless arm.

In the church, only the confessional had escaped destruction. Inside, a father found the bodies of his two small sons, clasping each other tightly round the neck. They had been finished off by machine-gun.

On the day following the massacre a report to headquarters was made by the men of Das Reich. It merely recorded that, in the course of military operations, the locality of Oradour-sur-Glâne had been razed to the ground. When a member of the SD visited what was left of Oradour, he alleged that reprisals had been taken because a German officer and his driver had been arrested by the Maquis and threatened with execution. The officer however had escaped and had organised a punitive action.

No evidence was ever found to support the story or to trace any link between Oradour and such actions.

It took nine long years before those – some of those – who were responsible for the operation were brought to book for their crimes. Nine long years before the world heard of the visit, shortly after the massacre, of the Bishop of Limoges who found the charred bodies of fifteen children in a heap beneath the burnt-out altar of the church.

In 1953 a French military court established that 642 inhabitants – 245 women, 207 children and 190 men – had perished in the massacre. Twenty members of the SS detachment were sentenced to death, but only two were executed, the remaining eighteen having their sentences commuted to terms of imprisonment. The actual commander of the detachment at Oradour, SS-Sturmbannführer Otto Dickman had been killed in action, since the massacre.

The Waffen-SS had always contained a freebooter element within its ranks; thugs who fought side-by-side with fanatically brave fighters on the battlefield.

The sadists of Der Führer were of the same stamp as those thugs who beat Jews to death in the streets during the heyday of Ernst Röhm and his brownshirts. Gangsterism was never far below the surface of National Socialism.

As for SS Das Reich, it had been given a particular job to do in the campaign against the French Resistance. The Division was told to stamp out every Maquis cell that it discovered – and to adopt whatever methods it thought necessary. To this end, Das Reich was attached to the German general in command of the Limoges district.

The Maquis lacked nothing in cunning, and trapping it was not easy. The men of the Waffen-SS, when frustrated, vented their spite on the local population. A deserter from Das Reich revealed:

'During these operations the officers wore no badges of rank, not wishing to be recognised. First we cleaned up the country around Agen within a radius of seventy kilometres. The population of many villages was searched and massacred and the officers raped the youngest women.

'After the operation was over, the officers searched the soldiers and took away all objects of value from them. All cattle were taken by the Divisional Supply Column, as supplies from Germany had been cut off.

'Some kilometres from Agen, when we were passing through a small hamlet of some twelve houses, a woman of about thirty years old was watching us from a window. Seeing a lorry halted by the roadside, our Company Commander asked her, "Are there any Maquis here?" "No," she answered. "Then whose is this lorry?" "I don't know," she replied. Without further questioning she was dragged down from the first floor, undressed, beaten with cudgels and hanged bleeding from a nearby tree.

Further on, our company stopped in front of a large house over which the tricolor was flying. Our Company Commander opened fire on the front of the building and the owner came out: the officer immediately shot him in the chest. All the occupants came out and five young women were taken away in one of our vehicles. The Company then left, all the men singing and firing their rifles as they drove through the village.

'Passing through the country after leaving the village, we fired at anyone working in the fields, and their horses, cows and dogs were all machine-gunned.

'From there we went to Limoges and the next day we continued cleaning up. Everything in our path was killed; and the women undressed, raped and hanged from trees. That evening, while the Company was searching for provisions, I managed to get away, unable any longer to endure such sights.'

Das Reich operated through hilly, deserted and difficult country, where the forces of the Resistance were well dug in and were able to receive intelligence of what was likely to happen well in advance. Petrol was becoming perilously short and rail travel was practically impossible because of Maquis sabotage of trains.

As the German forces were swept away and began retreating, the latent patriotism of the French burst forth. In towns and villages the tricolor was taken out of hiding and hoisted proudly from churches and town-halls.

One town, though, was premature. Eighty-nine kilometres from Limoges lies Tulle in a valley of the river Corrèze. In June 1944 it had a population of twenty thousand. On surrounding hillsides and on winding roads, the Maquis fought a running battle with isolated pockets of Germans. By 8 June all seemed calm. In triumph the local Maquis swept into Tulle and liberated it on behalf of the Free French. But everyone had reckoned without Das Reich.

German armoured vehicles descended on the town; the officer in charge, without discrimination, ordered the civilian population to be rounded up. Many were hanged, some from balconies and lamp-posts in the main street. Others, with a touch that Himmler would doubtless have approved, were herded to the municipal rubbish tip and slaughtered there. The men of Das Reich even turned on some of their own supporters and murdered them as well, either to stem waverers or remove unwelcome witnesses. With some perverted justice, a few Milice, the voluntary police force recruited by the Vichy government to collaborate with the SD and the Gestapo, were also wiped out.

Meanwhile, the war was coming home with a vengeance to the Third Reich. Those generals who dared to draw Hitler's attention to a military situation which was written a mile high in every report that reached him were brushed aside. The struggle, said the Führer, was to go on. Faced with the hopelessness of the military situation, he retreated into the past and into his beloved historical precedents. At a military conference on 31 August 1944 he launched into rhetoric tinged with a totally illogical optimism. There was tension, he was

218

sure, among the Allies; sooner or later they would crack under the strain. What was the western Alliance, anyway? Merely a coalition. Everyone knew what happened to coalitions. Eventually they broke apart. And even if every foot of ground that had been gained in the war was lost, that was by no means the end of the story.

The Führer proclaimed: 'If necessary we will fight on the Rhine. It makes absolutely no difference. Regardless of the circumstances, we will continue this long struggle until, as Frederick the Great said, one of our damned enemies becomes too tired to fight any more, and until we secure a peace that will ensure the existence of the German nation for the next fifty or a hundred years and which, above all, does not damage our honour a second time, as happened in 1918.'

This was the nearest Hitler ever came to admitting that the war could not be won by outright conquest. But this did not mean that a new mood of realism had descended on the Führer. Soon the gambler's instinct was reasserting itself – together with much of the old courage and resource.

Adolf Hitler was not broken yet. Immediately after the August meeting, he gave orders for the preparation of the final great gamble: the mighty Ardennes offensive in which the Waffen-SS was to play the key role.

13

If Heinrich Himmler had been asked to pick just one member of the Waffen-SS whom he considered to embody all the ideals of that élite organisation, it is highly probable that his choice would have fallen on Obersturmbannführer Jochen Peiper.

In Russia more than once this handsome, dashing Berliner had served SS Leibstandarte with noble élan; was this not the splendid SS officer who had swooped to the rescue of 320th Infantry Division before Kharkov? Was this not the man who, ardent Nazi believer, and iron soldier, had such a brilliant track-record in Poland and the east? Here surely was the one man in the Reich who could translate into action the Führer's latest plan for confounding the Allies? Both Hitler and the Reichsführer-SS thought so. With the battle of the Ardennes, the hour had surely dawned for Jochen Peiper!

Once stirring rhetoric and nationalism would have stirred the blood in Peiper's veins. But he had come a long way from those heady days of the 1930s when the Death's Head insignia had exercised its potent glamour. That had been back in the officer cadet school in Brunswick when he had heard the thrilling news.

He, Jochen Peiper, was to be adjutant to none other than Heinrich Himmler, the Reichsführer-SS himself. Peiper's family was particularly pleased. His father had been in the Army and secretly regarded the new élite as arrogant and upstart. But, surely, if it had the good sense to pick young Jochen, it could not be as bad as some people had thought. The SS was delighted to gain in its senior ranks an educated gentleman; Himmler, the chicken farmer, felt he had need of such people.

There had indeed been tinsel glamour in those early days of National Socialism. On the outbreak of war there was heavy adulation throughout Germany for the fine Aryan specimens who went off to fight the importunate Pole – particularly for the members of the Leibstandarte. At twenty-five years old, Peiper was marked out for promotion in the ranks of the world's hardest army.

And it *had* been a hard apprenticeship in the Waffen-SS. Peiper remembered vividly that business of the 320th Infantry Division and of the Soviet ski-battalion which had barred his way by seizing a village. There had been no time for ideological abstractions then; Peiper had wheeled his tank column off the road and surrounded the village.

The fight had been brutal, sharp and short; most of the Russians had died where they stood. That particular engagement and its successful outcome had put Peiper firmly up the ladder: SS-Sturmbannführer in mid-1942, SS-Obersturmbannführer in command of 1st SS Panzer Regiment in 1943.

He held the Knight's Cross and had been more than blooded in battle. But there had still been something of the schoolboy about him. In the summer of 1943 he had fired a grenade-launcher directly at a Russian T34. As the red and yellow flames licked greedily at the Soviet juggernaut, Peiper had grinned to his admiring comrades: 'I suppose that's enough to get me the combat infantryman's badge, eh?'

It had all been good recruiting-poster stuff, the sort of nonsense Dr Goebbels was fond of putting out. But aping the movies was scarcely what war was about. War was about command, having young, untried faces in your charge – faces that were a reflection of yourself a few years before.

When Peiper glanced in the mirror these days to see that his hair was still ruthlessly close-cropped in the prescribed Waffen-SS manner, he saw an old and set face staring back at him. Heroism had left its mark. Or rather the snow and ice of Russian winters had done that. You became a hero by driving the troops of the 1st Panzers deep into enemy lines and by knocking the stuffing out of Ivan. You destroyed four Soviet divisions, over one hundred tanks and seventy-six anti-tank guns. In Russia you had lived with violence and death and you had learnt to ignore the growing fear of frost-bite and blindness. No one gave you an Iron Cross to hang on a Christmas-tree.

News inevitably filtered through to Peiper that something big was being planned for the Leibstandarte. What it was he had scarcely a notion, but he confided to close colleagues that it had better be good if it was to reverse the course of the war.

That Peiper was kept in the dark about what was going on was scarcely surprising; only a handful of top staff officers was in the secret.

And the unveiling of that secret was conducted at a pitch of high melodrama. On the evening of 12th December 1944 a host of generals was summoned under the seal of secrecy to Rundstedt's headquarters. They were forthwith stripped of side-arms and briefcases. Then the generals, adult individuals in charge of men at the front, were ushered on to a bus and driven around like children on a mystery tour. When the driver was satisfied that they had no idea where they were, the generals were deposited at the entrance of a deep underground bunker – Hitler's headquarters at Ziegenberg near Frankfurt.

Each man, when he encountered his Führer, had to keep the look of shock out of his eyes. For here was a stunted figure, pale and puffy of countenance, his hands trembling, one arm kept rigidly on the table so that it would not be seen to twitch. The voice, however, was as strong as always, the strange mesmeric power burning on all batteries. And here was all the old rhetoric:

'If now we can deliver a few more blows, then at any moment this artificially bolstered common front may suddenly collapse with a gigantic clap of thunder, provided always that there is no weakness on the part of Germany. It is essential to deprive the enemy of his belief that victory is certain. Wars are finally decided by one side or the other recognising that they cannot be won. We must allow no moment to pass without showing the enemy that whatever he does, he can never reckon on our capitulation. Never! Never!'

What were those few more blows to be? In brief, one mighty sledge-hammer of an attack in the west. What had happened to the Allies over the preceding months influenced Hitler in believing that this new gamble would be successful.

In mid-September, Eisenhower's Army had become bogged down on the German frontier west of the Rhine. The United States 9th, 1st and 3rd Armies had found the going tough. True, Aachen, north-east of Liège in Belgium, had surrendered to 1st Army on 24 October; Eisenhower had expressed a hope of 'slogging' through to the Rhine but this had not been realised. The opposing armies had sized each other up like two reasonably-matched boxers. There was a danger that Germany would go on to the defensive, a state of affairs that was abhorrent to Hitler. Might there not be a way of recovering the initiative and hitting back with such force that the other side would be left reeling at the sheer weight of that aggression? To do that would mean splitting the American 3rd and 1st Armies, cutting through to Antwerp and thus depriving Eisenhower of his main port of supply. Then – assuming this was successful and the assumption was indeed a big one – the British and Canadian armies could be rolled up along the Belgian-Dutch border.

As the Führer spoke, his eyes glowed with their old fire. His listeners realised that in his mind he had already won the battle and was now turning back on the Russians, recapturing the Balkans and wiping out the failures of the last three years. The indignities of Moscow, Leningrad and Kursk could be reversed! The mighty new offensive would cut through the Ardennes forest.

What Hitler was oblivious to – or chose to ignore – was that he did not have the resources of 1940. They had been bled and slaughtered in Russia. There was no longer the comforting strength of the Luftwaffe to depend on.

The Führer, having outlined the scheme at least to

223

his own satisfaction, renewed his rambling historical harangue. Eventually the dazed generals were removed to collect their sidearms and briefcases and prepare for the coming offensive.

The task of assembling men, tanks, aircraft and supplies dictated that the earliest the battle could begin was 16 December. Three Armies were to be involved: 6th SS Panzer, 5th Panzer and 7th Panzer, all of which would attack along a front of seventy miles. The 60th Panzer Army (later 6th SS Panzer Army), under the command of Sepp Dietrich, would consist of the Leibstandarte, Das Reich, Hohenstaufen and Hitler Jugend. Hitler however had another trick up his sleeve; this particular campaign he vowed would not be played by the normal rule-books of war. His generals were not to be trusted any longer; there was far too much defeatist talk in the air. The Führer had use for someone who would obey orders – very special orders – without tiresome moral scruples. Not for the first time he thought of Otto Skorzeny.

But that was in the future. Meanwhile, Hitler had no intention of giving the generals too much say in the Ardennes offensive. An eye had to be kept on them, not so much because of likely insubordination but possible treachery. Ever since the Bomb Plot, Hitler had been increasingly wary, even to the point of persecution. However, he still trusted his Waffen-SS – so far.

The war-lord took over the role of dictating the movements of units, particularly that of 1st SS Panzer Division's Kampfgruppe (Combat Group) which was to be led by young Peiper.

Peiper's brief, even for such an experienced campaigner, was daunting. His greatest strength was not simply his prodigious forces, but the loyalty he was able to extract from his men. This was total; most of them were prepared to follow their Obersturmbannführer to the grave.

This Kampfgruppe had a strength of around five

224

thousand men, made up of 1st Panzer Battalion of 2nd SS Panzer Grenadier Regiment, SS Reconnaisance Battalion, Artillery, anti-aircraft guns, Pioneers, Engineers and Services. The route that they were all to take was worked out personally by Hitler and he made it clear that no deviation whatever would be tolerated.

The advance must be a steamroller. All threats to flanks were to be ignored. For the Führer, gazing at a map, it must have seemed simple enough. But the advance was across a frighteningly narrow region that was full of bends; and Peiper remarked bitterly at one point that an army of bicycles would have proved speedier and more effective.

The route to be taken would lead west through the village of Honsfeld and on to Baugnez. Then it would be south to Ligneuville, with a westward strike to Stavelot on the Amblève, with Trois Ponts as the final destination. After that, the countryside would be a great deal easier. A breather would be allowed at Werbomont, then there would be a dash for Huy, well south-west of Liège, on the Meuse. Here there was a good motor road which would be excellent for armour. The ultimate destination was Antwerp.

It was a terrifying schedule which Sepp Dietrich had drawn up on the direct instructions of the Führer: one day for breakthrough and penetration, one day to get the armour through the Ardennes, one day to reach the river. And all this in gigantic, lumberingly slow 68-ton King Tigers which would have to run the gamut of American units already entrenched in the Ardennes. Privately, some generals thought of the adventure as a suicide mission.

Nevertheless, it was indeed that powerful army that rolled forward towards the last major Nazi campaign of World War II. Once again that healthy talent for insubordination – nay, direct disobedience – came to the rescue of a Waffen-SS officer. Peiper had no intention of throwing away lives; get to the Meuse he would, but if it meant some deviation from the agreed route, then so be it.

Peiper's advance should have been along a road leading to Schoppen, but it was a mass of slush and mud. Far worse, fuel supplies were dwindling. A solution was at hand, though; to the north lay a road with a paved surface – and an American fuel dump not too far away at Bullinghen.

What was the good of a prescribed route if the armoured vehicles dried up and became sitting targets for the Americans as so much useless scrap metal? There were times when orders were made to be disobeyed; this was one of them.

Armoured vehicles were sent out on a speedy reconnaissance which paid dividends. Back came a report of plenty of fuel. Triumphantly, Peiper rolled into Bullinghen, overcame a small garrison of engineers, destroyed twelve American liaison aircraft on the ground and captured fifty thousand gallons of fuel. American prisoners were mustered to pour the fuel into the parched tanks.

Soon Peiper, his conscience not troubling him at all, was back on the route dictated by Hitler. The fuel problem was solved – for a while at least. Peiper's next decision was to divide the column to carry out a pincer attack upon Ligneuville, a small town to the west.

While he kept to the prescribed route, a second detachment of tanks and grenadiers advanced on Peiper's right flank along minor tracks and roads. This detachment took utterly by surprise some stragglers from the US 7th Armoured Division. At the Baugnez crossroads, the Germans opened fire, the machine-guns raking the trucks and causing the momentarily-dazed Americans to leap out and fling themselves in the ditches.

But the gunfire continued and in the barrage the Americans re-emerged, throwing down their weapons and raising their hands above their heads. By now the bulk of the German column had moved on – except for two armoured vehicles which ground to a halt, directly facing the group of some 150 prisoners who were promptly rounded up and herded into a field in the nearby hamlet of Malmédy.

Malmédy! A name to place in the annals of Waffen-SS atrocities alongside Le Paradis and Wormhoudt . . .

In the first German vehicle stood SS Oberschütze George Fleps, a Rumanian member of the Waffen-SS. Fleps, the 21-year-old private of Swabian descent, was to prove the equal of any native-born SS man when it came to brutality.

Now he raised his pistol, took careful aim and fired.

The driver of Second Lieutenant Virgil Lary of the US Army, standing in the very front of the prisoners, pitched forward, blood cascading onto the ground from a chest wound. The rest of the prisoners stood paralysed; those who survived said later that it was like watching a film of some atrocious carnage that was happening to someone else somewhere else, not here in a quiet Belgian village to American soldiers.

This feeling of unreality, of numbing detachment, did not last long. For now the machine-guns were speaking. The SS men, whipped into an atavistic fury, raked the defenceless prisoners. Hoping that at least some of his men could escape the relentless arc of fire, an officer yelled 'Stand fast!' in a desperate bid to avert a stampede.

Some men did not die. Virgil Lary, though badly wounded, was one. His mate Ken Ahrens was another. Lary dropped to the ground feigning death, hoping that the sweat pouring down his face would not betray him. After an eternity, the machine-guns stopped. Now there were just individual pistol shots as the *coup de grâce* was administered. But the danger was not over. The SS were walking among the bodies, giving many of them a testing kick – often not merely in the kidneys but full in the face with steel-tipped boots. One thing Lary registered above all: the SS men were laughing. 'They were like maniacs,' he said later.

On the nearby road, tanks squashed the bodies of those who had managed to escape from the meadow. As they rumbled off and a calm fell, Lary was conscious that the laughter was getting fainter. Some were shouting 'Wait for me' like children on the way home from the playground.

Ken Ahrens had been wounded twice in the back, but was still alive. He was frozen from head to toe after the long wait in the grass. God knows how long he had lain there. Then he was conscious of the dreadful pain from the two wounds in his back. Ahead of him he saw a wood and bolted towards it. And behind him the machine-guns of the SS spoke again.

Now his heart was thumping and his breath coming in gulps. For a moment, he allowed himself the luxury of leaning against a tree and he shut his eyes praying for the unconsciousness that threatened to overwhelm him. The trickle of his own blood along his feet woke him sharply and the message was clear: if you stay here you will either be shot by the Germans or will bleed to death. Half walking, half crawling, he headed for the nearest inhabited point – at Malmédy – to tell the world of an atrocious crime.

Lary, meanwhile, had clambered over a fence and run along a dirt road until he came to a shed. He lurched into it, gratefully taking shelter under a pile of sticks. Later, Lary and two other GIs found their way to the American lines. They were, in the words of an eye-witness, 'screaming incoherently . . . something about a massacre'.

The next day Lary and the two men told their dreadful story to two newspapermen, Hal Boyle and Jack Belden of *Time*. Appalled though they were by the revelations, the two newsmen realised that they had a story of a lifetime in their hands and they could barely conceal their excitement. As soon as they decently could, they drove off at high speed to file their story. By six that evening, it was in the hands of the Inspector-General of 1st Army.

From incredulous and outraged American commanders the order went out that the story of the massacre was to be given maximum publicity. The news that the Waffen-SS were shooting unarmed prisoners coursed through the front-line American divisions like a running fuse.

The contagion of brutality in this war was sharply demonstrated by an order issued by the 328th US Infantry Regiment: 'No SS troops or paratroopers will be taken prisoner, but will be shot on sight.'

Snow was falling at the lonely crossroads by now; the bodies, within hours, looked as if they were covered by a white shroud through which blood was seeping.

To Peiper's columns, the events at the Baugnez crossroads had been a mere diversion; there was the all-important objective of Ligneuville ahead. In fact Peiper and his men, after storming through the narrow streets, found the place empty and decided to give themselves a small treat. They scoffed the hot lunch which had been prepared for the American garrison.

The advance was going remarkably speedily, just as any adventure involving tanks should. But the sheer ease of it worried Peiper. In his experience, there was not such a thing as an easy conquest. Why was Ligneuville a ghost town, and might there not be something unpleasant waiting around the corner?

There was. And the damage was done by two Shermans attached to 9th Armoured Division. It was not so much the actual havoc wrought by the American tanks, but the fact that they seriously held up the German advance. Two personnel carriers and a Panther fell to the US Army. Peiper retaliated sharply and efficiently; the two Shermans were knocked out of action and prisoners taken. But precious time had been lost. The light of the short December day was receding rapidly.

Eventually the Germans found themselves on the high ground overlooking the Amblève bridge at Stavelot. Peiper looked gloomily at the narrow, fast-running river. Infantry would have laughed at it and practically paddled across. But here was a case of transporting tanks and other vehicles; Stavelot would surely be a great advantage captured intact.

But there was little to raise the spirits of the veteran tank commander: looking across the river Peiper spotted an ominous bunch of American vehicles. The position was obviously defended to the teeth. Had the tank columns rumbled into a specially prepared trap?

In fact, no. To have captured Stavelot would have been like the proverbial candy snatched from a baby. What Peiper was looking at through his field-glasses was some engineers hastily constructing a road-block. Tanks and anti-tank guns, there were none. The other American vehicles were trucks that had been given the mission of snatching the enormous supplies of fuel before they fell into the hands of the Germans.

In short, before Peiper stood a bridge that was not mined and a roadblock that was not finished. One determined thrust and Stavelot could have been his.

Naturally Peiper knew none of these things, but his puzzlement and hesitancy were to cost him dear. Suddenly, the air was full of explosions and a sheet of violet flame shot across his vision. One of the tanks had edged too far forward and become a victim of a hastily-laid daisy-chain of anti-tank mines.

As if on cue, a thin crackle of sniper fire came from the first row of houses on the north side of the Amblève. Then streams of white and green tracer bullets raked through the darkness from a slow .50 calibre machine-gun.

All this, of course, merely strengthened Peiper's belief that Stavelot was heavily defended. Stand and fight? Certainly if there was a prospect of winning. But Peiper was damned if the lives of his men were going to be sacrificed in an ignominious little engagement like this. No, the sensible thing was to withdraw and think again, but there must be an alternative workable plan. How about another bridge? There was a likely one further along the Amblève at Trois Ponts. If that could be taken there was no further point in worrying about Stavelot.

At that moment fatigue, which had been knocking persistently at the back of Peiper's brain, looked like breaking through at last. He realised suddenly that he was tired to distraction; for three days there had been no sleep for him and his men. Now it was as if cotton-wool had taken the place of his limbs.

His decision was to seek intelligence about the bridge at Trois Ponts and the safety of the approach. Any further action could be taken next morning. He could barely summon the energy to give the order for rest.

But, in fact, exhaustion produced not sleep, only worry. At one point around midnight he had reached that sweet margin between consciousness and slumber when an unexpected messenger arrived. His news was grim. He revealed that, in the early hours of 18 December, elements of SS Panzer Grenadier Regiment which had been travelling with the main Divisional group, had seized Recht, which lay to the south-east of Stavelot and was divided from it by the river Recht. The mass of these troops was stuck; frustratingly tangled in a chaos of traffic jams which were clogging the German rear areas. Peiper could therefore forget about any reinforcements.

In some strange way the news cheered Peiper. Reinforcements or not, he would push on. He had encountered many tighter corners than this. Besides, his men expected it and there they were in the early dawn miraculously rested and itching to get at the Americans on the Meuse.

On the German side of the bridge the dawn quiet was fractured suddenly by the roar of diesels and the winter air became abundant with fumes of thick blue. Peiper

231

and his legions swept forward in high spirits.

The short, sharp barrage which greeted them seemed not to worry the Germans at all as they made a dash for the bridge. The going was downhill, and two Panthers and a grenadier company rolled on, taking full advantage of the added momentum.

The Americans made do with whatever meagre reinforcements they had been able to gather in anticipation of the German move. The noise was deafening: the mighty roar of the tank engines, the clatter of metal tracks. To that was added the whine of the American shells and the crash as they found their target in the advance tanks.

An anti-tank gun crew opened up and the shells ripped into the steeply-angled glacis plate of one of the German tanks. Then the flames shot up like burning fat from a giant dish. A blazing inferno, the ungainly Panther rolled on into the path of two Shermans, damaging them badly.

The second Panther was luckier. In no time at all it was across the little stone bridge, followed by the lighter vehicle whose crews threw themselves over the side, rushing for the first row of American-held houses, firing from the hip as they sped along.

The full strength of the assault by Peiper's revitalised young comrades was altogether too much for the Americans. The tank guns were captured and their infantry driven back. Soon the whole of Peiper's forces were streaming into Stavelot and fanning out through the streets. The Americans were forced away to the north.

Trois Ponts was next – a vital crossing in a key area on the way to the Meuse. The Germans simply had to have it.

Trois Ponts, as it happened, was no better defended than had been Stavelot. Company C of America's 51st Engineer Combat Battalion had been involved in such gentle tasks as cutting up trees in the nearby forests to supply timber for bridges and logs for dug-out roofs. It had been a pleasant life up till now, far from the main battle-front. Many other troops scoffed at it as a civilian assignment, but still more were envious.

Such envy was to end with a vengeance at 1730 hours on 17 December 1944.

Orders came to stem a very real threat. Germany was threatening the entire Amblève line; armoured columns were already on the march. If they could not be stopped, they could at least be delayed. The engineers would have to turn their talents from building bridges to destroying them. This was all very well, provided the Americans were unmolested, but the men of C Company possessed just ten machine-guns and eight bazookas. Plainly, any destruction of bridges would have to be done *before* the arrival of the tanks. But how were the engineers to be alerted?

The solution fell by luck into the lap of Major Robert Yates, the resourceful commander of the engineers. A 57 mm anti-tank gun and crew, adrift from its unit, wandered into the area and Yates had no hesitation in snapping them up.

The gun was placed out on the Stavelot road, just past the highway under-pass with the purpose of covering a mined section of the road. Of course, Yates knew perfectly well that a 57 mm anti-tank gun was, to say the least, of limited use against formidable German armour. But that was not the point of the exercise; the virtue of the 57 was that it should make a *noise* and cause a diversion for the engineers to get on with their work.

Yates pushed one thought to the back of his mind: for the men who had to crew the 57 there could only be one fate. A score of Panthers against a single pop-gun!

It was just before noon that the Germans came. At the sight of the mines – the first delaying tactic – the Pioneers clambered down and shifted them out of the way for the mighty tracks. Under the railway line and around the corner came the leading Panther – and juddered to a halt. There, facing it, was the almost pathetically frail 57.

An order was rapped out from the men in the Panther. The tank fired and missed. Then David homed in on Goliath with sharp red and yellow bursts. And so the contest was on, uneven from the very first. The noise told the engineers what they wanted to know; the enemy tanks had arrived. Within seconds, the middle span of the vital bridge had caved in and there was a crash as the debris hit the water.

For Peiper and his tanks there was now no way across. The SS Obersturmbannführer stared at the four dead bodies of the crew of the 57 and cursed. If it had not been for them he would have been well away by now.

Peiper hunted desperately through the map for an alternative route – one that would stick as closely as possible to that originally laid down by Hitler.

But freedom of movement was one thing never to be granted to Jochen Peiper.

With Trois Ponts now out of the reckoning, the map told him that the most promising by-pass route and eventual exit to the west lay to the north through the mountain village of La Gleize. It was not much of a place; a clutch of small stone houses grouped around a little church at the end of a twisting hilly road. But there was a bridge that the Germans managed to capture, over it a route was possible back to Werboment, one of the first places on Hitler's itinerary.

With relief, Peiper made the crossing. Then out of the skies came chaos. It was heralded by the roar of four Thunderbolt fighter-bombers which zoomed towards the convoy, depositing its load of 500-pounders with deadly accuracy. It was not just Peiper's men at La Gleize who got the full brunt of the attack. Along a distance of twenty miles the aircraft swooped, attacked, pulled back to regroup, and returned for a fresh onslaught.

For two hours the hammering went on. At the end of it, ten vehicles lay shattered and useless. It was not just

234

that the column had been badly mauled. A good many of Peiper's troops had not been used to air attacks. Many had panicked and run in fear for the woods. Peiper was a man of iron nerve, unlikely to be shattered by the terrifying assault which had come out of the clouds. The older men likewise had taken the attack in their stride; Peiper himself, as a reflex action, had dropped to the earth where he stood, burying his face in the earth and allowing himself no other emotion but anger. When the attack was finally over, he found himself with a force many of whose younger members were white with fear. Slowly everyone picked themselves up and the advance went on.

This was by no means the last air attack of its kind; when the waves of aircraft kept coming, Peiper was forced to disperse the advance and resume after dark.

Another bridge loomed ahead, but that was blown right in the path of the leading tank crews. Plainly the present route was an invitation to annihilation. The whole method of progress had to be thought through again; Peiper ordered a return to La Gleize.

By now the awful prospect stared the Kampfgruppe in the face; it was not going to make it out of the Amblève valley. But the Leibstandarte, true to its traditions, was determined to stand and fight.

And it did – in every area of the offensive. Well to the south, a section of 2nd SS Panzer Grenadier Regiment struck out south-west from Recht, crossed the Recht river and made for the key road and rail junction of Poteau. The American tanks rumbled to the defence; the artillery and machine-guns of the Leibstandarte were there to reply. Among the few houses, tank-destroyers, assault guns and tanks dodged one another, but American superiority was never in doubt. Withdrawal could have been engineered without dishonour. But that was not the way of the Leibstandarte; its men stood their ground and were slaughtered.

Peiper, on the infrequent occasions when he slept, was

haunted by the command of Sepp Dietrich, speaking at the behest of Adolf Hitler. The progress must be maintained; the tank formations must keep moving, no matter the cost. Peiper by now began to pin his hopes on Stoumont, to the west of La Gleize. Would this be where he would break out at last?

He began laying his plans. They envisaged the deployment of two mighty columns in a classic manoeuvre which the Germans had used many times and which had enjoyed its fair share of success: the pincer.

Reinforced now by the King Tiger Battalion, Peiper had an immense advantage in armour. His men advanced through the winter mist with that assurance expected of an élite force. The efficacy of the tank-dash, which had always shown the Leibstandarte at its best, was demonstrated as it had been in happier times. American defensive fire was now puny; it was quelled before the gallant forces of Jochen Peiper. The US Army was out of its depth; by midday, Stoumont was in the hands of the Nazis.

But it was all, ultimately, to prove an empty dream; capturing Stoumont was one thing, holding it quite another. Peiper faced the old problem of shortage of fuel. A brief campaign would be acceptable, but if there was going to be a long protracted campaign then more petrol would be needed quickly.

The moment must come when Stoumont was lost. Kampfgruppe would need to press on: to Targon and Chevron which was now the decided route for breaking out of the Amblève valley.

Meanwhile, Stavelot had been seized by the Americans and the crimes there of some of the Waffen-SS – men of 2nd Panzer Grenadier Regiment under SS Obersturmbannführer Sandig – came to light. Groups had fought their way into houses in Stavelot and in surrounding villages, dragging out anyone suspected of the one crime calculated to raise SS fury: harbouring American troops.

Twenty-six people had crouched in the cellar of a house

belonging to M. Legaye. Teenaged Waffen-SS troops, bored by a hold-up in the advance, roamed the street above in disgruntled gangs. Eventually, they discovered the cellar and demanded its evacuation.

Up came the cry: 'We are all civilians here.' One by one, the occupants of the cellar were dragged out and summarily shot. When Madame Prince fell crying: 'My poor children without a mother!' the SS dragged out the three children and shot them, too.

Madame Gregoire survived miraculously, the only one in the cellar to do so. To one soldier she remonstrated: 'There was nobody there but innocent civilians.' This brought the riposte: 'The innocent must pay for those who are guilty. The people of Stavelot have been protecting American troops.'

It was later established that 130 civilians had been killed in and around Stavelot in a single day: forty-seven women, twenty-three children and sixty men. By evening there were few families who had not lost a member.

Peiper was now determined that Stavelot must be recaptured and the Americans driven out. The bid failed and in yet another desperate gambit to cross the Amblève, Panzer Grenadiers were made to take to the water. It was December – and an exceptionally cold one at that. The Germans died in great numbers under the hail of American fire. Those who did not disappear beneath the reddened river were driven back. Courage was daunting and typical: when one group of swimmers was decimated, another took its place. Those who did actually manage to reach the river bank were slaughtered as they clambered ashore. The attempt to form a bridgehead had failed.

The situation of Kampfgruppe Peiper had all the elements of desperation. The lack of fuel was chronic but no quarter was asked or given and now the Americans set out to destroy the Germans grouped in the Stoumont-La Gleize sector.

The thick fog hung like gauze over the three-column attack, but Peiper gathered such resources as he had.

The losses of US columns were, from Peiper's point of view, eminently respectable: the Americans lost eight tanks and the assault received a far more lavish mauling from the enemy than the Germans would ever have thought possible.

At Stoumont, fighting centred round a large sanatorium in which the Germans had established a strong infantry position. The attack was sharp and bitter, the movements of forces hampered by the swirling fog. The Germans were rooted out and the sanatorium became a fortress. But the SS was not beaten; some 300 yards away, 2nd SS Panzer Grenadier Regiment dug in for another assault.

Patients of the sanatorium, mostly sick children and the elderly, had been bundled hastily into a network of rooms deep underground.

Then the SS erupted from their cover and charged. To the Americans it seemed like the rush of some ancient barbarian army. The SS, grenades and pistols at the ready, shouted: 'Heil Hitler.' Grenades were thrown and pistols fired as a preface to grim room-to-room fighting.

Here was combat at its most elementary and savage; even if the Americans had been in possession of all the Shermans in creation it would have done little good. The slope outside the sanatorium would have impeded their progress. Three tanks were set alight, the Germans welcoming the sudden break in the reek of the fog. Slowly and surely the Germans gained the upper hand. For a full twenty-four hours they kept the Americans out of the building. But the sanatorium of St Edward was but a cosmetic sideshow; Peiper was still as far away from pressing on with the vital advance. And there the opposition was almost total. There was only one answer: a fall back from Stoumont to La Gleize.

La Gleize! Humiliation could scarcely be greater; the proud Leibstandarte, so used in the days of its glory to those splendid unchecked advances, now seemed doomed only to retreat or, at worst, stalemate.

Perhaps not quite. There was still a strong German outpost at Cheneux, on the southern side of the German salient, where there was a light bridge over the Amblève. Peiper was determined to keep the route open.

Across the damp winter ground and through the swirling fogs, Panzer Grenadiers grappled with the 2nd Battalion of the US Airborne Infantry. Tank tracks had difficulty in biting deep into the sodden terrain which played havoc with the deployment of the German armour.

Soon the tanks were stranded hopelessly. Men leapt from them and scratched and clawed at their opponents through choking fog. Casualties were heavy; true to its tradition, the Leibstandarte held its ground.

Two companies of parachute infantry of 82nd Airborne Regiment fought their way into the village of Cheneux on a mission which was bound to be a bloodbath. The Americans charged like avenging legions across open ground, only to be raked by the inevitable return fire. Peiper was not going to give up his only bridge across the Amblève without a struggle, and the price he extracted was heavy in American lives. But the Germans paid, too: the tough rearguard they left behind was killed almost to a man.

Elsewhere, disasters now crowded in thick and fast. Pockets of Germans who had succeeded in crossing the river near Stavelot were scooped up; engineers, attempting to build bridges, were effectively dissuaded.

At La Gleize, refuge point so often in this battle, there was now inferno.

Repeated attempts to drop supplies were a failure. Peiper requested permission to pull out. His men had been forced into the cellars of houses which were filled with both German and American wounded, and when permission for withdrawal came it was accompanied by an order for total evacuation of men and vehicles.

Characteristically, Peiper ignored the last proviso. An unreal order like that was obviously made by the top brass, secure and comfortable behind the lines. Plainly these were men who had no conception of the reality. What was the point of clogging withdrawal with all that excess baggage? Peiper's aim was to quit La Gleize as soon as possible and then turn round and fight.

Meanwhile, the prisoners could be let loose and his own wounded left to the Americans to look after. Peiper made up his mind to do exactly what he expected of his own men: he would walk out in the lead, his head held high. That was how the very best of the Leibstandarte conducted themselves.

A vignette – and an interesting sidelight, incidentally, on Peiper's personality – is worth recording, small incident though it was among the dispirited shambles of the withdrawal from La Gleize. When Peiper quit the village he was minus his own Iron Cross. Without hesitation he had unclipped his decoration and presented it to Junker, No 6 Company Commander in the Panzer Regiment, who had been severely wounded in the fighting. It was Christmas Eve 1944.

Next day, in La Gleize, the US forces captured twenty-eight tanks, seventy half-tracks and twenty-five guns. More than thirty tanks and one hundred half-tracks had been destroyed by fire. In all Peiper had lost ninety-two tanks, twenty-three artillery pieces (tractor-drawn), seven self-propelled guns, twenty-five armoured rocket projectors, ninety-five half-tracks, sixty-seven trucks and other vehicles.

At La Gleize alone, the Germans had lost two thousand men. What a shadow the brave SS legions had become! Was it to face this sort of fate that the bright-eyed young recruits had absorbed the parade-ground discipline of Keinschlag, Glau and Lichterfelde but a few years back?

What after all had been gained? Peiper's overall advance had been around thirty-five miles – twenty-five miles short of the Meuse. Over that short distance his combat group had a lot of the time been shuttlecocked.

Starved of fuel and ammunition, the Kampfgruppe had not been able to show of its best. As for the other columns of Dietrich's Panzer Army, they had frequently fallen victim to a terrain singularly inhospitable to tank actions: twisting, turning roads with frequent junctions which clogged up the traffic and frequently reduced progress to a snail's pace. The wooded country and the deep snows had not helped, either.

What honours had been carved out? Precious few, particularly when news leaked out of the massacre at Malmédy. Otherwise, all Peiper had to point to were the Swords on his Knight's Cross.

No success in the long run attended the special assignment given by Hitler to Otto Skorzeny, either. But Armoured Brigade 150 of the Waffen-SS has its bizarre place in the story of the Ardennes offensive.

Hitler had looked forward to his new meeting with the excellent Skorzeny. The rough-neck Austrian had distinguished himself yet again after the kidnap of Mussolini. He had gone ahead and abducted the son of Admiral Horthy, Regent in Hungary, and for that he had been awarded the German Cross in gold. Hitler reflected gloomily that the want of zeal in his generals contrasted sadly with Skorzeny's brilliance. The Führer had heard that Skorzeny had been furious at being kept out of the war until 1941 and the invasion of Yugoslavia, although he was by then a long-standing member of the Waffen-SS. After becoming seriously ill at the time of the siege of Moscow, Skorzeny had been offered a job in Section Six of the German Secret Service which specialised in sabotage operations. Altogether he seemed an excellent man!

Hitler didn't bother with the histrionics, but he was in his best mood when he greeted 'Scarface' Skorzeny and told him that he was now an Obersturmbannführer.

Abruptly, Hitler cut short the man's thanks, saying:

'You'll have to earn this promotion. I have for you probably the most important assignment of your career.'

Skorzeny was an uncomplicated character and Hitler recognised that a military exposition on the Ardennes offensive would be totally over his head. Instead the Führer came straight to the point.

'I want you to command a group of American and British troops and get them across the Meuse and seize one of the bridges.

'Not, my dear Skorzeny, *real* Americans or British. I want you to create special units wearing American and British uniforms. They will travel in captured Allied tanks. Think of the confusion you could cause! I envisage a whole string of false orders which will upset communications and attack morale.'

It was an idea worthy of Hitler at the very height of his powers. The astonishing reserves of energy still possessed by the Führer dazzled Otto Skorzeny and he forthwith went ahead to pick the specialist units needed for the job – Armoured Brigade 150 of the Waffen-SS. A team of language experts was assembled immediately to have a look at likely recruits. There were, unsurprisingly, not many convincing 'Americans' in Nazi Germany. Indeed, Skorzeny discovered precisely ten whose accent would pass muster. The remainder were capable of understanding English and saying 'yes' or 'no' but were likely to prove dangerous if garrulity was encouraged.

The supply of available American uniforms was scarcely generous. Dubiously, Skorzeny picked through the mound of greatcoats – indisputably American, but greatcoats were never worn by American troops in battle. The drab olive combat-jackets were just the right thing, but the letters 'POW' on the back were a distinct disadvantage. And what could you do with a single American Army pullover?

The hardware to hand was scarcely ideal, either. Certainly there were two splendid Shermans but one had transmission trouble and had to be left behind. Wood and canvas for purposes of disguise were then pressed into service on twelve Panthers. Skorzeny looked at them dubiously and commented: 'They might deceive very young American troops – far away and at night.'

Hitler's grandiose scheme translated into solid reality produced something that looked very like sets for a low-budget B-picture. Skorzeny realised that the whole thing was doomed to failure without better personnel. Soon he found himself with two of the new parachute infantry battalions, a company from a regular tank battalion and an experienced signal company.

Skorzeny did not lack energy, but he was badly let down by Army Intelligence – or lack of it. A few days after his briefing from Hitler, Skorzeny was staring in horror at a printed notice which had been pinned on notice-boards throughout Germany in Wehrmacht barracks. It was headed 'Secret Command Operations' and asked for the names of all English-speaking officers and men who would care to volunteer 'for special duties'. What a gift for Allied spies!

In a fury Skorzeny begged Hitler to call off the entire operation, only to be greeted with an icy refusal.

Some of Skorzeny's men had the ultimately useless distinction of actually getting to the river Meuse, but, as Skorzeny had feared, on 16 December a German officer carrying several copies of Operation Greif (code-name for the enterprise) was taken prisoner and the entire plan revealed.

But this was too late to stop Skorzeny causing endless, and at times humorous, chaos. German troops, posing as military police, took up positions at road-blocks and crossroads, misdirecting American traffic.

Genuine Military Police were nettled at being arrested suddenly by their own men and subjected to a catechism which included naming the capital of their home state and the identity of star baseball players. Matters were made even more confusing by home-grown American boys who did not know the answer to the questions they were asked, or had forgotten.

The official American view of this Waffen-SS tactic was anything but amused. Many Germans discovered in American uniforms were shot on sight, while others were court-martialled and executed.

Greif was a mere sideshow in the heroic story of the Ardennes. Heroism by the Americans in the lightning defence of Bastogne and Dinant; heroism by the Germans at Stoumont and La Gleize.

But for Jochen Peiper's men there was the crimson stain of the Malmédy massacre. At the crossroads, according to evidence produced at the trial at Dachau, 129 American prisoners died, although later the figure was amended to seventy-one. Eventually forty-three SS officers, including Peiper, were condemned to death, twenty-three to life imprisonment, and eight to shorter sentences.

Sepp Dietrich, Commander of the 6th SS Panzer Army, received twenty-five years; Kraemer, Commander of the 1st SS Armoured Corps, ten years; and Hermann Priess, Commander of 1st SS Panzer Division, eighteen years.

The trial, which took place before an American Military Tribunal, in 1946, aroused a storm of controversy. In the US Senate allegations were made, especially by the late Senator McCarthy, that the SS officers had been ill treated in captivity in order to extort confessions. Ultimately thirty-one of the death sentences were commuted to life imprisonment and the others were reduced.

There was also widespread uneasiness at the lack of direct evidence of an order having been given by Peiper to start the shootings, neither could it be proved that he knew about them until much later.

At the close of 1944, Hitler was to brook no mention of the closing of the campaign in the Ardennes. Rundstedt was all for pulling out the German forces, but Hitler was mesmerised by Bastogne. He was determined that it should be stormed yet again and the push to the Meuse resumed.

The offensive this time would be in Alsace, where the American line had been thinned out by several divisions of General Patton going north to the Ardennes. The Führer's faith in ultimate victory was as fierce as ever; the possibility of defeat was not to be entertained. He proclaimed:

'Gentlemen, you are not to conclude that even remotely I envisage the loss of this war. I have never learned to know the word "capitulation". For me the situation today is nothing new. I have been in much worse situations. I mention this only because I want you to understand why I pursue my aim with such fanaticism and why nothing can wear me down ...

'We shall smash the Americans completely. Then we shall see what happens. I do not believe that in the long run the enemy will be able to resist forty-five German divisions. We will yet master fate!'

On New Year's Day 1945, eight German divisions were flung into the attack in the Saar and followed it with a thrust from the bridgehead of the Upper Rhine. The spearhead was a Waffen-SS Corps made up of the 17th SS Panzer Grenadier Division Götz von Berlichingen and the 36th Volks Grenadier Division. Later the action was stiffened by the Divisions Frundsberg and Nord. What was chiefly interesting about this particular campaign was the identity of the man in command: Heinrich Himmler.

At last, when the Third Reich was all but shattered, the Reichsführer-SS had achieved his life's ambition. He was a *real* soldier – in a position to lord it over the Wehrmacht which had hated and despised him while grovelling to the SS. Very well, he was Commander-in-

Chief of the Reserve Army now, a job given to him by Hitler. Had he not always had this vision of himself as a titan of world politics? Had not the supreme *rightness* of his inflexible belief in National Socialism carried him, in ten short years, to be one of the masters of Europe? Everything he had done had been in preparation for this moment. He liked the title C-in-C Reserve Army. It had a ring to it. But then Himmler, with characteristic middle-class snobbery, had a weakness for titles.

In the early days of the Nazi movement Himmler had been childishly pleased when appointed Abgeordneter Ortsgruppenleiter (District Organiser), no less, of the party in Lower Bavaria. It had conferred some sort of status, but it was nothing compared to *this*!

The appointment had another advantage for Himmler. It helped him to forget the old feeling of inferiority that his master invariably induced in him. The shadow of madness now gathering around Adolf Hitler was causing the rages and the seizures to become more frequent. They invariably reduced Himmler to shuddering silence. Obviously the Führer had some faith in *der treue Heinrich*. Now it was a lot easier to endure even those stomach convulsions which the good Kersten was finding more and more difficult to allay.

The Army had its own views, of course, on Himmler's appointment, which many felt had been made by Hitler as a direct and calculated insult to those generals whose incompetence had lost the war. But, as was so often the case, the generals kept quiet; those who wanted to keep their jobs fawned as of old.

The New Year's Day offensive, code-named Nordwind and carrying Himmler's signature was, predictably, a failure; there was no breakthrough. Its only achievement was to delay the inevitable end, holding up the Allied advance. It was a measure of the seriousness of Germany's position that in normal times such losses as were sustained in Nordwind could have been shrugged off as of little consequence. But such losses now were intolerable for Germany.

By 5 January the Germans had given up all hope of taking Bastogne. The Armies of Model were trapped to the north-west of Houffalize on the river Ourthe and were given permission to withdraw.

The entire action in the Ardennes had cost Germany some 120,000 men, killed, wounded and missing. The Americans lost 76,000.

In just a month Hitler had thrown away a multitude of lives for precisely nothing, not for as much as a millimetre of ground. True to tradition, the Leibstandarte had done its duty without question. But even within the ranks of the élite, disillusion was becoming absolute.

That campaigns could not always be accompanied by victory was accepted as part of the rules of war, but that defeat should come in a series of inherently disastrous actions by a military commander rapidly losing control was intolerable. The 'good name' of the Leibstandarte – above all, the epic struggle of Kampfgruppe Peiper in the Ardennes – had become needlessly besmirched.

To Guderian, Chief of the Army General Staff and Commander of the Eastern Front, the dangers of Hitler's all-out attempt in the west were only too clear. As he put it succinctly: 'A sensible commander would on this day have remembered the looming dangers on the eastern front which could only be countered by a timely breaking-off of the operation in the west that was already, from the long view, a failure.' Guderian decided to face Hitler personally and try and persuade him that the battle, which was bleeding the Germans dry, should be broken off and that all available forces should be transferred forthwith to the eastern front.

Manstein had similarly braved the Führer's wrath when the question had arisen of withdrawal around Kharkov, and had won the day. But Hitler then had been a different figure to the crumbling war-lord of 1945.

Nonetheless, Guderian was determined to try, and on

9 January returned to the Führer's headquarters for the third time, taking with him his Chief of Intelligence, General Gehlen who, with maps and diagrams, strove vainly to demonstrate to Hitler the precarious German position on the eve of the expected renewal of the Russian offensive in the north. Hitler, according to Guderian's account, completely lost his temper, shouting and raving that the man who had assembled such evidence should be locked up in an asylum.

It was Guderian's turn to lose control. If Hitler wanted to commit Gehlen to an institution then he had better have Guderian certified as well.

Hitler ignored him, persisting in his insane belief that the eastern front had never looked more stable. Guderian retorted that the eastern front was like a house of cards: 'If the front is broken through at one point all the rest will collapse.'

Time – a short time – was to prove just who was right.

14

It must have seemed like a particularly crazy dream to the worn-out veterans of Army Group South. This was 1945; by all accounts total defeat stood like some dreadful spectre at the gates of Berlin; nothing could prevent the victorious Red Army from sweeping the Third Reich into oblivion. Germany was no longer supposed to have an army, to be desperately scratching around for the newest conscripts, yet suddenly in Hungary in the closing months of World War II it did not look that way at all.

Group South forces, holding a precarious line west of the Danube, found itself reinforced with train-load upon train-load of crack forces, wearing smart uniforms and armed to the teeth for the most sophisticated battle.

What did this mean? Surely things could not be quite as bad at home as was supposed. It seemed the Führer could lavish men and materials as of old. The truth was that Hitler had a fresh obsession: Budapest. The capital city of Hungary had fallen after a bitter siege and Hitler wanted it back.

After that, the Hungarian oil-wells were to be seized. The whole operation, to be known as Operation Frühlingserwachen, depended on surprise – a swift attack which would roll up the entire Soviet southern wing.

Things could scarcely have been worse in Budapest. For trapped in the city were fifty thousand men of the 9th SS Panzer Corps, which included men of the Division Florian Geyer and the 22nd SS Freiwilligen-Kavallerie Division.

The Führer was his old fiery and inflexible self: Budapest was to be recaptured and there would be no question of withdrawal. Guderian, to whom Hitler gave his orders, was astonished by the change in the war-lord, who had quite regained his old spirits and behaved as if the war was won. But Guderian recognised that Hitler was living out an illusion. In his memoirs the veteran tank commander wrote: 'I was sceptical since very little time had been allowed for preparation, and neither the troops nor the commanders possessed the same drive as in the old days.'

Guderian's forebodings turned out to be fully justified. The first in a series of assaults lasted nearly two weeks, but a decisive probe by the Germans through the Russian steel proved impossible. Events were now moving fast: on 8 January 1945 the hopelessness of the situation in the Ardennes could not be denied, even by Hitler. The 6th SS Panzer Army was instructed to pull out and rapid instructions were given for refitting. Of more immediate

249

seriousness was the fact that the Russians were literally knocking on the door of Berlin. By the end of January the Red Army had reached the lower Oder, a mere forty miles from the capital.

To Guderian the course of action seemed obvious. The threat on the Oder was surely what mattered; such forces as were available should be transferred to meet it. No, Hitler argued, what was needed was the broader vision. He then went on to make it clear that Hungary would be the objective.

'That way', Hitler argued confidently, 'we'll throw the Russians back across the Danube and then we'll have the initiative for other victories.'

It was sheer fantasy, but by then it had become obvious to most that the Führer was incapable of coming to grips with reality. The Waffen-SS, Hitler went on, would achieve these victories. Admittedly, things had not worked in the Ardennes, but Sepp Dietrich had the ability and ruthlessness to pull off this new feat. Orders were given for the immediate switch of the entire SS Panzer Army and four SS divisions.

Already engaged in the thankless task of trying to wrest Budapest for the Reich were the crack Divisions Totenkopf and Viking which, with the battered remnants of Army Group South, vainly tried to keep the front open. Eventually the supply trains, lamentably short of fuel and held up time and again by bad connections, began to roll out of the Rhineland. Panzer Grenadier Division Reichsführer-SS provided the bulk of the reinforcements which made for both sides of Lake Balaton. SS Panzer Army forthwith took part in a successful lightning assault on the Danube at Gran, where the Russians had established a bridgehead. Then between Lake Balaton and the Valence Lake came the main thrust; the first objective of the Leibstandarte and Hitler Jugend Divisions of SS Panzer Corps was to force bridgeheads across the Sio canal.

In other circumstances, such an operation would have

been meat and drink to the tank men of the élite SS. But this particular action was doomed to be a valueless bloodbath; the marshy ground turned out to be disastrous for tank operations and the Panzers were able to do little but wallow in the slime and take the punishment from the seemingly limitless number of Soviet tanks. Neither was the calibre of Waffen-SS fighting at the end of the war in the Balkans that which had characterised the early invasions of France and Russia: the old exclusive Waffen-SS was now stiffened with blatant riff-raff, most of it recruited by Himmler who by now was rejoicing in the increasingly meaningless title Commander-in-Chief, Rhine and Vistula Armies.

What was a man of Sepp Dietrich's stamp to make of human wreckage wished upon him: airmen no longer with aircraft to fly, superannuated sailors, cowardly deserters and useless factory workers? The answer was that Dietrich had to put up with them. He had given unstinted loyalty to Hitler, only to have the Waffen-SS demeaned and cheapened by a pseudo-soldier like Himmler whom Dietrich despised.

Nor was he the only one to turn his loathing on the Reichsführer-SS. For the truth was that Himmler, once he gained the supreme power which had eluded him for so many years, turned out to be totally unsuited for high command, incapable even of giving a straightforward order. Like most frightened men he hit out and, being Himmler, did it with conspicuous cruelty. Soldiers who were found guilty of cowardice in the face of the enemy could now be beaten: a barbarous revival of a custom unknown in the Prussian Army for nearly a century. Himmler went even further, extending to the Army the notorious Gestapo law of Sippenhaft: the arrest and possible execution of relatives of delinquents. He proclaimed: 'It is an act of racial duty according to Teutonic tradition to exterminate even the kinsman of those who surrender themselves into captivity without being wounded.'

251

In the past, the Waffen-SS had supported its Reichsführer. After all, it was he who had fought the Army over the years for a special status for the armed formations; it was he who had imbued in them their nationalism and fierce patriotism.

Now he was revealed as a badly frightened incompetent, prepared to turn the machinery of terror on his own people. Himmler had never been loved. Now he was hated.

At headquarters, subordinates reported that the Reichsführer-SS appeared sickly and listless, giving himself with increasing gratitude to the soothing ministrations of his physiotherapist, the sympathetic Balt Felix Kersten. This sickness of spirit was undoubtedly psychological: one half of Himmler was trying desperately to remain within the world of tortured fantasies where he had dwelt most of his forty-four years.

The other half, devoid of moral fibre in adversity, was seeking to escape. For Heinrich Himmler, Reichsführer-SS, Commander-in-Chief of the Reserve Army, Commander-in-Chief of Rhine and Vistula Armies, was at this stage making hesitant approaches to the Allies *via* Sweden for an Armistice. He reasoned that the Americans and the British would listen to *him* as a German statesman. Surely they could all come to 'an understanding'. Himmler's stupifying simplicity of mind could not grasp that the Allies knew of his reputation and abhorred it as much as many Germans.

Himmler had reasoned that all chances of even limited victory for Germany had gone. In that he was right. The net result of the forcing of the bridgeheads across the Sio canal by the Waffen-SS was an advance of precisely two miles. Soviet resistance stiffened and was to prove fatal.

But it is not the hopelessness of the military situation in the Balkans in 1945 which is recalled now by the veterans of the Leibstandarte. They remember the figure of their former Commander, Dietrich, up in his old place at the front, cheering on the exhausted Grenadiers as he had in the days of the lightning offensives through France. There were still some cheering prizes to be won: the fall of the town of Simontornya made a swing to the south possible, but the Russians, with mounting ferocity, put such gains at naught. Besides, it was becoming highly questionable how long an advance of any kind could be maintained: petrol, ammunition and spares were chronically short. But there could be no question of withdrawal. The Russians, keeping up sustained fighter-bomber attacks, harried the SS Panzer Army as it inched westward between the Danube and Lake Balaton – ninety-three miles of front. The Leibstandarte was there in the thick of it; like all the others it was now a Division only in name.

Worse, the Waffen-SS was speedily losing the confidence of the Führer. Hitler had experienced the first glimmerings of doubt during the Ardennes offensive. It seemed to him that his constant orders to resume the advance were being ignored. It was of no avail to point out to the Führer that the German offensive was over; all he could see were SS divisions in retreat.

The collapse of the Hungarian adventure threw Hitler into a rage to surpass all previous rages. When he managed to calm himself into some sort of coherence, he yelled for Keitel and dashed off a telegram to Sepp Dietrich as Commander of the 6th SS Panzer Army: 'The Führer believes that the troops have not fought as the situation demanded and orders that the SS Divisions Adolf Hitler, Das Reich, Totenkopf and Hohenstaufen be stripped of their armbands.' Here Hitler was referring to the insignia carrying the names of the Divisions, but in fact in many cases this insignia had not been sewn on replacement uniforms or else had been removed as a security measure.

This did not matter. It was the insult which stung. Sepp Dietrich is said to have summoned his divisional commanders, waved Keitel's telegram in their faces and stormed: 'That's all the thanks you get for all you've done in the last five years.'

That was by no means the end of the humiliation of the cream of the Waffen-SS divisions. Himmler was in among them all now with his cut-price thugs, raw recruits with a taste for blood who organised themselves into flying courts-martial with powers to execute suspected deserters and front-dodgers.

While on one hand he went ahead with plans to betray the Führer, Himmler clutched at every vestige of authority. Long an assiduous student of Soviet terror methods, he studied avidly reports that had come from the Russian front on Stalin's treatment of deserters. Soon he was thundering: 'I give you the authority to seize every man who turns his back, if necessary to tie him up and throw him on a supply wagon . . . put the best, the most energetic and the most brutal officers in charge. They will soon round up such a rabble. They will put anyone who answers back up against a wall.'

But by now not even the terrible repression of which Himmler was capable could do anything about stemming withdrawal; the Russian advance was unstoppable. The Panzers were all but spent, the superbly equipped Army of fresh-faced SS which had been sent to Hungary to put some fresh muscle into the tired Wehrmacht was being shoved back to the line of the river Raab and the Austrian frontier.

As an added twist of fate, the autumn weather turned particularly vile. Gone were the days when the Panzers could force their way through mud and rain and take it all in the day's slog. The equipment had been equal to the challenge then, and the crews ready for anything that weather in eastern Europe could offer, but it was a different story now. Much valuable equipment had to be abandoned or destroyed. The Soviet commander, Tolbukin, decided to press his advantage with a vengeance.

One characteristic held by both the Red Army and the

Waffen-SS was the willingness to expend an almost unlimited number of lives for objectives that some might have argued scarcely warranted it. This was such a time, and 267 tanks were lost in ten days as the Soviets struck home and carried the advance inexorably towards Austria, where defence was soon to be in the hands of a hastily conscripted Home Guard, the Volkssturm.

Despite the deadly insult which the Führer had heaped on the Leibstandarte, the élite legions fought on, their equipment gradually wearing away and the petrol supplies dwindling to a trickle. To conserve fuel, tanks began to tow each other, and with these an effort was made to reform the shattered companies.

Surveying the tattered remains of a once great force, Sepp Dietrich commented with grim humour: '6th SS Panzer Army is well named, all right. It's only got six tanks.' A slight exaggeration perhaps, but it was a pointed indication of the way things were going.

The condition of Dietrich's Army showed 1st SS Panzer Division as being totally burnt out and most of it with Army HQ. Four other SS divisions were of 'severely weakened' or 'weakened' strength; 356 Infantry Division consisted of precisely one Infantry-regiment. By early April the entire 6th SS Panzer Army had withdrawn well into Austria, and by the middle of the month Vienna had fallen to the Red Army whose progress continued unchecked along the length of the Danube.

The final campaign of 6th Panzer Army had soon degenerated into a messy, ignoble affair – of rearguards where handfuls of men fought and died in a whole series of conflicts against overwhelming odds. Seasoned campaigners of the Waffen-SS found themselves fighting side-by-side with barely trained Volkssturm and military academy pupils who had been hastily recruited by Dietrich.

While the Red Army coursed along the Danube, the US 3rd Army swept along to meet it. Between these two giants the battered, emasculated, disowned Leibstandarte was crushed, along with Army Group South.

In a fruitless attempt to regain some of his lost prestige as a military leader, Himmler had attempted an attack on the northern flank of Marshal Georgei Zhukov. Scraps of several divisions were sent into the attack, but the leadership was so inexperienced that it was an utter failure. Indeed, all it did was to give the Russians a little more ground to move in. Then a strong Russian force moved north along the Oder towards the port of Stettin, driving before it the outnumbered troops of Felix Steiner. Himmler's reaction was to move out of the possible path of the Russian advance; he smartly moved his headquarters to a camp near Prenzlau, twenty-five miles west of Stettin.

Himmler was plainly a dead loss; worse, he was a dangerous liability. Guderian was confident that Steiner's troops could do the job, but he badly needed reinforcements. Would it be possible to get some sense out of Hitler – and, more important, the extra resources that were needed?

Guderian was given a few leftovers, most of them of dubious use. He consulted his second-in-command, General Walter Wenck. He growled: 'What the hell are we to do with so-called reinforcements such as these?' Wenck shrugged: 'The best we can, I suppose.'

Himmler, jittery and indecisive, tried to hold on to his authority. He insisted that the attack be postponed until all the armament and fuel were to hand. All Guderian's instincts told him this was the wrong decision: surprise was of the essence. Guderian decided to send Wenck to Army Group Vistula as Chief-of-Staff with power to launch the attack. Then he told Hitler.

The Führer erupted, advancing on Guderian with fists flaying. He screamed: 'Out of the question! Himmler is man enough. Out of the question!'

Guderian stood his ground. Himmler remained silent, blinking through his spectacles and blushing with embarrassment. For two hours, Guderian repeated his proposals. Hitler's eyes bulged and the other men thought that he would have a stroke.

Then the Führer relaxed, all passion spent. He turned to Himmler: 'All right then, Himmler. Wenck will join you tonight. The offensive begins on 15 February.'

Hitler's next action was disconcerting. The man who five minutes before had raged at Guderian suddenly smiled and said softly: 'General, the Army General Staff has just won a battle.'

It was just about the only one that the Army did win. The attack lasted four days and was a total failure.

Fate was to kick Guderian with singular viciousness. At one point during the engagement, Wenck, dead tired, fell asleep at the wheel of his car, crashing into the parapet of a bridge on the Berlin-Stettin autobahn. He was seriously injured and was taken to hospital, out of the battle. His place was taken by General Krebs, an ardent Nazi and totally loyal to Hitler. Guderian reflected bitterly that he might just as well have held his breath.

On 16 April the Russians had burst through the line of the Oder and there was now a direct threat to Berlin. The Panzers, forced back on the beleaguered capital, found mostly puny allies; slave labourers, deserters, badly frightened teenage boys.

The SS may still have fought fanatically, the ordinary German soldier wanted only to survive. Those who lived in Berlin found the notion of desertion most attractive.

All a soldier had to do was melt away, walk home, hide or burn his uniform and put on civilian clothes. Some grew moustaches or beards and even dyed their hair.

But it was not without risk. The motley collection which had been assembled in a last fruitless effort to defend the capital of the Reich had these deserters for company – or, rather, their rotting carcases. From lamp-posts and trees they swung, the bodies of 'traitors'. Most of these were victims of the flying courts-martial of the Waffen-SS. Many of the dead were little more than schoolboys who had been dragged out of their homes after they had fled there in terror or to show off their uniforms.

The fate of all of them was identical: they were dragged away screaming, and strung up from lamp-posts. The placards pinned to their uniforms read: 'I hang here because I left my unit without permission.'

In 1944 Himmler had finished one of his speeches with the remark: 'So far the Waffen-SS has never under any circumstances caused disappointment and it will not – even under the most severe hardships to come – disappoint in the future.' In a sense it remained true. Defeats in battle there had certainly been, but the SS motto – *Meine Ehre heisst Treue* – was observed right to the end.

In Berlin itself the sullen rumble of the Russian guns was clearly audible that autumn. Ravaged, windowless buildings were reflected in the rain-soaked streets from which the snow of winter was slow to depart. Anarchy had long taken the place of even a semblance of civic law and order; if Berlin could be said to have a ruler at all it was Heinrich Himmler who kept order with his own terrible brand of discipline. The dregs of the prisons and the hospitals fought beside children of secondary-school age, many of whom, once given a uniform, were capable of showing their grown-ups a thing or two about brutality. Hitler Jugend was always full of apt pupils for the Waffen-SS.

All the spit-and-polish and pretention of élite formations like the Leibstandarte and Das Reich might later be recalled in the beery conviviality of the ex-servicemen's reunions. But it was the jail-birds and the psychopaths and the transferred concentration-camp guards that were to give the Waffen-SS an identity which the world was for many years after the war to accept as the true one.

It was indeed the sweepings of the Third Reich that lay between the Russians and the prize of Berlin. The Armies of Zhukov and Koniev were at the gates. In the west

258

Patton and Montgomery had crossed the Rhine.

Meanwhile, Adolf Hitler and his closest military colleagues huddled in a concrete bunker fifty feet below the marbled ruins of the Chancellery. The bunker was guarded, of course, by members of the Leibstandarte armed with automatics and wearing a cluster of hand-grenades in their belts. Originally, the Führer had planned to leave Berlin on 20 April, his fifty-sixth birthday, for Obersalzberg and there to direct the final glorious stand of the Third Reich. But events were moving too fast; the frontiers around Berlin were shrinking hourly. After the failure of the Ardennes, Hitler had returned to Berlin, where he was to remain until the last, directing real and phantom armies from the depths of his concrete cocoon.

Eye-witnesses have described Hitler's physical condition as fast deteriorating, the head slightly wobbling, the left arm dangling slackly and the hand trembling violently. The eyes, however, remained alert and that formidable personality still managed to hold the loyalties of many of his followers.

But not as many as formerly. Dönitz, Himmler and Speer were planning to flee north; Göring and Ribbentrop to the south. The Reichsführer-SS's leave-taking was formal, but Hitler showed a flicker of warmth towards his old party comrade of whose betrayal he still remained ignorant. Soon, the quintet had climbed the curved steps from the lower level of the bunker and passed through the passageways and corridors flanked by heavy protective bulkheads. The silence gave way to the sound of the guns and the earth trembled. Thus the five men separated, to make their way out of Berlin as best they could. Only Joseph Goebbels, Martin Bormann and the generals remained behind.

Now the curtain was about to go up on the very last military action of World War II – with a starring role for the Waffen-SS.

Hitler had one final card to play; the diabolical genius

who was still Germany's war-lord had a dazzling resilience and was still refusing to give up. The Führer was convinced that he had a magic formula for victory. Its name was Steiner.

On 21 April, Hitler unveiled the plan to his generals. Steiner had been ordered to move south to Eberswalde, break through the Soviet flank and re-establish the crumbling German defences south-east of Berlin. Hitler had told the SS Obergruppenführer: 'You will see. The Russians will suffer their greatest defeat, the bloodiest defeat of their history, before the gates of Berlin.'

In the bunker, the shaking Hitler moved his magnifying-glass uncertainly across the map, mumbling 'Steiner, Steiner' like an incantation. He remained oblivious to those around him, none of whom dared to tell him that he was pinning his faith on a handful of worn-out units. Hitler had also warned Steiner: 'It is expressly forbidden to fall back to the west. Officers who do not comply unconditionally with this order are to be arrested and shot immediately. You, Steiner, are answerable with your head for the execution of this order.'

But already Hitler was firmly installed in cloud-cuckooland where he moved imaginary battalions and nonexistent formations. The 11th Panzer Army existed virtually only in name: a small headquarters staff swelled out with freebooters.

Matters had passed beyond help in Berlin. By noon on 22 April the Russians had entered the city limits in Karow to the north and in Weissensee to the north-east. Other units were approaching in the east, making for Lichtenberg and Neuköln. And, in both north and south, Russian columns were by-passing the city, eventually to turn and complete the encirclement in the west. That anyone should still be on the Oder at all was nothing less than incredible: but holding on with tenacious bravery were the Frankfurt units and the 5th SS Alpine Corps.

Hitler, when he was not evoking the name of Steiner

with almost mystic reverence, spoke to anyone who would listen of the undoubted strength of the Waffen-SS 'volunteers'. These groups, such as they were, had been scooped up in a giant Russian dust-pan and shoved into Berlin where they were welcomed by the defenders. They were a grotesque bunch: the SS Panzer Grenadier Division Nederland and the 11th SS Panzer Grenadier Division Nordland were made up of Belgians, Dutch, Danes and Swedes. Here also were the SS Grenadier Division Lettische I which consisted of Estonians and Latvians. The SS Grenadier Division Charlemagne consisted of Frenchmen, Spaniards and Swiss, together with sundry conscripts and rejects from military schools.

Himmler had also opened the jails. At Tegel Prison convicts were told they would be pardoned if they fought for Berlin. To the Waffen-SS forces were added a convicted murderer and two men who were serving sentences for robbery.

Throughout 22 April the Führer waited anxiously for the great Steiner offensive he was sure would come. But Steiner had calculated the figures – 10,000 German fighters at most against at least 100,000 Red Army – and had vowed not to attack. But no one dared tell Hitler.

When the truth eventually dawned, the resulting rage was terrible. Hitler stormed on unchecked for five hours. His staff had betrayed him; it was made up entirely of cowards. The Wehrmacht had failed him, the National Socialist concept was no more. Shaken by sobs and howling, the Führer slumped back in his chair, crying that even the SS had failed to save the day.

Between paroxysms of grief, rage and self-pity, Hitler confided that he had given up the Wehrmacht months ago, but now for the very first time he must cast doubts on the Waffen-SS. Goebbels later confided in his diary: 'In general, the Führer is of the opinion that no high-class commander has emerged from the SS.'

Anyway, all that was academic now. The last hope had gone. Hitler rambled on about the 9th and 12th

Armies, but both were as good as lost. Hitler countered that there were plenty of reinforcements, later revealed as fewer than five thousand Luftwaffe personnel and a band of Hitler Jugend, armed only with hand weapons.

The Führer's most intensely loyal supporters who remained in the bunker now turned on the wretched Steiner, urging him to go into the attack as the last great patriotic act for Nazi Germany. Keitel even attempted to attack Steiner with his Field Marshal's baton, but the Waffen-SS man stood firm. 'The attack is worse than nonsense. It's murder,' he said flatly.

Most people had long ceased to be surprised by any aspect of Hitler's character. But even those who knew him best were astounded to see how calm he had once again become. With relative lucidity, he gave another order to Steiner – to establish a bridgehead across the Ruppihner Canal, on the route to Berlin. This order was obeyed, Steiner reasoning that it scarcely mattered whether the bridgehead was established or not. The Russians ground the offensive to a halt.

While Hitler was digesting this latest calamity, a fresh sensation was created in the bunker. It began at the listening-post of the Propaganda Ministry where engineers were monitoring a broadcast from the BBC in London. Suddenly one of the team, Heinz Lorenz, gave a gasp, snatched a pencil and began transcribing an item so incredible that he was briefly caught off guard. Once the entire message was in his hand, Lorenz, disregarding the danger of the streets, raced to the bunker.

The new dispatch was read out to the Führer and the assembly. Its contents were greeted at first in silence, then with a howl of rage from the men and fear from the women. The dispatch told of Himmler's secret negotiations with Count Bernadotte and his offer to surrender the German Armies in the west to Eisenhower.

Der treue Heinrich! Surely the one National Socialist who could have been depended upon above all others. Now Hitler saw it all as part of a pattern: the treachery of the SS and the Waffen-SS had been a carefully orchestrated affair. First, Sepp Dietrich had failed in Hungary. That, of course, had been deliberate. Then there had been the rank disobedience of Steiner.

The Führer, his face contorted with rage, looked around for a handy scapegoat. Anyone who had anything remotely to do with Himmler was now in danger of his life. Suddenly Hitler remembered Hermann Fegelein. Fegelein! He would do very well; had he not been the Reichsführer-SS's personal representative at headquarters? The man was already under arrest as a deserter; very well, he would be dealt with by a Leibstandarte firing-squad.

Of all the entourage surrounding Himmler, Fegelein was the most blatant main-chancer of the lot. Like Himmler, a Bavarian, he had originally made his living as a groom and prize-winning jockey, but had seen in the SS a way to some stability and security. In the Waffen-SS he had risen to command a cavalry division and attracted Himmler's attention by his successes on the eastern front. Fegelein was determined to look after his personal well-being as well as his career in the SS. A shrewd move had been to marry Eva Braun's sister, Gretl. A member of the family as well as the court – not bad for a former horse-coper!

However, Fegelein was prepared to put a limit on family loyalty. There was not going to be any of this nonsense about dying for the Führer. If his stupid sister-in-law was determined to die with her loved one, too bad for her. Fegelein determined to get out.

On 26 April he had left his station in one of the Chancellery bunkers and, in an act of singular foolishness, fled to his home in Charlottenburg district, where he took off his uniform. His plan was to hide. Hitler, by now thoroughly suspicious about the disappearance of the jockey, forthwith summoned SS Standenführer Hoegl and ordered him to root out the deserter. It was not difficult; with a party of armed guards, Hoegl drove through a thunderstorm of shelling to Fegelein's house and hauled him out of bed.

Fegelein may have been a political tramp without a single moral scruple, but he did not lack courage. To Hoegl he suggested that they should both find an aircraft and make for safety in the south. 'The war is lost and you know it,' Fegelein urged. 'Why don't we look to our own skins? Even Himmler has.' But Hoegl was not a policeman for nothing: everything must be done according to the Führer's orders.

Shrugging, Fegelein picked up a telephone, put through a call to the bunker and demanded to speak to Eva Braun. Surely, he pointed out, it made sense for him to try and get to his family in Bavaria?

The response sent a shiver of icy fear through the deserter. Eva screamed at him: how could he think of deserting the Führer at this grave hour? He must return to the bunker at once; she could not and would not do anything for him.

Soon ex-Obergruppenführer Fegelein found himself shoved into a small room in the bunker and guarded in case he committed suicide.

To Hitler, Fegelein's treachery confirmed what he had suspected all along. The entire SS was against him. Why had the Steiner attack failed? That was obvious. Himmler had countermanded the orders.

It did not take the Gestapo, well schooled in these matters, long to get what it wanted out of Fegelein. He admitted knowing all about Himmler's negotiations with Count Bernadotte, but he resolutely denied being involved in any plot against Hitler.

That was quite enough. Fegelein was taken out into the Chancellery garden and shot. The execution was carried out by members of the Leibstandarte. In this it fulfilled its original function of protecting the master. The one-time unit of the Verfügungstruppe and the child of the Stosstrupp had not failed Adolf Hitler.

The hunt was now on for the Reichsführer-SS, whose

men, Hitler insisted, had shamefully betrayed him and National Socialism. In fact, no such betrayal had taken place. Outside the bunker, the Waffen-SS fought on in the streets of the shattered capital.

Men of the 11th Panzer Grenadier Division Nordland, reinforced by the French Waffen-SS Charlemagne, together with a battalion of Latvians were reinforcing the Army Corps of General Mummert.

Himmler might have been preoccupied elsewhere, but the machinery of terror intensified. Now murder bands toured the air-raid shelters, announcing that any able-bodied man who shirked because of an air-raid was a traitor. Still more bodies swung from the densely populated lamp-posts of Berlin.

The remnants of the 9th and 12th Armies had all but been destroyed or encircled; the Russians were two streets away from the bunker. For the first time in months, Hitler was told the unvarnished truth and was prepared to listen to it. He made ready for the end.

In the early hours of 29 April 1945 the Führer married Eva Braun. After dictating his last will and testament, Hitler gave orders that both Himmler and Göring were to be arrested as traitors; the latter had made the mistake of attempting to push his claims as Hitler's successor while the Führer was still very much alive.

The newly-wedded couple finished their farewells to those remaining in the bunker. In a few moments a revolver shot was heard. The body of Adolf Hitler was found on a sofa, dripping blood. At his side lay Eva Braun who had swallowed poison. While Russian shells were exploding in the gardens of the Chancellery, the corpses were carried up and burned with petrol.

The Third Reich was to outlive its founder by but a week.

Even the news of Hitler's death did not stop the men of Nordland, who, reduced to less than one hundred, fought to the end. They at least never flinched in their loyalty.

15

In the north, Himmler, still free, roamed aimlessly around the headquarters at Plön, on the borders of Denmark, of Hitler's designated successor Grand Admiral Karl Dönitz. Himmler must have known in his heart that he was finished but he was loath even now to surrender his authority. He also persuaded himself that the titles of his various offices would give him some sort of prestige when it came to the interview with General Eisenhower which he felt sure he would be granted.

The illusions were chipped away one by one. The announcement of Dönitz's cabinet came as a severe blow: there was no portfolio for Heinrich Himmler. Dönitz reasoned that it was in his best interests to have a 'respectable' government to negotiate with the Allies; besides, there were few in Germany who would have been willing to serve with the Reichsführer-SS even in a rump administration.

Only the façade of power remained but that was still formidable. Himmler still had an SS escort and his Mercedes. Habits are not easily broken and Himmler was treated with all the old deference and fear as he moved around sulkily, like a child deprived of its box of bricks.

It was then that a seemingly promising offer of help came to Himmler from a totally unexpected quarter in the Waffen-SS. Leon Degrelle, the Belgian Fascist leader who had enrolled in the armed SS, made contact and proposed that his men should join up with Himmler's to form some sort of resistance group and proposed a meeting at Malente, near Kiel, north of Plön. Himmler set out, accompanied by his bewildered staff, on what was plainly a highly grotesque adventure.

Degrelle, driving a Volkswagen powered by potato schnapps, caught up with Himmler who was driving himself, a crash-helmet rammed down on his head. The meeting was ludicrous. Degrelle had no forces to offer worth speaking of; his Belgian SS units had long scattered.

While they were acting out their pantomime, both men had to take refuge when Allied aircraft swept down on the column, vanguards of a raid on Kiel. Suddenly Degrelle's resolution seemed to leave him. After the party had scrambled out of a ditch, the Belgian commander made good his escape. Himmler's ultimate destination was Flensburg which plainly could only be reached by running the gauntlet of Allied bombers.

Himmler's continual hanging around Dönitz's headquarters was both obstructive and embarrassing, but no one really knew how to deal with a totally useless Reichsführer-SS and some hundred and fifty hangers-on. But the dark mystique of Heinrich Himmler was such that none dared take any action. Himmler might only possess the shadow of power, but that shadow was formidable indeed.

On 5 May, Himmler decided to hold what he proclaimed as a key meeting on the future of the Reich. In the presence of SS Obergruppenführer von Herff and representatives of the Gestapo and SD, Himmler outlined plans for the setting up of an SS government in Schleswig-Holstein which would conduct independent peace negotiations with the western powers.

Warming to his theme, Himmler began distributing titles and jobs while his audience stood open-mouthed.

But Himmler was not allowed to live with his lunacy for very long. On 6 May he received the following communication signed by Grand Admiral Dönitz:

Dear Reich Minister,
In view of the present situation, I have decided to

dispense with your further assistance as Reich Minister
of the Interior and member of the Reich Government,
as Commander-in-Chief of the Reserve Army, as a
Chief of the Police. I now regard all your offices as
abolished. I thank you for the services you have given
to the Reich.

This was followed by an order which specifically
banned any resistance by the SS. The Schutzstaffel in all
its forms was abolished. And that included, of course,
the Waffen-SS.

The creator of the original armed élite bodyguard was
dead; the brain that conceived it rotted among the ruins
of the Berlin Chancellery. Only his sinister chief executive
remained, and here the fates were gathering.

On 10 May the time had come to move on again.
But where? The south offered the only possible route,
although Himmler seemed to have no plans or objective
beyond some vague idea of contacting the Americans.
Eventually, a party of four cars – Himmler had graciously
consented to curtail his motorcade – reached the mouth
of the Elbe.

From then on, Heinrich Himmler became indistinguishable from the scores of refugees wandering homeless
over the land he had done so much to help devastate.
Nights were spent sleeping rough in farm buildings. Over
five days, the party tramped on slowly, travelling through
Neuhaus to Bremervörde – a distance of a little more
than one hundred miles from Flensburg.

This strange party, which included a Waffen-SS
adjutant, Obersturmbannführer Werner Grothmann, had
removed the insignia from its uniforms and were posing
as members of the Secret Field Police, making its way to
Bavaria.

A psychiatrist would have relished Himmler's choice
of disguise: he had shaved off his moustache and wore
a patch over one eye which gave him a sinister piratical
appearance. Was it, perhaps, a manifestation of some

268

inner desperate need to draw attention to himself even at the price of capture?

He carried papers which had once belonged to a postman or policeman named Heinrich Hitzinger who had been condemned to death by the People's Court.

The Secret Field Police was an ill-advised organisation to have chosen for the disguise. Originally the creation of the Abwehr (Foreign Intelligence), it had been incorporated into the Gestapo in 1942 and was therefore very much on the Allied black-lists. Possibly Himmler and his entourage had seized on the quickest and most convincing disguise of uniform that they could find.

Had their papers been those of ordinary members of the Wehrmacht, it might have been a different story. Instead, the party was screened at three camps: Zeelos, Westertimke and Bremervörde. It was at the Bremervörde control point that the moment of truth came. Together with a number of other suspects, Himmler was rounded up and taken to 031 Civilian Interrogation Camp, Lüneburg. At four o'clock in the afternoon Himmler was paraded before the officer-in-charge, Captain Selvester.

The prisoner aroused little suspicion, since such a parade was standard routine. But later Selvester was told that three of the prisoners were demanding separate interviews.

Captain Selvester takes up the story:

'The first man to enter my office was small, ill-looking and shabbily dressed, but he was immediately followed by two other men, both of whom were tall and soldierly-looking, one slim and one well-built. The well-built man walked with a limp. I sensed something unusual, and ordered one of my sergeants to place the two men in close custody, and not to allow anyone to speak to them without my authority. They were then removed from my office, whereupon the small man, who was wearing a black patch over his left eye, removed the patch and

269

put on a pair of spectacles. His identity was at once obvious. He said "Heinrich Himmler" in a very quiet voice.'

Just why Himmler revealed his identity can only be guesswork; possibly he felt that his name might well entitle him to some extra consideration. Any illusion did not last long.

Speedily, Himmler was placed under armed guard and an officer from the Intelligence Corps summoned hastily. Then the prisoner was asked to sign his name so that the signature could be compared with one already in the records.

At first Himmler thought that he was being asked for a souvenir and only agreed reluctantly. The next stage was a body search and Captain Selvester again takes up the story:

'This I carried out personally, handing each item of clothing as it was removed to my sergeant, who re-examined it. Himmler was carrying documents bearing the name of Heinrich Hitzinger, who I think was described as a postman. In his jacket I found a small brass case, similar to a cartridge case, which contained a small glass phial. I recognised it for what it was, but asked Himmler what it contained and he said: "That is my medicine. It cures stomach cramp." I also found a similar brass case, but without the phial, and came to the conclusion that the phial was hidden somewhere on the prisoner's person. When all Himmler's clothing had been removed and searched, all the orifices of his body were searched, also his hair combed and any likely hiding place examined, but no trace of the phial was found. At this stage, he was not asked to open his mouth, as I considered that if the phial was hidden in his mouth and we tried to remove it, it might precipitate some action that would be regretted. I did however send for thick bread and cheese sandwiches and tea, which I offered to Himmler, hoping that I would see if he removed anything from his mouth. I watched him closely while he was eating, but did not notice anything unusual.'

Meanwhile there was a flurry of activity at 031 Civilian Interrogation Camp. Extra troops with tommy-guns and machine-guns were mustered hastily. Extra sentries were posted at the gates. Soon the cause of all the excitement was rumoured and then confirmed. More than one British soldier confessed to a sense of pride that *his* camp had netted such a notorious prisoner.

Himmler flatly refused to put on the only other clothes available, a British Army uniform, and had to be content with a shirt, underpants and socks. The rest of his body was wrapped in a blanket.

Captain Selvester was worried about the missing phial and was convinced that his prisoner was hiding poison somewhere. Himmler, though, was giving nothing away. The food seemed to revive his spirits and he became communicative and almost jovial. Throughout he made it clear that he wished to communicate with some higher authority and did not consider that his treatment was worthy of a senior Nazi.

Later in the day Himmler was removed to Second Army Headquarters for further questioning. Again he was searched, primarily in the mouth and buttocks. Nothing was found.

But still the authorities were not satisfied. At the interrogation centre Himmler was put in charge of Sergeant-Major Edwin Austin who was determined to prevent Himmler committing suicide.

It was well known that the top Nazis carried poison with them against capture, and Austin had already had one failure when he had been unable to prevent a senior SS officer crushing a capsule of cyanide between his teeth.

As soon as Himmler was shown in, Austin indicated a couch.

He spoke in German: 'That's your bed. Get undressed.'

The old Himmler reasserted himself and stared menacingly at Austin, seeking to win over the Englishman through sheer force of personality. But Himmler was no longer the Reichsführer-SS whose very name spelt power and terror throughout Europe. He was now merely a nondescript, myopic vagrant, trouserless and without dignity.

Himmler said to the interpreter: 'He doesn't know who I am.'

Austin replied sharply: 'Yes, I do. You're Himmler. Nevertheless, that's your bed. Get undressed.'

Himmler attempted to wield a non-existent authority. But Austin was a no-nonsense British sergeant, not some quaking SS subordinate. He merely stared the prisoner out. Himmler sat down dejectedly on the couch and started to take off his underpants. Yet another examination was made. The armpits, hair, ears and buttocks were searched as Himmler stood naked.

Then the doctor ordered him to open his mouth. For a moment, Himmler stood meekly. Then he wrenched his head aside and his interrogators caught a glimpse of 'a small black knob sticking out between a gap in the teeth on the right-hand-side lower jaw.'

The doctor shouted: 'He's done it.'

Colonel Michael Murphy, Chief of Intelligence on Montgomery's staff, and Sergeant Austin leapt on Heinrich Himmler, turning him on his stomach to prevent swallowing. Colonel Murphy yelled for a needle and cotton. Himmler's tongue was soon pierced and the cotton threaded through to hold it out.

Normally, the action of the Zynkali capsule of potassium cyanide was fast. But there was nothing speedy about Himmler's death because of interference with the progress of the poison into his system. The capsule had been of thin metal, sufficiently strong to withstand careful swallowing of food and liquids, if only one side of the mouth was used.

And so, in circumstances that could scarcely be more sordid, the former Reichsführer-SS went into a death agony that lasted twelve minutes. His body lay twisted on the floor, surrounded by a grisly litter of swabs and basins.

Soon the photographers and the cine-camera operators were doing their work, recording for posterity the end of the twentieth century's most terrifying Grand Inquisitor.

Two death masks were taken. Both were, in their different ways, appropriate. The first showed features twisted into a pained grimace of pure evil: illustration of a godless soul whose monstrous crimes had not yet been revealed to the world he had done so much to destroy. The other mask was peaceful: it was of Himmler the bourgeois, the ever-dedicated clerk, the nine-to-five suburbanite rather than the spiritual descendant of the Teutonic knights.

At least, Hitler had been granted a Wagnerian funeral of sorts. In contrast, Heinrich Himmler's body was bundled into an army blanket secured with telegraph wire. Sergeant-Major Austin, who in civilian life had been a dustman, buried him in an unmarked grave.

The macabre death of Heinrich Himmler was for a long time to cast a blight over the carefully-nurtured image of the Waffen-SS as an élite fighting force which held itself aloof from the more loathsome excesses of the rest of the SS.

An élite? Brave fighters who wanted nothing more than to be regarded as the right arm of the Wehrmacht? Himmler's chosen method of death did not help the case.

One Waffen-SS officer, a holder of the Knight's Cross, who committed suicide because he felt that his Reichsführer-SS had betrayed his men, seemed to sum up the feelings of many in immediate post-war Germany.

This officer left a note saying: ' One of my best comrades parted from life because he loved his wife so dearly that he could not endure her unfaithfulness. My Reichsführer forbade him burial with military honours and after his death erased his name from the SS with insult and shame. And yet he himself tried to slip through the cordon, dressed as a character in a bad detective story. And when he was caught, he swallowed Zynkali instead of accepting responsibility before the victor's court and saving from the gallows a hundred poor devils who had done nothing but carry out their duty.'

Himmler, it was clearly inferred, had himself betrayed the Waffen-SS, whose true role in the war would now never be believed by anyone.

A final order came from OKW that the Waffen-SS was to surrender. It was obeyed with scrupulous rectitude by the élite formations. With a final formal parade, the bulk of the Leibstandarte surrendered in Austria to the Americans. But Sepp Dietrich's men did not shamble dejectedly into the prisoner-of-war cages in the manner of so many of their 'masters' in the Wehrmacht. A touch of arrogance remained even in defeat. On 9 May, SS Panzer Grenadier Regiment Deutschland sent the following communication to 2nd SS Panzer Division Das Reich:

'The Regiment Deutschland – now completely cut off, without supplies, with losses of seventy per cent in personnel and equipment, at the end of its strength – must capitulate. Tomorrow the Regiment will march into captivity with all heads held high. The Regiment which had the honour of bearing the name Deutschland is now signing off.'

A former SS officer described the final ride, the vehicles maintaining 'a more exact formation than usual. The Grenadiers sat stiffly at attention. With exemplary bearing we drove westwards. There were the Americans.'

Not surprisingly, most Waffen-SS groups surrendered

to the Americans or British rather than the Russians. Occasionally, there were shocks. A unit would surrender to a group of Americans confident that it would be well treated. But often prisoners were guarded in rotation by Americans, British – and Russians. To be captured by the Red Army meant a sure sentence of death in the labour camps of the Soviet Union.

Here and there were gestures of defiance. Perhaps Hitler Jugend, whose members constituted some of the bravest fighters of the Waffen-SS, could be forgiven for disregarding the 'demeaning' orders of the Americans to drape their vehicles with white flags. A brief final review was held before the commander. Thus, with discipline and proud bearing, the bulk of the thirty-eight Schutz-staffel Divisions passed into captivity and history.

TABLE OF SS RANKS AND THEIR
APPROXIMATE EQUIVALENTS

SS	British Army	US Army
Reichsführer-SS	Field Marshal	General of the Army
SS-Oberstgruppenführer	Lieutenant-General	Lieutenant-General
SS-Obergruppenführer	General	General
SS-Gruppenführer	Major-General	Major-General
SS-Brigadeführer, SS-Oberführer	Brigadier	Brigadier-General
SS-Standartenführer	Colonel	Colonel
SS-Obersturmbannführer	Lieutenant-Colonel	Lieutenant-Colonel
SS-Sturmbannführer	Major	Major
SS-Hauptsturmführer	Captain	Captain
SS-Obersturmführer	1st Lieutenant	1st Lieutenant
SS-Untersturmführer	2nd Lieutenant	2nd Lieutenant
SS-Sturmscharführer	Regimental Sergeant-Major	Sergeant-Major
SS-Hauptscharführer	Sergeant-Major	Master-Sergeant
SS-Oberscharführer	Quartermaster Sergeant	Technical Sergeant
SS-Scharführer	Staff Sergeant	Staff Sergeant
SS-Unterscharführer	Sergeant	Sergeant
SS-Rottenführer	Corporal	Corporal
SS-Sturmann	Lance-Corporal	Corporal
SS-Oberschütze, SS-Schütze	Private	Private

PEN & SWORD MILITARY CLASSICS

We hope that you have enjoyed your Pen and Sword Military Classic. The series is designed to give readers quality military history at affordable prices. Below is a list of the titles that are planned for 2003. Pen and Sword Classics are available from all good bookshops. If you would like to keep in touch with further developments in the series, including information on the Classics Club, then please contact Pen and Sword at the address below.

2003 List

PEN AND SWORD BOOKS LTD
47 Church Street • Barnsley • South Yorkshire • S70 2AS
Tel: 01226 734555 • 734222